CROSS-CULTURAL ESSENTIALS 1

GOD'S NARRATIVE: GENESIS TO CHRIST

A WALK THROUGH THE BIBLE FROM GENESIS TO CHRIST'S RESURRECTION

54 TUTORIALS WITH DISCUSSION
POINTS AND ACTIVITIES

God's Narrative: Genesis to Christ
A walk through the Bible from Genesis to Christ's resurrection
Biblical Foundations, Module 1 of the Cross-Cultural Essentials curriculum

Copyright © 2019, 2016 AccessTruth

Version 1.2

ISBN: 978-0-9944270-3-8

All Rights Reserved. Except as may be permitted by the Copyright Act, no part of this publication may be reproduced in any form or by any means without prior permission from the publisher. Requests for permission should be made to info@accesstruth.com

Unless otherwise indicated, all Scripture quotations are taken from the Holy Bible, New Living Translation, copyright © 1996, 2004. Used by permission of Tyndale House Publishers, Inc., Wheaton, Illinois 60189. All rights reserved.

Published by AccessTruth
PO Box 8087
Baulkham Hills NSW 2153
Australia

Email: info@accesstruth.com
Web: accesstruth.com

Cover and interior design by Matthew Hillier
Edited by Simon Glover

Table of Contents

About the Cross-Cultural Essentials Curriculum 7

TUTORIAL 1.1 9
The Master Storyteller

TUTORIAL 1.2 17
The stories we tell

TUTORIAL 1.3 21
The whole story

TUTORIAL 1.4 27
Every story starts somewhere

TUTORIAL 1.5 33
What's so great about Foundational Teaching?

TUTORIAL 1.6 41
Preparation for Creation to Christ

TUTORIAL 1.7 43
The Bible is God's message to all people

TUTORIAL 1.8 47
The Bible tells us what God is like

TUTORIAL 1.9 51
God created angels, the heavens and the earth

TUTORIAL 1.10 55
God revealed through His creative acts

TUTORIAL 1.11 59
God created Adam and Eve

TUTORIAL 1.12 63
God placed Adam in Eden

TUTORIAL 1.13 67
God created a wife for Adam

TUTORIAL 1.14 71
Lucifer rebelled against God

TUTORIAL 1.15 75
Adam and Eve disobeyed God

TUTORIAL 1.16 79
The curse and the promise

TUTORIAL 1.17 83
God provided clothing for Adam and Eve

TUTORIAL 1.18 87
Cain and Abel's offerings

TUTORIAL 1.19 91
God punishes the world, but saves Noah

TUTORIAL 1.20 95
God remembered Noah. God scatters at Babel

TUTORIAL 1.21 99
God chose Abram. Lot choses Sodom and Gomorrah

TUTORIAL 1.22 103
God's promises to Abram. God destroyed the twin cities

TUTORIAL 1.23 107
God gave Isaac and delivered him from death

TUTORIAL 1.24 111
God chose Jacob to be the ancestor of the Deliverer

TUTORIAL 1.25 115
God promoted Joseph. God took Jacob's family into Egypt

TUTORIAL 1.26 119
God preserved the Israelites and protected Moses

TUTORIAL 1.27 125
The Lord sent plagues on the Egyptians

TUTORIAL 1.28 131
God delivered the Israelites & continued to provide for them

TUTORIAL 1.29 137
God's agreement to bless the Israelites if they obey Him

TUTORIAL 1.30 141
God gave the Ten Commandments

TUTORIAL 1.31 147
God told the Israelites to build the Tabernacle

TUTORIAL 1.32 151
The Israelites did not believe God would give them Canaan

TUTORIAL 1.33 155
God took the Israelites into Canaan and chose their king

TUTORIAL 1.34 161
God sent His prophets to the Israelites, they are refused

TUTORIAL 1.35 167
God foretold the birth of John and fulfilled His promises

TUTORIAL 1.36 171
God was about to fulfil His promises concerning the Deliverer

TUTORIAL 1.37 175
The Deliverer was born and grew into manhood

TUTORIAL 1.38 181
God sent John to teach & to baptize. John baptized Jesus

TUTORIAL 1.39 187
Jesus resisted Satan's temptations

TUTORIAL 1.40 191
Jesus began His ministry

TUTORIAL 1.41 197
Jesus taught the necessity of the "new birth"

TUTORIAL 1.42 201
Jesus had power to heal & forgive. Jewish leaders plotted

TUTORIAL 1.43 207
Jesus calmed a storm & released a man from the control of demons

TUTORIAL 1.44 211
Jesus fed 5,000 people

TUTORIAL 1.45 215
The Pharisees rejected God's way

TUTORIAL 1.46 219
Jesus is the Christ, the Son of God

TUTORIAL 1.47 225
Jesus is the only door to eternal life

TUTORIAL 1.48 229
Jesus raised Lazarus from the dead

TUTORIAL 1.49 235
Jesus taught that we need to humbly admit our guilt

TUTORIAL 1.50 241
It is foolish to give material things pre-eminence over God

TUTORIAL 1.51 245
Jesus rode into Jerusalem. They celebrated the Passover

TUTORIAL 1.52 251
Jesus was arrested by His enemies

TUTORIAL 1.53 257
Jesus was crucified

TUTORIAL 1.54 263
Jesus was buried and was raised from the dead

About the Cross-Cultural Essentials Curriculum

It's no secret that there are still millions of people in the world living in "unreached" or "least-reached" areas. If you look at the maps, the stats, and the lists of people group names, it's almost overwhelming. The people represented by those numbers can't find out about God, or who Jesus Christ is, or what He did for them because there's no Bible in their language or church in their area – they have *no access* to Truth.

So you could pack a suitcase and jump on a plane, but then what? How would you spend your first day? How would you start learning language? When would you tell them about Jesus? Where would you start? The truth is that a mature, grounded fellowship of God's children doesn't just "happen" in an unreached area or even in your neighborhood. When we speak the Truth, we need to have the confidence that it is still the same Truth when it gets through our hearer's language, culture and worldview grid.

The *Cross-Cultural Essentials* curriculum, made up of 10 individual modules, forms a comprehensive training course. Its main goal is to help equip believers to be effective in providing people access to God's Truth through evangelism and discipleship. The *Cross-Cultural Essentials* curriculum makes it easy to be better equipped for teaching the whole narrative of the Bible, for learning about culture and worldview and for planting a church and seeing it grow.

More information on the curriculum can be found at *accesstruth.com*

Introduction to Module 1: God's Narrative: Genesis to Christ

God's Word is one entire, seamless description of what He has revealed about Himself, about the Spirit world, about Creation, about humans and His intentions for them. God's Narrative: Genesis to Christ (Module 1) covers the first part of God's Narrative. Beginning in Genesis, it gives an overview from His Word of His interactions with men and women throughout history, right up to the life of Christ. This begins the One Story: a seamless description of all that has been, is, and will be, with God as the Master Storyteller.

ABOUT THE CROSS-CULTURAL ESSENTIALS CURRICULUM

How to use this module

Read / watch / listen: Read through the tutorial. If you have an online account at *accesstruth.com*, or the DVD associated with this module you can watch the video or listen to the audio of the tutorial.

Discussion Points: At the end of some tutorials there are discussion points. It may be helpful to write down your answers so you can process your thoughts. If you are doing the tutorials in a group, these points should prove helpful in guiding the discussion.

Activities: Some tutorials have activities that involve practical tasks, worksheets that need to be completed, or may just ask for a written answer.

Primary Contributor

Paul Mac and his wife, Linda, spent 11 years in Papua New Guinea involved in pioneering church planting in an isolated people group. They were privileged to see God plant a number of churches in that area that continue to thrive today. During the time there, they headed up a translation team that produced a New Testament in the local language. After leaving PNG, Paul and Linda worked for 12 years in leadership and consultative roles with an international mission agency. Today they continue to provide church planting guidance for a number of different teams engaged in some of the world's most challenging contexts. They are passionate about seeing churches planted that are well equipped to carry on for future generations.

1.1 The Master Storyteller

 OBJECTIVES OF THIS TUTORIAL

To engage with the real and relevant issues of God's inherent right and desire to communicate with man.

The first and final word

The capacity of words, spoken or written, to actually contain truth, has widely been brought into question in the last few decades. Whether there *is* even such a thing as Truth - an overarching Truth - has been hotly debated. We live in a world where, in many places, absolutes are no longer popular. As individuals, and as a society, making definitive statements that our ideas should be listened to is no longer a comfortable position to hold.

These debates are not just academic - maybe because people have too much time on their hands - the denial of absolute Truth has already profoundly changed and seriously reshaped many societies. In part, the move away from belief in an absolute and unalterable truth has resulted from what is essentially a reasonable challenge; the question was asked, 'Who has the right to say what is true?' and 'Why should your version of things, or mine, be the accepted one?'

Today, more than ever, that challenge must be met with a relevant and adequate response. A premise of all that will be said here is that there is an answer, and that it is more than adequate. Someone does in fact have the right to be speak and to be heard, and that Someone is God. Because He spoke truth, there is Truth, and it is Truth that can be communicated in human language, in real words, and can be clearly understood. As the source of everything - the world, us, our ability to conceptualize and to communicate - He is the One worthy of being listened to. Everything we see around us in the natural world; animals, plants, people, the earth and its environment – in fact all of the foundational elements of the reality in which we live – are created by an all powerful, all knowing, personal God. The Jewish and Christian Scriptures - what we call the Old &

New Testaments - were written by real people, in real words, using real languages, and they communicate what God wanted to say. The Bible is God's Word.

When you honestly dig down to what is underneath the reality in which we live, you will find God. Starting with any other foundation than God - or perhaps trying to deny the evidence completely and imagine that there is nothing other than a physical reality - eventually leads nowhere, no matter how simple or how sophisticated a description is given along the way. The logical end to beginning without God, is that there is no Truth, no words that really mean anything of value, no one who can really say anything, no one who can understand. But the good news is that God has spoken. He has spoken Truth into the world, and His words are our source of Truth. So because God has spoken Truly, we also are able to speak truth and to say things that are valuable, meaningful and powerful. It is possible for our words to be worth listening to, if they are founded in what He has established as Truth.

This aspect of God - this speaking truth, telling it like it is - that's not just something He chose to do at some point - a whim. It's not just a nice, agreeable side of God. In fact, this speaking, communicating, relating aspect of God is so essential to who He is that it is not possible to talk accurately about God if it's not consistent with this aspect of who He is. It's also not possible to speak accurately about the world and us within the world without acknowledging this foundational characteristic of God - as willing Communicator.

Speaking truth is part of who God is, but we should not understand that to mean that He is forced or compelled to speak by anyone or anything outside of Himself. God is completely and ultimately free. The concept of freedom, and even our ability to understand it - freedom to decide anything, to believe, to act, to speak - is founded on the fact that God is completely free. And so God, acting from His character and being, freely chooses to speak, to communicate, to tell His Story.

His account of creation - the only first-hand account, as He was there - says that He spoke everything into existence. The Bible says that Creation itself is a kind of speech - a story about God.

> **GENESIS 1:3** Then God said, "Let there be light," and there was light.

> **HEBREWS 11:3** By faith we understand that the entire universe was formed at God's command, that what we now see did not come from anything that can be seen.

Later, when God came to the world in the person of Jesus Christ - both God and man - He was called The Word - an identity which expresses so eloquently God's desire to communicate with us.

> **JOHN 1:1** In the beginning the Word already existed. The Word was with God, and the Word was God. ² He existed in the beginning with God. ³ God created everything through him, and nothing was created except through him. ⁴ The Word gave life to everything that was created, and his life brought light to everyone.

The creation of the world, its history since creation and our existence today as part of that history, has the idea of *Story* at its core. God's Story. It is a narrative which revolves around the Word - His birth, life, death and the events beyond that. God is the Master Storyteller, because it is who He is in His very being. He initiated the Story, and we are there as part of the story, but the Story is His and it is ultimately about Him. He began it and He will take it to the conclusion that He has decided on. The first and final Word are His. He *is* the first and final Word.

Who's listening?

It comes as no surprise that as the all-powerful, personal Creator - the Master Storyteller and Narrator of Truth - God also fashioned beings who are able to listen to Him. What would be a surprise is if He had created the world then left it to chance that someone who could listen would eventually come into being. But God did not leave it to endless chains of blind chance, through countless millennia - He expressly fashioned a living being with the ability to listen and understand.

God created, and His creation is the setting and the context for Him to tell His story to us as human beings. But we are not simply passive listeners, because He intentionally made us like Himself - in the sense that we are free. He made us and gave us freedom - the ability to listen, to hear, to understand His Story - and incredibly He also gave us the capacity to respond: to be able to know Him, to love Him, to obey and to worship Him. Of course the other side of this gift of freedom is that we also have the capacity to turn away and to refuse to listen, even to the point of telling our own stories, and to make ourselves the focus and heroes of those stories.

As a race, of course, that is what we have done and what we continue to do. In fact, not listening to God is a defining feature of our identity as a human race. As a group, it's who we are in our very being. We've turned not listening into an art form - we do it well, and we do it with enthusiasm - and we delight in our chosen role of not listening to the One who made us and gave us that capacity. On the whole, we have become obsessed with talking so loudly that we hear only our own voices.

A commitment without limits

God began by creating a place for us so that the very reality of the place itself expresses important things about Him every single moment. He followed-up by making us exactly as we needed to be to hear and know Him and then He gladly offered, and continues to offer, to be our Story Teller - to write us into His grand, sweeping narrative - and even to collaborate with Him in it.

When we decide to tell our own distorted versions of His Story, our real potential is wasted and our victories are hollow. Our inventions harm as much as they help, we worry that many of the things we've made are actually devouring the world that He made to be our safe haven. We suffer from the lack of Him and search desperately for what prove to be inadequate replacements. And in response to our predicament we either shake our fist at God or perhaps we even stop listening altogether and try to entertain ourselves into spiritual oblivion.

But here is the most incredible part of the whole narrative: God's commitment to speaking with us remains unchanged. He is saddened - he takes no delight in the terrible consequences of our rebellion - but He is not put-off at all by our arrogance. It might seem reasonable for Him to simply leave us to suffer the consequences of our chosen path, but instead, the unspeakably holy and powerful Creator actually doggedly pursues us - His lost race of Listeners. He uses every means available to draw our hearts and minds to Himself.

His pursuit of us - His rescue effort - is at the heart of His Story. It is what He is about, who He is and what He does. His incomparable love and mercy, demonstrated in the face of our rebellion, is a theme that dominates the entire Story that He so urgently wants us to understand. This unprecedented rescue effort brought Him from all that is rightfully His as God, down into time and space, to earth, into the limitations and weakness of a human body, and ultimately it took Him to death, to the very depths of Hell. Now that's a story that must be told. This book is all about those who've been rescued, telling God's story to others in such a way that they will be compelled to listen, and hopefully, will choose to become active participants in telling His Story themselves.

❓ DISCUSSION POINTS

1. Do you agree with the statement that "absolutes are no longer popular" in our society? Give some examples from your own experience.

2. In what way do you think that creation is revelation ("a kind of speech")? What are some of the things that the world around us tells us about God? Do you feel that, in general, you are conscious of God communicating through Creation?

3. Why do you think God gave us as humans the capacity to listen and understand his communication – his Story – while at the same time giving us the freedom to reject, to not listen?

4. How does it make you feel on a personal level to think about the absolute commitment God makes to communicate with us? On a daily level, are you conscious of His presence and desire to interact with you?

➡ ACTIVITIES

1. Spend at least an hour somewhere in natural surroundings (without any electronic devices active) simply being conscious of and enjoying the reality of God "speaking" through Creation.

1.2 The stories we tell

 OBJECTIVES OF THIS TUTORIAL

To begin to think about and discuss the importance of cultural relevance in the presentation of Biblical Truth, and to see how different cultures have very different views of the world.

Life - a tale of survival

There is something very compelling in accounts of survival, to someone beating the odds and pulling through despite terrible and desperate circumstances. Ernest Shackleton led his expedition, incredibly without loss of life, after their ship was crushed in the Antarctic ice or, more recently, mountaineer Joe Simpson lived to tell the tale of his fall into an abyss while climbing in the Peruvian Andes. (Book and movie 'Touching the Void'). Perhaps these stories resonate with us because for all of us to some degree, life itself is a tale of survival.

Every one of us comes into this world in the same way, with very few resources for survival - equipped with little but our skin and one or two highly effective ways of demanding attention from our parents. And we need every bit of help we can get, because the world that we find ourselves in is in many ways a harsh one. There are many things that jeopardize our survival. As we grow, the things we need become more sophisticated and complex. We need companionship. We need to feel we belong. We look for acceptance. We want to be valued, and we all need some reason to get up in the morning, some reason to keep going - to survive - to make sense of it all.

But we humans have a massive dilemma. Our senses are constantly receiving data, bits of information, from the outside world. And we're specifically designed to have all those bits of experience tie together - we were made to try to make sense of it all - we need to make sense of it all to face life and death. That need is at the core of being human. Remember that we were designed by God specifically to hear Him tell us His Story and for us to understand our story within that framework. It was always His intention to tell us why any of this matters - why we find ourselves alive - why we exist - but our understanding of the world and our place within it can only be correctly or truly understood when it is placed within His narrative. So what is our dilemma? We were designed to listen, but we have rejected God who made both us, and the world we live in. And we rejected His over-arching narrative that actually does make sense of it all.

So how have we, as a human race, tried to resolve this dilemma? Our very design leads us to seek the Narrative to explain life, but having rejected the true story, we really left ourselves with no choice but to make something up. To a degree we do this as individuals, but we also pass on these stories to each other - we make an agreement to accept a certain version of a story so that we can survive together as communities, or as societies. It's actually what a culture is, and a language is the verbal communication of that common story among a group of people. People who share a language often share quite a lot of the story or stories they tell to try to make sense of their common experience of the world.

Two very different stories

Let's briefly explore two examples - which are about as far apart as they can be - to illustrate the need we humans have for making sense of it all, and in what way we hold stories in common to do so.

Scientific Humanism

The first example is a cultural context that most of us are familiar with - modern, scientific, humanism. What do we mean by those terms? If we had time, we could trace the origins of this particular story - or worldview - much further back, but we're using 'modern' to mean the last few centuries. So we will say that this particular story began at the time of the Renaissance - when people began to challenge an assumption held up to that point by Western societies, that everything we can know comes from the Bible as interpreted by the so-called universal or Catholic Church. As a result of that challenge, human rationality - our thoughts - became the guiding principle. Humans claimed the right to tell their own story. That's why we call it 'humanism'.

Science - the way in which humans investigate and describe the world around them - took over as the chief storyteller. Its version of the world became the narrative of choice. For a time God was given a small role as a distant Creator, but with so little to do He eventually disappeared from this story. This led to the view that all reality, everything we experience or can think of, human behavior, human history, the way everything came into being - all could be explained in purely material or physical terms.

It seemed for a time, that this was a pretty good, tight storyline and that the human race would go on to solve its problems and plot out its own glorious future. But as time went by, cracks began to appear. There was widespread unrest, endless armed conflicts, including the two global wars. The modern nations founded most directly on those humanist principles ended up being some of the most vicious and murderous in all of recorded history. And what's more, it became obvious that this story did not live up to its billing - it was supposed to explain absolutely everything. But the fact is, the scientific, humanistic version just doesn't account for things like beauty and justice, nor answer the deep questions of people's hearts.

Thousands of different solutions to this failure in the plot have been attempted over the years, with all kinds of twists, theories and trends. Room has even been made for religion or a vague 'spirituality', but the scientific humanism that defined this story from its beginning is still there as the dominant theme in most so-called modern societies today.

Animism

A second, very different, story is often called animism. Actually, like our first illustration, there are some things that we can say to describe an animistic worldview, but in reality it is a broad term for a great many stories that share some major features. Animism is the worldview of many traditional or 'tribal' societies - usually those who've had the least contact with others.

The story of animism in many ways is the opposite of the scientific, humanistic story. For animists, the material, physical world is closely intertwined with the unseen spiritual world. The worlds of the living and the dead are not clearly distinguished, and because ancestors remain active in the physical world, it is up to the living to appease or find ways to solicit their help for survival. Without traditional access to the technology of reading and writing, animistic beliefs are often passed down in the form of myths, chants, incantations and dramatic dance. While the scientist in a lab coat or the reporter for the nightly news is the storyteller for scientific humanism, animism's narratives are told by the local shaman or healer. Power, and therefore the right to say what is true or not, is held by those who are seen to have the answers for survival in a perilous physical/spiritual world.

Animistic beliefs are fluid and adaptable in order to explain events and incorporate new ideas that come along. For this reason we often find animism mixed (syncretism - a combination of different beliefs) with other dominant worldviews. Many traditionally animistic societies have taken on the overarching stories of a world religion to take care of the big questions of life and death, but have retained their smaller, traditional animistic stories to try to make sense of their day-to-day human needs.

So what can we say about these two seemingly very different worldviews or Stories? And what general lessons are there for us as tellers of God's true Story? We can see, first of all, that having some way to explain and make sense of life is a compelling need for everyone: it's the same for a person surrounded by cutting-edge technology in a modern city or someone whose culture has changed little in hundreds of years. Having rejected God's Story, humans take it on themselves to tell their own versions of reality - they really have no choice but to do this. Stories that are accepted widely are based on some claim to authority; dreams and visions, ancient writings, religion, science or even human reasoning itself. But regardless of their starting point, they fail. Gaps always appear. They always fall short of claims to make sense of it all, to answer the most important needs of human beings.

At the beginning of Paul's letter to the Christians in Rome, he vividly describes the process of people rejecting God and His Account of reality - what Paul calls 'trading truth for a lie' - and he talks about the devastating results in every area of human existence. But in that same passage, Paul also talks about the Answer. This Answer is what drives him, motivates him, and gets him up in the morning. He has been entrusted with God's True Story - a Story that, in the very telling, has the power to convince and change people's thinking and lives.

As tellers of God's Story we must first of all be convinced that it can back up its claims. That it has the inherent authority and power to replace all other Stories that humans have told. We must feel the same obligation Paul describes - of telling God's Story clearly and carefully to anyone who will listen, regardless of who they are or where they come from. And we must be willing to understand the narratives of their lives - to respect, empathize and care for them as those for whom God has given His All. Because they are those He is seeking, so He can tell them His Good, True Story that will answer the deepest needs of their hearts.

❓ DISCUSSION POINTS

1. Picture describing yourself within your cultural setting to someone from another planet. Start from the "widest-angle" and gradually narrow it down to observations about any cultural sub-groups you would say you're a part of.

2. Briefly describe some of the most important points about the "Story" our culture has accepted and tells itself. (1) Who or what are the Main Storytellers? (2) What is accepted as the purpose of our lives? (3) What are the really big problems we face? (4) Where do we look for the solutions? (5) What happens after death? Do you feel that, in general, you are conscious of God communicating through Creation?

3. Do you have any friends who are not believers with whom you regularly discuss the "deeper things" of life?

If so, describe the kinds of conversations you have with them: e.g. Are they interested in what you tell them about your faith or are they antagonistic towards Christianity? How do you respond?

If not, what do you think the reasons are? Is it because you don't have friends who are not believers? Or you do but they, or you, are not comfortable talking about those kinds of things?

➡ ACTIVITIES

1. Watch a successful movie from the last 10 years taking some notes about the underlying worldview that comes through in the storyline and dialogue.

1.3 The whole story

✓ OBJECTIVES OF THIS TUTORIAL

Learners will think about the fact that in contrast to all other "stories" - which are fragmented and inconsistent - the Biblical narrative provides the framework for an understanding of the way things are.

Fragmented stories

Different cultures - our own included - have lost the true account of the way things are, but it has not happened all at once, it has been a gradual process, often taking centuries. This process of losing the True Story has been slowed down by the fact that the natural world tells part of the Story about God - it's as though creation has been speaking truth to the vague echo of truth that each man is born with.

> **ROMANS 1:19,20** They know the truth about God because he has made it obvious to them. [20] For ever since the world was created, people have seen the earth and sky. Through everything God made, they can clearly see his invisible qualities—his eternal power and divine nature. So they have no excuse for not knowing God.

Many groups still retain fragments of the Biblical account. There are stories that talk of creation, of a flood, of a time when languages came to be. But as each group turned away from worshiping the One True God and began to replace the truth with their own stories, there was a gradual forgetting and turning away from what they knew to be true - a continuing replacement of truth with fragments of other stories - either their own or from other religions. The stories that people tell to try to make sense of the world are often disjointed and self-contradictory.

Reality in the Biblical narrative

How have we responded to the confusion that exists - how have we tried to tell God's Story? We have often only added to the confusion by telling parts of the story, by taking pieces from here and there, assuming the listeners will make a cohesive story out of it all. We might tell a story about Daniel and the Lions, then Peter & John healing a lame man, add a sermon from some verses in Luke and then another from Nehemiah. There has been little continuity, or sense of historical truth. Many times our listeners come away with no understanding of this being a story with a beginning and a middle and an end - a narrative of God's actions in real space and time - His Story.

For people to understand the enormity and significance and Truth of the Story, we need to tell it from the beginning and then continue on to its conclusion. It is a Story that is tied firmly to reality, to history, and to real events. It has progression like any story or narrative does, and it moves from logical cause to effect. Disjointed and confused stories need to be replaced with a comprehensive seamless story of reality, because that is what it actually is - and the truth must sweep away the fragmented story people have come to believe.

The way we present God's Story needs to demonstrate the difference between people's confused and fragmented views of reality with the historical Truth we find in the Biblical narrative.

A focus on God's character

Presenting Biblical truth with a focus on man's felt needs, keeps man at the center of his world and at the center of the story. The other mistake that we can make is to focus our teaching on man's sinfulness. Of course people need to realize their sinfulness and their need, and this should be one of our most important teaching goals, but it isn't the focus of the Story.

The primary purpose of any Bible teaching should be, not to elevate the sinfulness of man, but to elevate God - to bring glory to Him, and to bring out His character through the things He has said and done. This is the purpose for which we are created. This is the purpose of His Word. It is His Story.

> **1 CHR 29:11** Yours, O Lord, is the greatness, the power, the glory, the victory, and the majesty. Everything in the heavens and on earth is yours, O Lord, and this is your kingdom. We adore you as the one who is over all things.
>
> **ROM 11:36** For everything comes from him and exists by his power and is intended for his glory. All glory to him forever! Amen.
>
> **COL 1:16** For through him God created everything in the heavenly realms and on earth. He made the things we can see and the things we can't see - such as thrones, kingdoms, rulers, and authorities in the unseen world. Everything was created through him and for him.

>**REV 4:11** "You are worthy, O Lord our God, to receive glory and honor and power. For you created all things, and they exist because you created what you pleased."

Reality for man can only come into focus when he understands who God is. This is the basis for all truth. We need to tell His Story which focuses on Him. Only then can man know who He is and understand the world in which he lives.

>**PROVERBS 9:10** Fear of the LORD is the foundation of wisdom. Knowledge of the Holy One results in good judgment.

The main focus of our teaching should be the nature and character of God and His glory.

The story of grace in response to man's sin

As we tell about the fall and the sinfulness of man, the important focus will not be on "So what are you going to do about it?" rather it will be "OK, listen to the story of what God has done about it."

God's Word is centered around the story of what God has done about the problem of sin. It is His response to man's rebellion and how He has brought about reconciliation - the plan of salvation. It is about Him redeeming - buying back out of sin - people who are lost and unable to help themselves.

Christ is the center

The Bible tells about the coming of the Messiah, God's Son, within a real historical setting and as the fulfillment of God's plan of reconciliation. The whole Story has led to this point. It is God's next and greatest action in the ongoing response to the problem of sin. It was certainly the greatest event in all of history - but it was not an isolated event.

The story of God's redemption plan begins in the Old Testament and then culminates in the New. When we teach only the last part of the story there is the great risk that people will not understand. They hear the solution but they don't understand their true dilemma. Because their fragmented confused "story" remains unchallenged, they don't see how the events of Christ's life and death relate to them. It's a story, but not the story.

When Christ's life and death are not placed within the historical context, there is the risk of it being seen as just another story among many stories.

Answers to difficult questions

The cruelty of man, the issue of pain, the question of how a loving God can allow war and suffering - these are things that many people raise as objections to Christianity or are confused about. The answer to all of these things is interwoven in the Biblical narrative. Issues such as these can only be understood within the whole framework; as God, without a single exception, acts righteously and justly but also lovingly and graciously.

And the answers to those difficult issues can only be understood when man's depravity is seen in its historical perspective. When people understand that the human condition is a result of the fall, and that this was not God's intention for man, but actually the logical result of man turning his back on his Creator and on the purpose for his creation.

When we tell the whole story, we are answering peoples' questions as God has answered them - from the basis of the Biblical narrative. We are not presenting a religion, or selling our own particular interpretation of the world. And if people choose not to believe, then it is God's story they are rejecting. We should teach so that God's nature is clearly seen through his actions, and on the basis of his redemption plan. Then He will be glorified and people will have the opportunity to respond to truth - rather than what they might say is just "one religion among many".

❓ DISCUSSION POINTS

1. Describe your formative experiences of hearing Bible stories and being taught from the Bible. Who or what, in general was in focus? Has it been your overall experience (without being unduly critical) that although God was mentioned, the "heroes" of the stories were often people? David, Samson, Peter etc. What implications do you think this has for our view of God's Word and God Himself?

2. When you are reading or studying a portion of God's Word, how much do you usually think about things like: Who was writing or saying this? To whom? What was their physical setting? What was their worldview like? etc. OR, do you tend to think just about what God is saying to you personally at the time you're reading the passage? Do you feel there is a conflict between these two approaches to the Bible?

➡ ACTIVITIES

1. Read the book of Ruth through in one sitting. Then;

- Briefly note any observations you have, or questions that come to mind, about the historical and cultural setting for the narrative.
- Comment in any way you like about God's role in the events recorded.
- Reflect on how this particular story fits into the whole of the Biblical narrative and God's Purposes.
- Note anything about this part of God's Word that encourages, inspires or challenges you personally.

(Note: Keep it brief. You should end up with no more than a page of notes.)

1.4 Every story starts somewhere

 OBJECTIVES OF THIS TUTORIAL

Learners will begin to think about the benefits in presenting the Gospel within the context of God's historical actions.

Careful master-builders

Many evangelism methods and church planting models have developed out of the push to speed things up - to get quick results and ever larger numbers of converts in a shorter amount of time. This is an understandable response to the great needs in the world and the urgency of the task. Unfortunately however, over time the results of much of this effort do not last because they are built on poor foundations. Building in this way is not God's way: He does things carefully and builds things to last. He is in for the long haul - right to the Finish.

> **HEBREWS 3:4** For every house has a builder, but the one who built everything is God.

> **PSALM 33:6,9** The Lord merely spoke, and the heavens were created. He breathed the word, and all the stars were born. ⁹ For when he spoke, the world began! It appeared at his command.

God is the master architect of His Work - His Church - and He has called us into partnership with Him in that work.

> **1 COR 3:10** Because of God's grace to me, I have laid the foundation like an expert builder. Now others are building on it. But whoever is building on this foundation must be very careful.

We are responsible to, and would be wise to, follow the instruction the Architect gave for building his Church. But do we? Much mission work focuses only on evangelism. But what we are actually called to is to make disciples and to teach all that Christ entrusted to the apostles. God wants to see groups of His disciples raised up who will in turn reach out to teach, disciple and plant churches themselves.

Where will we start?

So with a desire to do things according to his plan, we must lay careful foundations. But how will we go about it? Where will we start? Which parts of God's Word will we choose? What will we focus on? What principles can guide us?

Preparing the ground

> **JEREMIAH 4:3** ... Plow up the hard ground of your hearts! Do not waste your good seed among thorns.

A principle we see throughout Scripture is that human hearts in their natural, fallen state are not good soil for God's Word. People have willingly told their own stories and found their own solutions to life's dilemmas. Man has believed the great lie that he can determine his own path (as gods), and it is the tendency of every human being to see things from their own perspective.

We are not naturally worshippers of God.

> **ROM 3:11,18** No one is truly wise; no one is seeking God;... "They have no fear of God at all."

> **ROM 8:7,8** For the sinful nature is always hostile to God. It never did obey God's laws, and it never will. [8] That's why those who are still under the control of their sinful nature can never please God.

Everything in the fallen nature of man wants to reject the idea of his need - he does not want his sin to be exposed - he wants to believe that he can DO something to get through and that he can make himself right in God's eyes.

Felt needs - an incorrect foundation

There has been a great emphasis in mission circles on culturally felt needs as a starting point for developing a plan for teaching. The Gospel is often presented as the answer to these felt needs - with the priority being to make the message seem relevant, and above all, acceptable, to the listeners. Cultural issues will have to be addressed at some point, but they should not be the starting point or shape the message.

When the focus of Bible teaching is on human beings' need for happiness, belonging and security, it puts man at the center of the Story - it becomes all about us, not all about God. As we've said, man has chosen to tell his own stories, and those stories are based on felt needs; the things he assumes are important, solutions he has arrived at for the dilemmas he faces.

Not only are the solutions wrong, but the dilemmas are also not the most important ones.

Jesus did not come to meet felt needs

The Lord Jesus Christ Himself said that His prime purpose in coming into the world was not to make people happy, peaceful or secure. He came to settle the problem of sin - something that many of the people He spoke to were not even aware was a problem. Their aspirations were political, they wanted deliverance from oppression.

After feeding the 5000 He refused to feed them again, and the result was that many who'd been following him turned back. He refused because He knew that their real need was to understand that they could only find eternal salvation in Him.

God does care about what people are going through. We see the compassion of Jesus many times. But His primary response and the purpose for which He came was to give His life in payment for sin - to meet the real needs of the people He cared for so deeply.

Offering cures to those who don't know they're sick

> **MAT 9:10-13** Later, Matthew invited Jesus and his disciples to his home as dinner guests, along with many tax collectors and other disreputable sinners. [11] But when the Pharisees saw this, they asked his disciples, "Why does your teacher eat with such scum?" [12] When Jesus heard this, he said, "Healthy people don't need a doctor – sick people do." [13] Then he added, "Now go and learn the meaning of this Scripture: 'I want you to show mercy, not offer sacrifices.' For I have come to call not those who think they are righteous, but those who know they are sinners."

Jesus did not invite the self-righteous Pharisees to come to Him. He said "Go and learn" because He knew that they could not offer anything to God which would satisfy His holy, righteous demands.

> **JOHN 9:40,41** Some Pharisees who were standing nearby heard him and asked, "Are you saying we're blind?" [41] "If you were blind, you wouldn't be guilty," Jesus replied. "But you remain guilty because you claim you can see..."

They were in great need, but they didn't know it. But what does He say to those who sense their heavy burden?

> **MATT 11:28** Come to me, all of you who are weary and carry heavy burdens, and I will give you rest.

A God who is too small

Not only have most people come up with their own solutions, they have also decided themselves what God is like, and therefore what He will be satisfied with.

It is a basic human mistake to 'shrink' God down until He is someone we can understand, someone we can please, someone manageable, and someone who can be manipulated and deceived. So how can people see who God really is and what their real need is?

A knowledge of God is the only starting point

In the beginning God existed, before time, before anything else. For people to truly get to know Him we must start by clearing the stage of everything else that might draw people's eyes away. His Story must focus on Him - the pre-existent One, from the very beginning.

> **PSALM 111:10** Fear of the Lord is the foundation of true wisdom.

The importance of knowing God's absolutes

People may recognize God as Creator, as Judge, as Provider - even as someone who needs to be feared - but for a correct understanding of the way things really are, people need to *really* know who He is...

If God is not absolutely holy and righteous - then man could still use his own standards to judge himself morally,

If God needs anything at all there may also be some way to manipulate God for man's own ends.

If God is not absolutely powerful then there may be someone else who needs allegiance or there may be ways of avoiding His judgment.

If God is not all knowing there may be some way of deceiving Him or there may be things we can do, say or think which He does not understand.

If God is not omnipresent there may be somewhere to hide from Him.

God's Enemy works very hard at taking away all absolutes, because it is the knowledge of who God really is that leads to an understanding of man's greatest need.

Apart from a true knowledge of God, a person will never truly repent, believe and be saved.

God is revealed in the Scriptural narrative

So where should we begin? Where God himself begins - in Genesis.

"In the beginning…"

God introduces Himself to people in his Word - as God in the beginning. Before the stars, before the sun and moon, before any spirits, before man, before trees or anything else…this is God, this is what He was and is like.

As we follow His Story through his Word, we are able to listen as He tells it, and as He tells us the things He has done. We can see His characteristics consistently shown as we see Him in action, as we hear what He has made, and as He acts in relationships. We see His righteousness in the way He reacts to anything that violates that righteousness.

The Old Testament Scripture provides the foundational revelation of God as man's sovereign, omnipotent, omnipresent, holy, loving, righteous, merciful and immutable Creator, Lawgiver, Judge and Saviour. It makes sense to start a story at the beginning, following a logical sequence so that the whole story is understood. A journey begins at one point and goes to another. Buildings start from the foundations.

? DISCUSSION POINTS

1. What comes to mind when you consider the idea of God valuing things done carefully, with good foundations laid and then built on meticulously? How do you think He has already been equipping you to work in this way? What areas do you think represent the biggest challenges for you personally as you consider contributing with excellence to His Purposes?

2. What do you think about the idea that people are very ready to "shrink God down", to make Him someone/something they are comfortable with? Do you think that even as believers we try to make Him someone we can understand, please, manage and even manipulate? Give some examples.

➡ ACTIVITIES

1. In less than a page, describe a particular evangelism approach that you are familiar with. (If you have been personally involved in something choose that one to focus on. If you aren't familiar with any then do some research.) Include these points:

- Is any attempt made to present the Gospel within the narrative of God's Word?

- How much, and what *kind* of, effort is made to prepare people's hearts before the Gospel is presented?

- Where does the primary focus seem to be? On:
  (a) felt needs and possible benefits of becoming a Christian OR their real state before God as righteous Creator and Judge.
  (b) *their* response and what they have to do to be saved OR God's response to their need and what He *did* for them through the Cross?

- Is there any plan for taking someone on beyond salvation to understanding more of God's Word?

1.5 What's so great about Foundational Teaching?

 OBJECTIVES OF THIS TUTORIAL

To give an overview of Foundational Teaching and how it is used as a part of the equipping process for church planters in the *Cross-Cultural Essentials* curriculum.

Introduction

You'll be hearing a lot about Foundational Teaching in this course. As a matter of fact, you could say it's the **core** of the *Cross-Cultural Essentials* curriculum.

You might have heard of "Chronological Teaching"… That is usually used to refer to a set of materials – *Firm Foundations*. That material will be a resource for us in the Church foundations part of the *Cross-Cultural Essentials* curriculum. But when we say "Foundational Teaching", we are thinking even wider than one particular set of materials. We are really talking about a whole way of viewing God's Word.

A Biblical Foundation for Equipping

The description of the first of the four foundational areas of the *Cross-Cultural Essentials* curriculum is:

> Biblical foundations – understanding, living and teaching God's Word as a cohesive whole.

Our desire is for you to develop a view of God's Word as one entire, seamless description of what God has revealed, about Himself, about the Spirit world, about Creation, about man and about His intentions. God's revelation comes to us in different discourse styles or genres - some is Narrative, some is Poetry, Rhetoric, Polemic etc. But in the bigger sense, it is important to think of it as one Narrative – One Story: a seamless description of all that has been, is and will be, with God as the Master Storyteller.

Stories are part of who we are; part of our idiom; *It's a long story, Don't tell stories, That's the story of my life, The same old story, So the story goes, To make a long story short…*. Every culture and language tells stories; creation myths, legends, epics (sometimes in dance, chants etc.), books, novels...favorite tales, and just every day anecdotes. Just about everyone loves to hear stories and most of us like to tell stories, and each person has their own story.

But, there is ONE STORY that gives meaning and relevance to all those individual stories.

There is ONE STORY through which we need to interpret every story we hear, every story that is told...This idea that there is a Single overarching Story that makes sense of everything is something that has been attacked in the last 50 – 60 years:

Modernism – beginning in the Enlightenment (18th Century) gradually rejected God and the Church as the Story Teller and put Man (Humanism) and all that Man could discover and make (Science & Technology) in that role.

Post-modernism or post-structuralism (in the mid-twentieth century) challenged this – described these "meta-narratives" (Science, Freudian psychology, political structures, economic theories, history, religion) as ways of maintaining power. Language, the very words we use, were drained of their validity. Each person tells their own story. Each sub-group, each culture, etc.

Post-modernism says that words are only sounds, or symbols, without meaning. So the commonly held belief (although no one can function consistently like this) is that there is no universal meaning, no truth, no Story... that makes sense of language, or gives it meaning.

Words/Language have become separated from Meaning.

Post-modernism itself has been criticized as self-refuting, because it is a whole way of viewing things (a meta-narrative). Post-modernists reply that this critique is a modernist, one....the arguments go round and round.

The One who communicates

The One who communicates and makes sense of everything was there all along with God – was, in fact, God himself. Everything owes its existence, its reality, to Him. It was through this One who communicates and makes sense of things, that God gave everything its existence and life; and through His life God showed us clearly all the things he wants us to know.

> **JOHN 1:1-4** In the beginning the Word already existed. The Word was with God, and the Word was God. He existed in the beginning with God. God created everything through him, and nothing was created except through him. The Word gave life to everything that was created, and his life brought light to everyone.

As we have heard in previous tutorials: There is a Story-teller - He created a race of listeners - He is committed to telling us his Story - His Story is complete and cohesive.

So everything in the *Cross-Cultural Essentials* curriculum hangs on this reality. We want to help you understand this more fully – the way God's Story hangs together...the way it makes sense of everything... and that it is the absolute authority. That He has Spoken, and continues to Speak, to tell His Story.

How is the curriculum structured to help you understand God's Word as a cohesive whole?

Module 1

From Tutorial 1.7 onward Module 1 Tutorials tell God's Narrative from Creation to Christ. There will also be Discussion points, some research and study, some practical assignments to go along with the Biblical Narrative as part of each Tutorial.

We'll spend time talking about the foundational truths, how it relates to your own experience. How it contrasts with our culture, how you would try to share those things with someone you know. We will discipline ourselves to stay with the Biblical Narrative...to see how Truth builds, one truth upon another. How it ties together. How the solutions to important questions, moral, ethical, spiritual issues have their foundations and roots in the Biblical narrative.

Module 2

Looks back at the Biblical Narrative from Creation to Christ from the point of view of the identity change that has taken place for a believer - a new identity, access to God, coming together with other believers, looking back at the Biblical narrative from a totally new perspective.

Module 2 also covers Acts (our history, identity, mission, the Spirit's work, the Task, the completion of God's Revelation in the New Testament.

Module 3

Covers the Biblical Narrative from Romans (how we are to live, how we deal with sin, the basis for our service), and Ephesians (God's plan for His Church, what we have in Christ, His plan for marriages and families)

So what are the distinctives of "Foundational Teaching"?

It presents God - not man - as the central character in His Story.

1. It _tells_ and _teaches_ God's Story from the beginning...and from "the ground up", layer by layer, truth upon truth.

2. It focuses on what God says are peoples' real needs, rather than on their *felt needs*.
3. It presents Biblical Truth within its historical, geographical, cultural and linguistic context.
4. It applies Truth at a "heart" and worldview level.

Foundational Teaching is our shorthand way of talking about a whole view of God's Word, of Truth, not just how we teach 'people overseas', but how we understand Truth works, how it fits together, how it is meant to be viewed, and how it builds foundationally, piece by piece, block by block, idea by idea. And it is about us needing to begin with God himself…that knowing anything, and understanding how things are, understanding ourselves, other people, the world around us, having purpose…these only happen when we've first of all understood God.

God tells his Story to the world, not only through *words* but also through the *lives* of His people.

But Stories are not just understood, they are LIVED out. They shape how we feel we need to survive and therefore our view or who we understand we are, how we relate to others, what is important to us, and how we spend our time and energy. They are not just external Stories about we have to place ourselves within them and so they also determine our behavior.

> **1 THESSALONIANS 2:7** We didn't just share the Gospel with you, but our lives.
>
> **2 CORINTHIANS 3:3** …you are a letter from Christ showing the result of our ministry among you. This "letter" is written not with pen and ink, but with the Spirit of the living God. It is carved not on tablets of stone, but on human hearts.

Ultimately, our desire is for you to equip yourselves to contribute not just to people accepting the Truth in a theoretical way, not just to become adherents of a particular ideology, a religion, to become Christians….but to be living examples of the life of Christ for others. Once this Identity change takes place for people – they become different people to who they were before – then God wants to continue to tell them His Story, His True Version of Reality, so they;

- are able to enjoy their relationship with Him,
- appreciate Him and worship Him as He deserves
- understand their Identity, their History, their place in His Story
- become useful members of His family

- be light and salt in their communities
- contribute effectively within their local bodies as part of the Great Commission

That's what we want to help you equip yourselves to contribute to. To do that effectively, you need more than just to understand God's Word in a theoretical way. You need more than just to have insights into your own worldview and culture or an understanding of other worldviews. You need even more than knowing how to share Truth in those contexts…

If we're going to be the catalyst for other people to be willing to put aside their survival Stories, to go against the assumptions of their culture and community, to go through painful changes and adjustments, to actually change their values and beliefs at a fundamental level – then for us, this has to be more than an external set of facts or doctrines.

As you work to equip yourself with this understanding of God's Story, you will find that impacts the way you relate to your Friends and Family, the way you interact in the wider Community, and the part you play in your Church.

Understanding the other stories

The *Cross-Cultural Essentials* curriculum is all about helping a generation of church planters to equip themselves for the world's neediest contexts. The Biblical, Communication, Church Planting and Contextual Foundations areas of the program are designed to work together to equip you to tell God's Story to people who need it most, who for whatever reason don't have opportunity to hear His Story in a way they can understand.

But as we discussed in previous tutorials, no society, no culture, no community or individual is without some kind of Story already. The universe has a feeling of order about it. It works. Things clearly have a purpose, some kind of meaning. There's a sense too that human life must be about something. At a deep level people want some kind of answers. To know why. In order to survive the big scary universe we find ourselves in, we put ourselves at its center and gradually work out how to make everything work for us. Moving out from our local space and time…from the purely physical, the most basic needs of food, sleep and comfort. We have an inbuilt need to make sense of things, to survive - so we build our picture, we learn to tell a Story, that answers our emotional needs, our need for security, our need for companionship, to feel "at home", to feel loved… And we're told a Story by the people we interact with. Our parents, siblings, friends… gradually being affected more and more by the wider society. When we watch TV, cartoons, have books read to us, when we see the way other people behave, the way society functions (lines on the road, frames around doors, windows, boundaries between gardens and lawns, certain kinds of music, particular food... we learn what's normal, what's clean, what's not, what's nice)

This is what a Culture is, a society's Worldview. What we call a "culture" is a way of roughly grouping together people who share a similar "Story"; a common description of the world and how to survive in it... also of what lies beyond it. By definition, Stories other than God's comprehensive description of reality are not coherent... they don't tie together, they have gaps, they are mixed together... So don't picture people or culture's having well-defined, tight storylines. So for you to be equipped to contribute to church planting efforts among the neediest people, here are the steps the *Cross-Cultural Essentials* curriculum will take you through;

1. Understand God's Story in its entirety, "from the ground up".
2. Understand our own Worldview (the assumptions, what we take for granted, what has built into our values, beliefs).
3. Compare the two and adjust our views.
4. Begin to picture other worldviews... other Stories.
5. Begin to consider how to share God's Story in a way that will resonate and allow people to accept it as *their* Story, the true version of reality.
6. Be equipped to recognize and overcome some of the barriers and challenges involved in that task - language, culture, identity, relationships, communication, etc.

Summary

A *foundational* view of God's Story – is the core of the *Cross-Cultural Essentials* curriculum. It is about us helping you equip yourselves to;

- understand God's Word as one comprehensive, authoritative "Story" – His true version of how things are.
- live out of that Story, i.e. To take the opportunity to see how much it shapes your lives, and to adjust what's necessary
- teach His Story... to know how to listen to and understand people, and then share His Story in such a way that it grips their hearts, changes their lives and becomes their Story

TUTORIAL 1.5

? DISCUSSION POINTS

1. How would you describe the Story of our culture? Write out some points about the questions people ask and how you think many people answer those questions.

1.6 Preparation for Creation to Christ

✓ OBJECTIVES OF THIS TUTORIAL

This is for learners to prepare for the next set of tutorials that cover God's Narrative from Creation to Christ, to understand the process of working through the tutorial material, and the purpose of the discussion questions.

Steps to working through the Tutorials

Work through the rest of the Module 1 tutorials in the following way;

1. Read the **Tutorial** as you listen to the **Audio** or watch the **Video**.

2. Read and think through the **Discussion Points** (at the end of each Tutorial) and be prepared to talk about these questions. You could take notes on your thoughts or write out a longer answer if you like. For those doing the full *Cross-Cultural Essentials* curriculum with a facilitator this will be the basis for your discussion.

3. Do the **Activities and Assignments** (at the end of each Tutorial) and submit any written material to your facilitators.

What is the purpose of the Discussion Points?

The discussion points will be used as a basis for discussion with a facilitator, if this is the way chosen to use the material. Read the following notes so you might better understand the purpose of the discussion points that are included with each tutorial.

The Discussion Points in the Biblical Foundations Tutorials were developed with these things in mind;

1. To help people to engage with Truth in such a way that their own worldview assumptions are held up to the light of God's Word.

   - This is done *chronologically* (following the narrative of God's own story) and *foundationally* (each layer of Truth being added only after the previous, more basic strata are solidly in place).

- The discussion points are intended to help in the process by prompting people to consider the influences and building blocks that have shaped their own worldviews, and those of the culture they are most familiar with, as they engage with the narrative of God's Word.

2. Some of the suggested discussion points are more theoretical and objective: about what people "out there" think and say. Others, as already mentioned, are more about the participant's own preconceptions and worldview assumptions. Some are more subjective and touch on our emotional or personal responses to the Truth about God, who He is and what He does. Discussions should cover the whole scope of these different areas.

3. Discussions in many "Bible Studies" can quickly lose focus and therefore their effectiveness. The discussion points are intended to help generate discussion while keeping it relevant and clearly connected to the material covered in the tutorial itself. It is important for people to become familiar with this kind of discussion, so they become equipped themselves to teach material and then encourage discussion that is relevant to the foundational truths that a passage of God's Word is bringing out.

4. Although the purpose of these discussion points is to raise questions and issues which are not directly covered in the tutorials themselves, they are (as has been stated) still very much related to the part of God's Word being covered. So in that sense, just like the tutorials themselves, any ensuing discussion should also be foundational. In other words, even though the participants are believers and no doubt very familiar with the Bible, as an *equipping* process the discussions will be most effective if they engage with the "layer" of Truth being covered at that point, rather than moving on. So any applications to their lives should be made as much as possible *in light of whatever Truth has already been covered up to that point*. Again, this models for them, and therefore equips them also, in how to have fruitful discussions with people without jumping prematurely to Truth *for which no foundations have yet been laid.*

1.7 The Bible is God's message to all people

 OBJECTIVES OF THIS TUTORIAL

This tutorial introduces the Biblical Narrative, what it actually is, and how we are going to be covering it in the rest of the Module 1 tutorials.

Focused on God

So much of our lives are focused on ourselves. We think about our time, money, energy, emotions and our own thoughts. We are primarily concerned with our needs, desires, appetites, worries, etc. This is our default as human beings, like a compass always pointing back to ourselves.

Because of this compass that points to ourselves, we often come to God's Word to see what we can get out of it. Or perhaps what we are meant to do.

As we go through the Biblical Narrative over the coming months, we need to come to it putting all of that aside and honestly seek to find out what God wants to tell us. Let's let the focus be on Him. We want Him to be the One to tell us about Himself. From there we can more clearly see His view of the world, and also learn His view of us. Let's take the opportunity to work against our self-seeking default and allow this to be about Him. His Story.

Tracing the Biblical narrative

Instead of jumping around and grabbing what we want to from the Bible, we'll trace the flow of history as God tells it. We'll try to discipline ourselves to think in terms of the truth-foundations covered up to that point. Following the main story line - chronologically - or in the order in which those events happened and in the way He told it.

The Biblical Narrative is the Story of Him dealing with people. We will not be covering every detail, but will be touching on key events. This should serve to give us a fresh view of how things tie together - of God acting in time and space. Interacting with His Creation, with human beings.

Threads and Themes

We won't try to cover everything in the Bible. To do that would be years worth of material, incredibly, endlessly deep. Instead, we'll be looking at the major Themes, motifs, big subject lines. We will look at how they run through stories, books, lives and events that are included in the Narrative of God's Word. Our focus will be the themes that begin with who God is, and then play out in history, and finally play out for us. We don't want to get sidetracked into many possible subjects.

Foundations

As we go, we'll consider the underlying Truth, and truths. We'll ask God to teach us, firstly, more about Himself than we already know. Also about the way He sees reality, the universe. What are His views & perspectives – the way things actually are. We'll try to draw our attention to those things as we go. And we'll ask ourselves where we might have gaps or need to readjust our view. And ask Him to correct those things at the very foundation of the way we see the world, the way we relate to Him and the way we deal with others.

God's Word, God's Voice

We want to remember the incredible privilege we have of having God's Word. Of having His Voice speaking to us. We don't want to take that for granted - a possible danger for those of us brought up in Christian families or in a culture where His Word is freely available to us. We have the privilege of having this record of what He gave to His prophets to write.

> **2 TIMOTHY 3:16** All Scripture is inspired by God...

"Inspired" means - of extraordinary quality, as if arising from some external creative impulse, e.g. *Her singing performance was inspired*.

But God's Word is much more than that. In a way that only God could possibly do, He guided the thoughts of the prophets so they wrote down exactly what He intended. They were real people, using real language, that was culturally appropriate, but they wrote God's very carefully intended message.

So we can truly say that the Bible is a book (the only one) authored by God. And now, no less amazingly, He is speaking to us through those same words written down by those different men so long ago. In our language, just as culturally relevant to us.

Historically accurate

The Bible is not intended to be a history textbook as such. It isn't bound to the conventions of "history" as a humanities subject. It doesn't have to prove itself, defend its own viability and authenticity. But the Bible is historically accurate. Any perceived historical and scientific gaps, are in our understanding, not in the Bible. It is historically accurate, because it is God's true account of how things actually were, are and will be.

God is speaking to each of us

Most of all, let's remember how amazing it is to have the eternal, Creator God speaking to us. Let's continue to remind ourselves of what it means that He graciously speaks to us. As humans, and most personally and specially, as His children.

 **DISCUSSION POINTS**

1. In general terms what has been your experience of hearing and engaging with God's Word? What are the similarities and differences in that experience with the way the Firm Foundations overview is described?

2. What are some of the things in society that work against the idea that God's Word has authority...even against the idea that there is Truth?

3. Consider the issue of commitment that is required to study God's Word in this way and talk in practical terms about how you think you can find time to engage at the level that is needed.

 ACTIVITIES

1. Watch some clips online about the accuracy with which the text of the Old Testament Scriptures has been preserved over many centuries.

2. Listen to the song "Ancient Words" by Michael W. Smith and think about the lyrics. It can be found on YouTube.

1.8 The Bible tells us what God is like

 OBJECTIVES OF THIS TUTORIAL

This tutorial will help us to think over what God - our Storyteller - is like and how He has chosen to reveal Himself.

Last time
We thought about how we'll approach this study of God's Word. We thought about the incredible fact that God has spoken to us through the narrative of His Word. It is a factual, reliable record of His interactions with us as the human race. His voice speaking to the world, and to us, His children.

Knowing the One who is telling the Story
Before jumping right into the Biblical narrative, we'll briefly consider what God - our Storyteller - is like. For us these things are a reminder of stuff we've no doubt been taught. It provides reference points for things that the Narrative is going to show us about Him. All of us have wondered about what God is like. God doesn't provide a list, a set of propositions, about Himself. People have come up with those "Doctrines of God" to systematize their understanding. But those things come out of His revelation, which is the record of the things He's done, said, thought, events in which He's played a part, His interaction with people, and their thoughts about Him. We should be gripped by the possibilities, excited by the journey.

Unlike everything else, God just is
It's something of a paradox to have finite minds trying to understand the infinite. Time-bound beings trying to picture someone eternal. It doesn't fit with anything we've seen and experienced. God knows that, of course. He doesn't try to prove his eternality with logical proofs. In His Word, as our Storyteller, He just says that's the way it is. It's His true version of how things are, including who He is, and He just says that. That also means, that unlike everything and anyone else, He is not dependent. Not contingent – one of the arguments for the existence of God that goes back to Thomas Aquinas in the

13th century. Everything and everyone is contingent on something or someone else – this would extend back endlessly...except that we always come to God. His existence is the great reality on which every other part of reality hangs. For us who know Him, that's solid rock under our feet. A sure place to stand and learn more. Become more. Also good to remember that He doesn't need anything from us.

He delights in His children, loves to interact with us, is thrilled when we depend on Him, praise Him, but He doesn't need us. We, on the other hand, desperately need Him.

No limits in time or space
So He's unlimited by the confines of time. We live at the point (the present) of the past becoming the future. He exists at all the points, all the moments...

Another thing to note about our Storyteller - He is Spirit. A word we use for describing a personal existence not contained within a physical body. So He's not tied to a given place. We can only speculate in a feeble way about what that means. And the implications for His understanding of how things tie together. To experience all events simultaneously is to understand them fully – what is cause, what is effect, how one thing relates to another. We see from a limited, narrow perspective... His perspective is limitless. It's not always a comfortable thought though, is it? – being unable to escape from God's presence – even for those who know Him well. Note: This reality of God being present everywhere in the universe simultaneously is quite different to pantheistic thinking that God is everything in the universe.

Our Storyteller is a real person who speaks to us as people. His voice resonates in our ears. We know Him. Yes, He's Spirit. Yes, eternal. Yes, limitless, but He knows us, and He speaks so that we can know Him.

The trinity
Of course in our brief reminder of Who is speaking to us, we should remember that He is Three. The mystery that we call "the Trinity". God being One and yet Three. Something else we accept by faith, knowing that we come from a human viewpoint. But we know the Father, the Son and the Helper – the Spirit.

He is the Master of it all
Finally, as we consider who He is, we should put into perspective the fact that this One is over everything. He knows everything, He's more powerful than anything or anyone. He made it. He made us. All the powerful beings. All the energy wrapped up in the universe. He owns it. It is His. In His Story, His Word, He calls himself things like "The Most High", "The Lord". He gets to say how things are, what's right, what's wrong. How things ultimately turn out. But He is not "out there" the detached Storyteller about the

universe. Not the distant clock-maker who set things spinning on its own. He's invested, personally involved, fully engaged. That's the amazing thing, isn't it? This three-in-one Ruler over everything, who is everywhere, all the time and who always was, totally without need… He actually cares enough to tell us about Himself. He wants us: poor, frail, needy, disfigured, rebellious people to know Him, because He cares about us.

DISCUSSION POINTS

1. Is the picture of God revealing Himself through history something that has been part of your experience?

2. In Sunday school, youth group, church etc. did you hear the Bible stories taught in a way that tied them together as one entire narrative – God's Story?

3. Think of some people who are not believers that you know and describe their view of God. What are some of the major influences that have shaped this view?

4. What do the things said about God in this lesson mean for you in a day-to-day sense: that he is eternal, a spirit, not limited by time and space etc.?

ACTIVITIES

1. Read at least the initial definitions (more if you like) of the following terms:

- Pantheism
- Deism
- Theism

2. Choose one of the Discussion Points above and write an extended response (limit it to around a page).

1.9 God created angels, the heavens and the earth

 OBJECTIVES OF THIS TUTORIAL

Learners will continue to explore and discuss the themes and the truths presented in God's Narrative. The portions of Scripture referred to in this tutorial are: **Genesis 1:1-2, Job 38**

Last Time
Before launching into the flow of the narrative, we reminded ourselves who our Storyteller is. He is Eternal, experiencing past, present and future. No limits in time and space. Not dependent, the great Reality. He owns everything, He's over everything. He writes the Story as well as telling it.

The spirit beings that existed before the universe
Before starting into the narrative, we'll remind ourselves about who, apart from God, was there. God had brought into existence an enormous number of beings. The Biblical narrative doesn't focus on these beings that predate our world, but we get glimpses and clues which we can piece together into a composite picture. We'll do that briefly now, because they play an immediate role in the narrative itself. And they play a role today – any time someone is hearing God's Story.

They are "spirits" as a collective term – again, all we have for referring to *personal beings that are not limited to our physical world, to bodies*. The Narrative often refers to them, or to some of them, as "angels". It's always worth stopping and thinking about words, terms we use and the ideas, assumptions that cluster around them. Think about terms, words, "spirits" and "angels" and the images, concepts that have been attached to those by popular culture. Try to identify and put aside those assumptions so that the Biblical narrative itself shapes your understanding of the role of these beings.

A few things we *do* know about them from the Bible:

As we've said, they predate the world, the physical universe we live in - we're told the angles were witnesses to its creation.

We know that there are lots of them, perhaps millions.

They don't have bodies like ours, but at least some have the ability to appear in our physical, material dimension.

Because they were created, like us, they're dependent, contingent… not eternal.

Of course, because it was God creating them, they were all originally perfect.

They have personality - not robotic or controlled.

We'll see this emerge from the Narrative. To personal beings He creates, He gives real freedom to choose whether they'll listen to Him as God or go their own way.

And he gave them varying capabilities to fit the roles He had for them. A whole range of power, and knowledge and capacity to rule. How, or exactly what, is not entirely clear to us, but some at least have what's called "dominion", influence, some level of control.

The greatest among these servant angel beings was called Lucifer. Also created perfect and given incredible abilities to lead in their responsibilities. These beings, multitudes of them, were there at *the beginning*.

The Story begins

…with a straightforward statement that when it all started, was when God created "the heavens and the earth". Not "once upon a time", but "in the beginning", or, "To get things started". Of course there is eternity as a backdrop, if you like, but really the Story which God wants to tell us – which we can relate to, His interaction with us – begins then. We're all only too aware of the starting points of stories, as told by others…for our society, that is primarily "Science". We need to note that that story along with its starting points, is the product of predetermined stances – a materialistic, closed system. The trajectories of their assumptions, a kind of faith, logically points to that starting point – big bangs ("short-hand" for saying "A beginning without a personal God").

God's Story, the only one qualified to tell the Story, begins with Him creating when there was nothing physical, material, in existence. A very difficult concept for us from inside that physical, material world to grapple with. But that's what this Story is – God acting in a "God way", from outside the bounds of what is, otherwise, possible. Remember, it's His Story. His reality.

So He made stuff where nothing existed. That's part of being God. Being able to do that. Unique, of course, to Him. Not even angels with all their "spirit-world" understanding and abilities can do that. Job 38 describes this creation, and says the angels actually shouted for joy as they observed Him doing it.

What does it take to create?

It's beyond our human language's capacity – which reflects our minds' inability to begin to understand – what power and knowledge, this represents. To bring something into being where nothing existed. It involves knowing what *stuff* is, an exhaustive understanding of energy and light, motion, matter. If we could bring all together for one instance, all the information contained in all the websites and servers, all the power in all the nuclear reactors, the electrical grids, the ships it wouldn't be a blip on the radar of his knowledge and power. It wouldn't bring something out of nothing. It's His Story.

Things weren't yet put in order

God telling the story (Gen 1:2) describes the earth as created – the raw substance was there – but without order. Swirling chaos, dark, empty and lifeless. Water covering the planet. Uninhabitable. Not yet a fit place for anything or anyone. But His Spirit there, ready to do what God - the Three in One God - had planned *from before the beginning*. God knew where He would take this. Where His Story would go next.

GOD CREATED ANGELS, THE HEAVENS AND THE EARTH

❓ DISCUSSION POINTS

1. How does the idea of there being spirits and a spiritual world fit into your view of things and your daily experience of life?

2. What is your view of creation and the whole issue of whether the Genesis account is literal or not?

3. Were you taught science and other subjects in school/university from an evolutionist, old-earth perspective?

4. Do you feel there is any tension between the fact that God is all-powerful and the pain and suffering we see in the world?

➡ ACTIVITIES

1. Ask someone you know who is a Christian, and also someone who isn't, these questions and record their answers (try to keep it well under a page of notes):

- What do you think of when you hear the terms (a) "spirit" (b) "spiritual"?
- Do you believe in angels? If so, do they have bodies?
- Do you think the spirits of the dead can influence this world?
- What are your ideas about spirits and angels based on?

1.10 God revealed through His creative acts

 OBJECTIVES OF THIS TUTORIAL

Learners will continue to explore and discuss the themes and the truths presented in God's Narrative. The portions of Scripture referred to in this tutorial are: **Genesis 1:3-25**

Last time

We reminded ourselves who other than God existed. He had created a huge number of spirit messengers to do His will, equipped with the knowledge and ability to fulfill what He gave them to do, lead by the most able, the most powerful of their number, Lucifer. They were witnesses to the incredible beginning of all things as we know them, the "beginning", when God began His creation, from nothing… no matter, no energy. We left the story with the Spirit ready to bring order out of the uninhabitable chaos, darkness and emptiness.

Light

So in Genesis 1:3 the Narrative starts into the specifics of God creating the universe as we know it. And significantly, creation is described as an action of communication, "Then God said…", speaking things into existence, immediately and exactly as He intended. The first thing He spoke into existence, of course, was light. In that swirling, chaotic, darkness… light, with all its implications. Illumination yes, but energy, potential for life and growth. And all it symbolizes about God's revelation of Himself, through creation. Knowing He would create beings with eyes that would need light to see. Light for warmth, a world of light… for us. And as for each of His creative acts to come, God noted that the light He'd spoken into existence "was good" (Genesis 1:4). He's telling us in His Narrative that everything He made was that way. *"It's who I am, I am good, the things I make are good, what I speak into existence is good in every way, good and perfect to me and for you. I cannot do things otherwise. I don't make flawed things. It's not who I am".*

Day and night

Continuing the Story in Genesis 1:5 God divides light and darkness. The planet which would be home to the human race, which would mean so much to Him (and also cost Him so much) would spin in space for as long as He wanted it to, half light and half dark. Significantly, there were no other planets yet, no sun, moon, or stars. So light, now ordered into its designated time to illuminate the earth, was not the product of any source. God, right here at the beginning of His narrative, is letting us know that He is not subject to even the most fundamental laws - thermodynamics. He is their author. Humans only discover and describe whatever systems He embedded. So He could make light without a source. He could have the earth partially dark and partially light, without a sun and planetary rotation as a cause. He's the great Cause. The Light-maker. The Initiator. The Story Writer and Teller.

The atmosphere

God continues bringing order from the chaos, which is something that He does. Who he is. He commands – declares – that there will be a space... with water below (still covering the planet) and a layer above.

Dry land and plant life

Each day, more order. Now, on the third day, the oceans are pushed into place by his command and dry land appears, mountains, islands, slopes and plains.

The planet is starting to look a bit more habitable. God declares that everything is good, perfect... just what He's after. But it's barren. There's no life, and as well as being a communicating God and a God of light, He's also a God of life. Life is what He's about. He gives life and delights in life. So now, as recorded in Genesis 1:11 He describes plant life. But in words that are themselves alive and productive, fruitful.

So that by the end of the third day of creation, the planet is covered in plant life, trees, shrubs, flowers...and importantly, with seeds that will reproduce the same genera, species and families. The potential for self-propagating life contained in each. Each a small testimony to the creative power of God's voice. No blind chance here... careful, planned, intentional creation.

The rest of the planets

Now, on the fourth day of creation, the planets. From the small and specific detail of plant life, some on a microscopic scale, to the mind-blowing scale of the universe... containing billions of stars and perhaps infinitely big. We simply don't have scales to measure or scales of reference that make any sense. In all of that, the sun and moon and stars were created that are exactly what is needed for life to flourish on this little planet we call earth. Because God the communicator, the light and life-giver, is also loving. He was preparing a place for us, for humans. Somewhere orderly and habitable. A home.

Marine life and birds

Continuing His Story, He fills the oceans and rivers and lakes with creatures, and birds that fly above the planet. The variety and beauty are astounding. When we see these things and call them beautiful, that's because God created them, and us to see them in that way.

"Beauty" is a concept without meaning unless it is something invested by God in both the object and the subject. The story of Science sees no beauty. The physical world, and we in it, are reduced, in that story, to systems of particles and blips of energy… the product of chance or some incoherent survival force.

Animal life

So this first part of the story ends on the sixth day with the creation of animals in Genesis 1:24, 25. Again, with the inbuilt DNA models that will reproduce themselves generation after generation, unique and consistent. An incredibly diverse, wonderful world of creatures of all shapes and sizes.

So this part of the narrative of who He is was told, and continues to be told day after day, in every corner of the world… sometimes seen by humans but often carried out in the depths of oceans, in the far-reaches of the universe, on a scale too small for us to see, or in jungles and deserts with no human witnesses. A testimony to the creative power and brilliance of our God.

But for all its diversity, beauty and complexity, and though God said it was all good – all perfectly what He wanted… all of this is just background for what is about to come. God is about to create a race of beings for which the planet was now ready. That's where He chose to take His Story.

DISCUSSION POINTS

1. Trace some of the results different starting points have on someone's worldview (e.g. the purpose of the material world: a "closed" system without outside influence vs. a reality defined by an involved, ever-present Creator. How do you think these things relate to current issues like the drive for us to "preserve the planet"?)

2. Describe some of the factors (a) external, i.e. in our society and culture (b) internal, i.e. in our own thinking and attitudes that might be obstacles to us appreciating God's creation. As believers, how do you think we develop a greater sense of wonder and worship of God as our Creator Father?

ACTIVITIES

1. Other than the Biblical Genesis account and Scientific Materialism's version (Big Bang, Darwinian evolution), in approximately half a page describe another version of "Origins" that you have heard about or are familiar with. e.g. Hinduism, Buddhism.

2. Spend at least 30 minutes outside on a clear night observing the sky. Note down anything that you feel is reflected there about who He is and what He is like.

1.11 God created Adam and Eve

 OBJECTIVES OF THIS TUTORIAL

Learners will continue to explore and discuss the themes and the truths presented in God's Narrative. The portions of Scripture referred to in this tutorial are: **Genesis 1:26-31, 2:1-7**

Last time

Through the words of the writer of Genesis, God gives us His true account of His creation of the universe. He did it carefully and intentionally, and everything came about just as He wanted it to be… perfect in every way. Speaking into existence light, day & night, air and everything else needed to nurture life. The sun, moon & stars. The oceans and areas of dry land. Then plants and animals… life bursting out and able to reproduce itself.

"In our image…"

Now we come to the climax of the whole of this Creation account. Everything else was preparation, a backdrop, a dwelling without inhabitants… the plant and animal life each in their way containing life, but the true life of God would only be given to these, the final created beings. The rest of Creation was about fulfilling their physical needs and pointing them to God, so they'd see evidence of Himself all around them. But to appreciate and respond to that, and most importantly to Him, they'd have to be a certain kind of being… one that could know God and relate to Him.

In the part of the Narrative recorded in Genesis 1:26, God gives us an amazing and tantalizing glimpse at the interaction of the Three-in-One God. As He, they, plan the creation of this special kind of being, a race, human beings it says, "in our image, to be like us". Not the product of endless chains of blind chance, from the primeval sludge, through the primates and eventually something appearing "in the image of God". From the outset these beings would be something quite different from the rest of life on the planet. Different in creativity, in intellect, a capacity for wisdom, ability to communicate beyond the physical, having aesthetic capacity (appreciating beauty), a moral dimension (knowing right from wrong), relational, and with a spiritual dimension. This – the spiritual – is the real point.

God created a race of beings who have the capacity to hear His communication, to understand what He is saying, who He is, to be influenced emotionally, "in the heart", to have praise and worship well up spontaneously, and to want to do things that please Him, to decide in "the will" to align their actions with who He is. These beings would not be robotically programmed to obey. Clearly God wanted beings with real wills, who would resolve to love and obey Him.

With real responsibility

As well as being made *in His image*, God's narrative (Genesis 1:26) also makes another hugely significant point here. As the Writer and Teller of the Story, He would give these beings – humans – a genuine role, with real responsibility. The enormous potential – creatively, aesthetically, relationally etc. – would be given scope to flourish in the context of managing, caretaking, His Creation. And, most importantly, it would provide scope and opportunity for these humans to do everything in relationship…we could say "in community" with God. A perfect context in which to look to Him for guidance and encouragement. To use the capabilities He'd given them, but under His tutelage, His gracious leadership. Looking to Him as Father.

The first man and woman

A synopsis of the creation of the first man and woman is given (Genesis 1:27-30) then a bit later (Chapter 2), in more detail. First of all, the man – Genesis 2:7. The familiar description, forming him from the earth itself. From the most basic ingredient – dirt, soil – God creates the race that would be His image bearers. God is always interested in the substance, the essence, of life.

The form, moulded from the earth, was just an empty shell. Incapable of doing anything or fulfilling any purpose… Until God – the Giver and sustainer of Life - breathes His own life into it, and it becomes a *him*, a person. A living, breathing, communicating, responding being with intellect, emotions, a will and moral responsibility. And this person, this man, (who we know as Adam, from the Hebrew for "man") was the ancestor, the progenitor, of the entire human race.

God only created this one man, and one woman (whose creation we'll hear about). Part of their responsibility of caretaking the earth as God's representatives, His caretakers, was to reproduce so that the world would be populated by people. They were to found a race, the human race. In them, humanity existed in seed form, as it were. In those two lives, all the enormous God-given scope and potentiality was encapsulated. Created,

God says in 1:31, perfect. Exactly as He intended. Fashioned just as He wanted for them to play their appointed role in His Story.

Remember who was there witnessing all of this? The enormous number of spirit servants – angels – that God had made. Watching and wondering at the Creation of God.

Eager, no doubt, to see how the rest of His Story would unfold. Keenly observing the beginnings of this new race of beings – fashioned in the image of God Himself.

DISCUSSION POINTS

1. How does it impact you to think about the Bible's description of God carefully and systematically preparing a home for humans, and then placing them there - the best possible place for them?

2. Consider the implications of humans being created by God in his image (with all that entails) as opposed to some other starting point; evolutionary, non-personal, unknowable.

3. Take a moment to consider the significance of every person who has ever lived being the descendants of one man and one woman.

4. What are the implications of God giving a very real and enormous responsibility to human beings of caretaking the earth He created? What does this say to you about the kind of relationship God intended (and intends) to have with us, his image bearers?

ACTIVITIES

1. In about half a page write, in your own words, how the angels might describe what they saw and felt as observers of God's Creation, including the creation of man.

1.12 God placed Adam in Eden

OBJECTIVES OF THIS TUTORIAL

Learners will continue to explore and discuss the themes and the truths presented in God's Narrative. The portions of Scripture referred to in this tutorial are: **Genesis 2:1-17**

Last time
We were following God's Story of His Creation, how He, the Three-In-One God, decided to make a race of beings in His, "their", image. With intelligence, creativity, aesthetic appreciation, emotions, will, the capacity to know God, to communicate with Him, to love and obey Him. God planned to give human beings a responsibility of managing the earth and overseeing the lesser beings. And so He formed Adam and breathed life into him.

Unlike us, God doesn't leave stuff half done
So in His Narrative, God makes the point in Genesis 2:1 that Creation got done. He completed everything He had planned to do. This is no insignificant point. For one thing, it is very different to most humans.

We tend to start lots of different things in our lives, and leave quite a number of them half done. We make resolutions and commitments that we don't follow through on. In our society that is almost expected. And we don't necessarily hold ourselves accountable… perhaps a mild pang of guilt, but hey, that's "just what we're like". Not trying to exhort us to follow through on things, just drawing a contrast with God. He doesn't get discouraged, lose heart or interest, get into something else, and walk away… He always completes things He starts. And He does them right. They take as long as He intends and get finished exactly when He intends them to be done.

It seems a strange thing – the idea of the all-powerful God resting as described in Chapter 2. Of course we know it wasn't weariness. He hadn't run out of steam. The point here is that Creation, the entire universe and its inhabitants, were made, complete. He'd set in place the physical laws, the in-built balances, the systems, the capacity for ongoing propagation... with all its breathtaking beauty - the evidence of His power, His life, the things He wanted to say about himself, and the people to appreciate it and Him. And so, because it was finished, He stopped. The way that He describes it in His Narrative to us is that He rested. This idea of rest from work, to stop from effort when it's the right time...will come up again in the Story. It's an important concept and He highlights it for us here at the beginning.

The Creator who seeks relationship

An important thing to note here... The things God calls Himself as He's telling His Story are always worth considering. Up to this point the Genesis narrative, throughout the Creation events, has referred to Him as God. Now – in the 2nd chapter of the Story, He calls himself *the Lord*. This is a much more personal term that is all about relating to His Creation, and particularly to the humans created in His image. Because that's also who He is. He always seeks relationship with man. Having created someone to know, love and follow Him, He reaches out "in person" to man... as we'll see, He doesn't wait on man to initiate this. And there's an echo of that in Him now calling Himself by this more personal name, Lord. Still in charge, still holy and righteous, still the Creator God, but also wanting to know and be known by human beings.

In the garden

God now tells us about how he placed the first man in a special garden He'd prepared (Genesis 2:7-8). You suspect that the word "garden" doesn't communicate very well to us, but then we've nothing better. We can only imagine that it was an incredible place, full of all the amazing growing things...there for their beauty and to be eaten.

Having prepared it as the best possible place it could be, He puts him there. No record of consultations and committee decisions. He knows what's best for him and He puts him there. He's God, "the Lord", and Adam belongs to Him, at least rightfully, belongs to Him. He puts him there as His caretaker manager of this place. Everything is as it should be.

The two trees

As we know, among the thousands of different amazing trees, plants, shrubs, grasses, flowers etc. were two trees that were hugely significant and which would play pivotal roles in the ongoing Story of God's interaction with humans.

The first - what the Narrative (Genesis 2:9) refers to as *The Tree Of Life* - he was given free access to along with all the other fruit in the garden. The second, with the portentous name, *The Tree Of The Knowledge Of Good And Evil*, he was expressly forbidden to eat from (Genesis 2:17). In fact, God stated clearly and unequivocally, if he did eat the fruit from *The Tree Of The Knowledge Of Good And Evil* he would die. As simple as that! Well, not quite so simple. The full, terrible, horrendous meaning of what would be involved in this "dying", this "death", would not play out fully until later. In fact, it's still being played out today, as we know and see every day and feel in our own lives. But that's in the Story to come.

For now, Adam has a choice. A real choice. God, again, giving freedom to the personal beings He creates to choose whether they'll listen and follow Him or not. Adam's choice is between Life – remember there's no death yet in this world - or, He can choose this thing called 'knowing good and evil', but that – so God has stated – will result in death. That tree and its fruit were not inherently evil or bad because God doesn't make anything bad.

There's also nothing inherently wrong in knowing good from evil – God does. But that's the point. God wanted this man - who He'd made in His image, who He'd placed in the best possible situation and to whom He'd given an incredible responsibility - to come to Him with his questions. God knew that would be best for Adam. He didn't make him to work out his own Story. No one can do that. There's only One Story Writer and Teller. This was the relationship God, the Lord, wanted with this man and with all humans who would come after. It's what he was, and we are, made for. For man to write his own narrative of how things are, or how he might think they should be would no longer be life. God wouldn't be able to relate to someone who'd gone his own way like that. And with God being who He is, there'd be no coming back. No whining second chances. The result might still look something like life, but once cut off from God, the Source of life, it would actually be a kind of living death. Eventually, when physical death would take him out of time and the physical world, it would mean eternal separation from God.

But for the time being, Adam is in the garden with all the wonderful potential still before him if he chooses life and the relationship with God that he was created for.

? DISCUSSION POINTS

1. Comment on the picture that emerges from the Creation account of God finishing, down to the last detail, everything He sets out to do.

2. What is your reaction to the thought that God has the absolute right to determine what is best for us and to put us into circumstances of His choosing? How does that relate to the concept of personal freedom that is so strongly held in our western societies?

3. What are some of the common assumptions that you hear people make about where their dead loved ones have gone? Think about how those assumptions have developed, where they come from etc.

1.13 God created a wife for Adam

 OBJECTIVES OF THIS TUTORIAL

Learners will continue to explore and discuss the themes and the truths presented in God's Narrative. The portions of Scripture referred to in this tutorial are: **Genesis 2:18-25**

Last time

We saw in the Narrative that, having completed His work of creation exactly as He wanted it to be, God simply stopped, or "rested". We noted that, in contrast to humans, He never leaves things half done or poorly done. He gets it completely right the first time. Also how God, "the Lord", using a more personal, relational name, described where He put the man, Adam – a perfect context in which he could flourish, fulfill his responsibilities and relate to God as Father and Guide. And about the two trees, and the life or death choice that they represented for Adam, and, therefore the human race.

God notes Adam's need

In the Narrative, the Three-in-One God already mentioned that He/They made a male and female version of human beings. But then, in the chronology of events, Adam is created – formed from the soil as we know, coming to life when God breathes His life into him.

God places Adam into this wonderful place – this garden – and then clearly instructs him about the two trees.

At this point, Adam is the only human being...we haven't yet heard the account of how the previously mentioned female is made. The Story (2:18) picks this up now and describes God, the personal, relating Lord God, observing that the man shouldn't be alone as a human.

He needs a companion, a helper.

God knows Adam completely. Knows his needs. He should, right? He planned, then made him after creating a world for him to live in. Significantly, He doesn't consult with Adam on this point. How could Adam know in what way he was lacking, to even begin to imagine a solution, much less set about supplying it? But God does know, He cares deeply, and He sets about providing what Adam really needs... God also knew what was needed for the accomplishment of His purposes - the thing which He'd put Adam here for, and tasked him with. Again, even though he'd been told the general scope of the task, he couldn't possibly know how to set about it or what was needed for its completion. But God knew that a female companion helper for Adam was essential if the planet was to be inhabited by a human caretaking race, bearing the image of God and relating to Him as their Guide and Father. A principle and pattern is being established which we'll see repeated numerous times in God's Story of Him relating to us as humans.

Naming the animals

We come to this fascinating part of the sequence of events - recorded in 2:19,20 – in which God brings the animals to Adam for him to name. Imagine the scene, as the appointed caretaker of the earth is introduced to its non-human inhabitants and gives each animal a name. This is not a cute Sunday school pantomime but a significant event whose full import we can only glimpse or speculate about.

The connections perhaps to God's creative speaking "and God said" and now, the man, made in His image, naming each animal. Or how the essence of things, of identity, is somehow tied up in their linguistic labels. And also the symbolic aspects of Adam taking a supervising ownership for what he has now seen and named himself. But we must let the Narrative, God's Story, provide its own balance. There is a healthy speculation and wonder, and there is an unhealthy and dangerous going beyond, and an inappropriate *reading into* what He has revealed.

God provides the perfect companion/helper

Despite observing closely and coming up with a linguistic description - a name - for each different animal. And no doubt marveling at God's creativity in the vast variety of the animal kingdom... It's apparent that in all that variety none of them is anything like Adam in the most basic essence of who he was. None of them could begin to fill his need for human companionship. None of them could possibly share in the life-essence of one created in the image of God... the animals were clearly something other, lesser than that. This seemingly simple account of events and the sparse commentary is profound in its implications.

There are no sophisticated arguments here about ethics or theories on macro-biology, but in God's true version of how things are, lay the foundations for complete and satisfying answers to all the troubling questions of mankind. Even as those who know Him now, we too are faced with the simple choice of whether to accept His version as the solid place from which questions are answered, OR to forever grope about in the sludge of our own self-perpetuating doubts.

Marriage an important part of God's Story

So the Narrative (2:21-22) completes the details of how God miraculously brings into existence the perfect companion helper for Adam. Taken from his body, his "flesh and bone".

And she is all that God intends. All that Adam needed. All that, as humans, they need for each other. They are equal - it was made clear earlier - in being made in the image of God with all that means. Adam, understandably, is delighted with this woman. "At last" he says…this is who he'd been looking for even if he didn't know it. The completion, as it were, of himself as a person.

And that, of course, is what marriage is. Not a human invention. Not an outmoded Christian convention or tradition. This is part of God's Story itself. An integral part of what He was and is about. Bringing two individuals together, leaving their former identity and primary loyalties within their birth family, and creating a new entity, a new family - a unit within which God's purposes (for them and the wider Creation) were to be fulfilled. And this picture, a marriage as God says it should be, will feature a number of times in His Story, a powerful picture, in fact an actual description, of Him relating to His people…but that's for later.

So without any evil in their hearts, without any sin to confuse or impinge on their delight together, it says (2:25) that their nakedness wasn't an issue. They were innocent in the most innocent of ways. Not foolishly naïve like innocence is often depicted, but innocent because they did not think, had no reason to think, about things in any other way. The relationship of the man, Adam, and the woman, Eve, and their companionship together and before God their Maker, was pure, was just as He intended it to be.

❓ DISCUSSION POINTS

1. As you think about the account of God bringing the first man and woman together as companions in this new world, what aspects of His character stand out to you

2. Consider the true freedom from guilt and fear that Adam and Eve enjoyed in the beginning. With that still in mind, comment on the rejection of personal accountability to God that is a hallmark of our society today.

3. In what ways (if any) do you feel the Genesis account of Adam and Eve's creation is at odds with society's current view of marriage, gender and sexuality?

➡ ACTIVITIES

1. Do some research on current trends in marriage, divorce and the family. In approximately half a page, describe the picture you get of marriage and what our society's view is on marriage and the family (provide statistics if necessary but mainly write in your own words). If you have time, note any contrasts you come across between the predominant western view and for example, Asian, Latin American or African perspectives.

1.14 Lucifer rebelled against God

 OBJECTIVES OF THIS TUTORIAL

Learners will continue to explore and discuss the themes and the truths presented in God's Narrative. The portions of Scripture referred to in this tutorial are: Ezekiel 28:12-19, Isaiah 14:13-15

Last time
Through the Narrative of His Word, God told us the details of how He had completed the creation of the image-bearing race He had planned. Knowing that it's not best for the man, Adam, to be alone, God says he'll make him a companion. Having seen and named all the other, lesser, animal beings, Adam finds no companion among them. When Adam meets the woman, made from his flesh and bone, he recognizes in her his perfect companion.

This, the first and archetypal marriage, is pure and perfect as God intended.

The angels and their leader, Lucifer
Before continuing with the Narrative, we need to fill in some background, which would have been familiar to the original Hebrew audience at the time these early parts of God's Story were being recorded. A tragic, calamitous event – a series of events, in fact, a chain of terrible choices - that would have enormous significance for the lives of Adam and Eve, for creation, and the future of the human race.

You'll remember that before we jumped into the Narrative, God's Story, as recorded in the Bible, we noted that He'd created a huge number of servant beings, messengers - angels - to undertake His purposes. As created beings they were, of course, inferior to God, but nonetheless had the necessary understanding and capabilities, real power and authority, to fulfill the tasks and responsibilities given them.

Lucifer - meaning Morning Star - the greatest among them (and like them created, of course, perfect by God) was a being of enormous authority and power. His position was pre-eminent among all created beings, the closest in fact to God's throne itself.

Rebellion

But here's the astounding thing. Instead of continuing faithfully and gratefully to serve God, the One to whom Lucifer owed all his authority, wisdom and capabilities in the first place...Lucifer rebelled.

As part of His Narrative, God would include a description of these events written by His prophet Ezekiel many centuries later. Ostensibly a funeral song for the King of Tyre, verses 12-19 of chapter 28, are also a tragic account of Lucifer as he was and as he became.

It describes him becoming entranced with his own "exquisite" beauty and corrupted by his own splendor, consumed with his lofty position...until he freely chose... (remember how God always give free choice to personal beings He creates)...he freely chose to rebel against God,

Forgetting his created, contingent, dependent existence, he even aspired to equality and perhaps dominance over God as supreme ruler of all things.

Another prophet, one of God's appointed storytellers, Isaiah, would give an account (Chapter 14:13, 14) of Lucifer making ridiculous, outrageous, statements that he would go up to heaven and be "like the Most High". Also remarkably, numerous other angels followed Lucifer in his rebellion.

God's response

Of course, it goes without saying that none of this took God by surprise. As we noted earlier, His knowledge of all things is complete, exhaustive. Likewise, God's sovereign rule was in no way threatened by this rebellion. Later, again through the words of Isaiah, (14:15) God would dismiss out of hand even the slightest possibility of success for Lucifer's plan. Asserting that, far from ever reaching the unattainable position Lucifer aspired to, he would be "brought down to the place of the dead, down to its lowest depths".

So the former leader of God's spirit messengers, trusted and favored, was stripped of his position and, along with the other rebellious angels, expelled from God's holy presence, from Heaven.

Satan, present and future

From this point on in God's Story he would usually be called *Satan* - the Enemy - and his spirit followers *demons, devils, unclean or evil spirits*. So even as God writes His Story - the way things were, are and will be - Satan became the self-appointed leader of every effort to write a conflicting Story or stories. He and his fallen spirit followers are implacably committed to their original goal of usurping God's sovereign rule. Their hatred and enmity inevitably extended to the race of humans, created in God's image and given that original caretaker role over the earth.

Later, God's Narrative tells us more about Satan's activities, depicting him in one place as a vicious, wild animal, prowling the earth for victims to consume. Indeed, Satan is about to enter the Story of God's interaction with human beings in a way that would prove to be earth-shattering in a quite literal sense.

Taking a brief glance ahead, it's worth noting here where the Story will end for Satan and his hordes of demons. God's Word tells us that a place of punishment, a "lake of fire" has been prepared for him, for them. If God truly is writing the Story as well as telling it to us, as we know He is, then the future for His Enemy and enemies, is grim to say the least.

Is this for real?

As we hear these stories about angels, demons, attempts to supplant God, places of punishment and so on, how are we to take them? Should we in the 21st century be expected to take them seriously – even as believers? After all, they do sound not unlike the plot of a movie, or a video game, or some science fantasy book. Or perhaps we've heard these things dismissed as myths and legends, on the level of the epic tales of other cultures and religious traditions. But let's consider this. Wouldn't a cunning, malevolent Enemy want people to think that about God's Story? Wouldn't he want it dismissed as just one among many stories? Wouldn't he want people to feel clever and sophisticated so that they'd see it as symbolic, a religious cautionary tale perhaps, but not to be believed as a true account of actual events?

And wouldn't a clever adversary of God's see to it that there were many other versions in all kinds of media, so that God's True Story would sound vaguely familiar, just without the special effects and good cinematography?

At the end of the day, like Lucifer, like Adam and Eve, on all different levels each of us is faced with the choice of whether we'll put ourselves in the role of our own storytellers, whether we'll listen to others wanting to do so, or if we'll simply and humbly be listeners to God's Story.

? DISCUSSION POINTS

1. In what ways, if any, do you think that popular culture – TV, movies, video games etc. – might affect how many people would relate to the Bible's portrayal of angels, Satan, demons etc.?

2. How much impact would you say it has on your daily life that, as God's Word tells us, a whole domain exists which is inhabited by spirit beings?

3. Have you heard about any religions or worldviews that portray reality as an endless battle between good and evil, positive and negative etc.? If so, comment on any similarities or differences you see between those ideologies and the Bible's account of God's relationship to Satan and his rebellious angels.

1.15 Adam and Eve disobeyed God

 OBJECTIVES OF THIS TUTORIAL

Learners will continue to explore and discuss the themes and the truths presented in God's Narrative. The portions of Scripture referred to in this tutorial are: **Genesis 3:1-8**

Last time
We reminded ourselves of some important background to the part of God's Narrative we're about to hear. How Lucifer, lifted up with unbelievable arrogance led a rebellion of many angels against God. How they were expelled from God's presence to await their terrible eventual fate… but, far from being remorseful or repentant, to this day he, they, remain committed in their hatred, their antipathy toward God and His image-bearing human race.

Life in Paradise
So we return to the Narrative where we left off. Adam and Eve in their true, pure innocence, relishing the place God had made for them, delighting in their companionship, growing – we can safely assume – under God's tutelage, in their grasp of what was involved in their caretaking responsibilities over Creation. And enjoying their relationship with God, as their Guide and Father.

Remember the freedom they were given to enjoy the produce from the garden…we can only imagine the sights, sounds and tastes that were available to them – the variety of decorative and edible plants, the animals around them. Senses perfectly tuned to appreciate them.

Satan in disguise
One observer of all of this found no delight in the life of these humans in Paradise or their relationship with God. We can only begin to imagine the bitterness, the hatred that must have consumed Satan as he watched these image-bearers of the One whose

position he coveted…and the jealousy over their God-given caretaker roles in Creation. Watching and waiting he hatches a plan to try to bring about the death, the separation, that God had said would result from the humans going their own way and eating of *The Tree Of The Knowledge Of Good And Evil.*

In Genesis chapter 3, God's Narrative describes the day when he enacts his plan. We aren't told specifically why Satan chooses to disguise himself a snake, although the text gives a hint by saying that it was the "shrewdest" of the animals. A pattern is established here that continues to the present time – of God's Enemy carefully, cunningly, viciously, finding ways to disguise himself, and wrapping his deception in attractive or seemingly benign packaging.

And, as we'll see, finding our points of vulnerability, using our pride, our desires for fulfillment… whatever he can, to whisper his false story to us. His intent is not to frighten, but to deceive. And he, and his servant fallen angels, are masters of their craft.

Eve, willingly deceived

Certainly, from the Narrative (Genesis 3) when he finds Eve alone she is not alarmed, and very willing to conduct a conversation. It's significant that he begins with questions. Questions often seem neutral, but it's always important to assess the premise from which they come. His line of questioning will effectively cause her to doubt God's good motives toward them. And, by implication, to create for the first time a glimpse of another more independent and self-determining approach to life. Why should they after all, is the implication, not make decisions for themselves? Surely God's warning about death resulting from eating fruit from a particular tree was exaggerated! What was all this about death, anyway? Could it be that God had selfishly kept something agreeable back from them? Were His intentions toward them so perfect after all? Had they been naïve in believing and obeying Him so unquestioningly? Might there be an unexplored and desirable dimension to life less dependent on Him?

And so, gladly buying into Satan's deception, being enticed now by the appearance of the tree, and suddenly hungry for the independent wisdom he said would result, she ate some of the fruit. (3:6) And then, as we know, Adam willingly ate some as well.

The resulting death

The results of their decision were immediate and catastrophic. The Narrative says nothing about any physical changes to them or their surroundings, but everything had changed.

They *saw* everything differently. Indeed, it says (3:7) that their eyes were *opened*; but it was not the pleasant, liberating experience Satan had intimated and which they'd imagined. They suddenly found themselves ashamed, naked, exposed, no longer at home in the world God had created for them, no longer comfortable with who they were, or with each other.

So had God exaggerated when He said they'd die if they ate from that tree? They were still breathing, their senses still functioning.

But God had, of course, spoken truly. Death, inevitably, tragically had now become part of who they were. They had chosen to cut themselves off from God, the source of their life.

Physical death had now become the end point of their lives on the earth, their trajectory. And ultimately, they were destined eternally for the place prepared for the Enemy, all the enemies of God. That's who they identified with, and they would share their fate.

The broken relationship

The Narrative makes it clear that the amazing God to God-image-bearer relationship was now broken… and that is the real essence of death. Where formerly they were innocently pure, now their nakedness brought a sense of shame, of dissonance in God's world. And now they are forced by their own choice to seek their own solutions, to provide for their own needs.

Feeling shame and wrongly assuming this is an external problem, a matter of form, they try to hide their shame with leaves, to make themselves presentable again, according to their own standards. According to their own perceptions of "good and evil". But this is no solution. Their problem is inner, of the spirit, it's way out of their control, their ability to patch things up.

Now, when God comes to the Garden (which sounds, from the Narrative, like a regular point up to this time) they hide. Fear has displaced harmony and delight. Everything is wrong, out of kilter. Shame and fear were, in fact, the right response for them. They had much to be ashamed of and much to fear. They had listened to God's Enemy, and identified with his rebellion. They had become rebels and enemies themselves…in their very being. This too is death. They were now facing the righteous anger of a God who will not, cannot, ignore anyone who arrogantly tries to write their own story. It's His. He's the Author. Anyone who doesn't acknowledge that, who listens to any other voice, will suffer the eternal consequences.

ADAM AND EVE DISOBEYED GOD

? DISCUSSION POINTS

1. How does it make you feel when you think about the reality of a powerful, and crafty being, Satan, who is determined to stop people from knowing God and to spoil the relationships with God of those who do know Him?

2. Describe some of the biggest influences on this society which you suspect are actually put there or at least manipulated by Satan so that he can influence people away from Truth. (Think of those things which most people tolerate, or even support as right and fair, but which seem to be against what we've seen of God's character so far in this study.)

3. Think about some of the famous people and celebrities you know of and the well documented problems in their relationships. Trace that rather sad picture back to the separation and isolation that resulted from Adam and Eve rebelling against God.

4. How big a part do you feel that fear plays in our lives, and how much of that can we relate to the fear that Adam and Eve felt after they'd sinned?

1.16 The curse and the promise

 OBJECTIVES OF THIS TUTORIAL

Learners will continue to explore and discuss the themes and the truths presented in God's Narrative. The portions of Scripture referred to in this tutorial are: **Genesis 3:9-20**

Last time
We picked up God's Narrative again, with Adam and Eve enjoying the life God had given them in the garden of Eden and their relationship with Him. Then Eve being willingly deceived by Satan disguised as a snake. The man and woman eating from *the tree of the knowledge of good and evil*, and the immediate disastrous results in the form of their shame and fear within God's creation, with each other, and most importantly, before God. Evil and death, in all its dimensions, had now entered and become part of who they were, just as God had warned them that it would.

God the Communicator called out to them
So we left Adam and Eve, ashamed, pathetically trying to cover their naked bodies with leaves sewed together, and now, hearing God's approach, hiding from Him in fear. Never before had this been their response, every time before they had been grateful at His approach, glad for His presence, eager to talk with Him. In His Narrative (Genesis 3:9) God recounts how He called out to Adam, asking where they were. Of course God knew where they were, knew all that had taken place…so His calling out like this had a purpose other than to seek information. In fact, God was declaring, revealing important things about Himself, as He always, tirelessly does. He is the Communicating God who speaks. It was His Voice that He had made Adam and Eve to hear. And even though now it produced fear and other responses we'll see, He knew that it was His Voice they needed to hear.

They'd been deceived, bought a lie, and it was – it always is – the Truth, God's take on things, His true Version, that they needed. Even now, having turned away from Him, joined in Satan's rebellion, even with death and the fractured relationship stamped all over them, God reaches out to them. He takes the initiative, knowing they are unable. As we'll see, God wanted them to acknowledge that He had spoken truly. And He wanted them to understand their desperate need of Him at this, their first and darkest moment.

His questions and their answers

Each of God's questions (Genesis 3:9-13), beginning with "Where are you" are not intended for Him to find anything out but rather to reveal things to them… about Him, about themselves, about realities. And to give them opportunity, even at this late stage to humbly acknowledge their culpability. One thing that His questions reveal too is where the real authority lies. Not with the Enemy, certainly not with them, but with God Himself. He had, has, every right to demand answers and they knew it.

Adam admits their fear that they were hiding because of being ashamed at their nakedness. When God asks if they know this from having eaten of the forbidden tree, Adam gives his famous answer, whining that it was his wife's fault. She, in turn, of course, blames the serpent. Here another pattern is set in place, sadly…our human tendency to try to shift blame: to someone else, to circumstances, to their upbringing, the "bad crowd they fell in with". And modern psychology plays along with this, encouraging a culture in which those who claim the victim label are no longer responsible for their thoughts, words or actions.

No one, of course, was fooling God. No one was going to crawl out from under their responsibilities. Everyone was, and always is, held responsible for their choices and actions.

With Him all attempts to manipulate, to deflect, or to spin things are futile.

The curse and the promise

Because the Narrative doesn't tell us, we've no way of understanding all the implications of the curse God now puts on the snake for being Satan's chosen disguise in his deception of Eve. (3:14) It's tempting to speculate, but all we can safely say is that it was reduced from that moment to the legless slithering we're familiar with today.

God will go on to pronounce other terrible results of the rebellion of His image-bearers and, until now, Creation caretakers. But first, in this, the darkest of times, when hope would otherwise have been extinguished in their hearts, God allows a small but bright pin-point of light to shine. A hope. A life-line to be grasped even as they're realizing that they've rejected everything that was real and solid in their lives - hope in the middle of the cold terror that must have been gripping their hearts.

A promise, not clear in detail, but real and solid nonetheless. In the form of a revelation to the snake, really to Satan, he's told that his apparent recent victory will be fleeting. A man, an offspring of the woman, will come, who'll do battle with this one who has sworn enmity with God and His created beings. Satan will inflict pain, but His will be the ultimate victory. Satan's temporary reign will be brought to an end with his defeat. God is letting the man and woman know that although their story from now on will be full of pain and sorrow, His Story is still being written. No one but He, the Lord God has the right to decide how it will end. This is who He is. Unwilling, unable, in His holy being, to relate to anyone on their terms. To tolerate offence to His perfection. But at the same time, always reaching out, reaching down, in love.

This kind of reaching down for no reason other than His loving choice can never be effectively labeled in human language. In English, the best we have is the word grace - a word that has lost its coinage in common usage. Something to be constantly grateful for though is that we, unlike many other language communities, have His Story available in our language. We have the wonderful opportunity to hear His Story of how He reaches out *in grace* to rescue humans from their predicament. So we're not restricted to theoretical propositions, to dogma, dry doctrinal statements. He wants our understanding of who He is - in this and every aspect - to grow within us as we listen and observe Him, in action, in real circumstances, contexts and relationships.

This part of the narrative (Genesis 3:17-19) concludes with God giving them some insights into the results of their disobedience. Of the pain in childbirth Eve would experience. The earth from which Adam had been formed, and over which he'd been given responsibility, was itself cursed. Changed. It was now a harsher environment. A tougher place to live. Life would be difficult and painful. Their needs would only be met with great challenge, hard, physical work.

And because they are the ancestors, the antecedents, of all the human race (Genesis 3:20), the dire results – the great curse – would come on all. Having chosen to try to write his own story, in many ways it would not be a pleasant one for man. Thankfully God did not walk away. He will still have the final say in how things unfold for His lost image-bearing race.

THE CURSE AND THE PROMISE

❓ DISCUSSION POINTS

1. Consider Adam and Eve's initial response to God after their disobedience in light of the way many people in our society blame their problems on something or someone else. From what we've seen of God so far in the Genesis narrative, what do you believe is His perspective on people's tendency to paint themselves as victims rather than taking responsibility for their own choices?

2. Think about your own responses when your faults and wrong actions are exposed. How have you typically handled that kind of situation in your life? What insights does this perhaps give you about the way you view (1) God (2) yourself?

3. Keeping in mind that Adam and Eve had just, as it were, thrown back in God's face all that He had done and all He intended for them, what do you think about Him now making a promise to send a Deliverer? In human terms would that kind of response by a sovereign ruler be seen as a sign of strength or weakness?

➡ ACTIVITIES

1. In no more than a page;

- list some of the evidences of God's grace that He has already demonstrated up to this point of the Narrative.

- explain how you think grace might differ from generosity or even love.

- describe some ways you're aware of that God has shown His grace to you, personally.

1.17 God provided clothing for Adam and Eve

 OBJECTIVES OF THIS TUTORIAL

Learners will continue to explore and discuss the themes and the truths presented in God's Narrative. The portions of Scripture referred to in this tutorial are: Genesis 3:21-24, 4:1-2, Psalm 100:3, Acts 17:25

Last time
We listened to the part of God's Narrative that describes the immediate aftermath of Adam and Eve choosing to listen to the Enemy's deception. Their shame, fear and excuses as God came and asked them questions. Then the Curse and the Promise…the small light of hope in the gathering dark… One who would come and break the Enemy's temporary hold.

God provides Adam & Eve clothing of His choosing
We'll remember how after having lost their purity and innocence, and becoming ashamed at their nakedness, they stitched some clothes from leaves. God's Story draws attention to this matter again by recording (Genesis 3:21) that God covered them with animal skins He had made for them.

Once again, we see how the seemingly simple Narrative is embedded with the things God wants to draw our attention to about Himself, and how everything else – including us – stands in relation to Him. The point here is one that will be hammered home over and over in the continuing Narrative as God stresses the fact that any efforts humans make on their own – based on our assessment of a situation, our ingenuity, energy, resources, devotion…whatever – never come close to His standards…never can, never will. It doesn't even make it onto the radar in terms of satisfying Him.

It's significant that it was the skins of animals that God says He used. This is the first record of animal death in the Narrative. Innocent animals, with no moral responsibility of their own, paid with their lives to hide the naked shame of God's image-bearers, now corrupted. Adam had been given the awesome responsibility of caretaking God's creation including its other lesser inhabitants. He'd named them one by one. They were under his oversight and care.

Now, one - perhaps a number - had to die because of the humans' choices. Innocent blood has been shed for them, for sin. We'll see this pattern emerge continually throughout God's narrative.

And one final observation about this incident… this is another poignant example of a part of who God is that we've noted, a golden seam we want to mine from His Narrative. This thing, that in our limited linguistic choice, we call "grace". Rather than walking away in disgust from these whining, ungrateful, pathetic semblances of himself, he reaches out and replaces their pitiful attempts to cover their shame, with something that He says is right. That's a picture of His grace worth pondering and asking Him to make very real to us.

Shut out of the garden

Now (end of Chapter 3) another fascinating glimpse of the three-in-One God interacting… as before, their topic is the humans. The beings made in their, in God's, image, have become their own moral arbiters…have set a course of deciding for themselves what is good and bad – what they want to do.

The problem now becomes the possibility of them living on eternally in this state. (Remember that Adam and Eve *symbolically represent* the human race. But also, as the progenitors of the human race, in very real, tangible ways, their choices will play out for, will directly impact, all their descendants.) They've chosen the way of death, of separation. God will not allow them to eat of the Tree Of Life and live forever in a half-life existence, a mockery of the life He'd wanted them to enjoy with Him forever. Everything has changed. A different plan is now in place, and He acts in accordance with that.

So God sends them (the Narrative gives the feel of them being forcefully ejected) from the garden. In fact, the way back in is entirely blocked by powerful angel servants of God.

There will be no return to the perfect environment He'd prepared for them – a home for them to live in, a base from which to carry out their work, and a context in which He could interact with them and they could learn from Him. Now life will be tougher, harsher…any joy will be hard won. And the interaction with God will be in light of those realities, not the previous pure, innocent, harmonious and very direct relationship.

With death in their bodies and evil in their hearts, God cannot allow them back to the garden, to the tree of Life. Nor to the easy access they've had to Him there. Another footing will have to be established…and, as we've already seen, it will have to be of his design, his doing, from his grace, if there's any hope at all.

Cain and Abel born outside the garden

The Narrative continues now with their lives outside the garden. Eve becomes pregnant and gives birth to a son, Cain, then another, Abel. Although sin and death are an ever-present feature of this new existence, God allows them the opportunity to bring more life into it.

He's the life-giver. Life, even our lives under the curse, is a gift from God. Many other parts of the Narrative will reinforce this.

The words of one of God's songwriters (Psalm 100:3) for example tell us to "Acknowledge that the LORD is God! He made us, and we are his." And centuries later one of his chosen mouthpieces, Paul, would state that "He himself gives life and breath to everything, and he satisfies every need." (Acts 17:25) It's a hugely significant point, because our lives, every life, comes from God. So, as the songwriter said, we are His. He rightfully owns us, lock, stock and barrel. The response though of humans to his authentic claim on their lives will consistently be part – often a very sad part – of what He chooses to make a part of His Story.

Something important to note is that these new human offspring have come into the world outside the garden and all it represents. They never experienced the life God intended them to have – in the place He'd prepared for their parents and for them.

Their interaction with God (and they did interact, as we'll see) was never inside – with its pure, innocent, easy, direct access to the Creator-Father. They were *born* with death stamped all over them. And evil, sin, was their constant companion… part of who they were. Part of them, in fact… card-carrying members of those who always tend to want to write their own stories, who tend to reject God as the true Story Writer and Teller.

As we've already noted, this group has a self-appointed leader, eagerly pointing the way toward rebellion. Tirelessly enticing, deceiving, entangling. Making people think they're free to tell their stories, determine their destinies. When in fact they're being led constantly deeper into bondage. God's Enemy. This was Cain and Abel's situation. And that of course, is the situation, the condition and the ontological reality for every human born since.

GOD PROVIDED CLOTHING FOR ADAM AND EVE

❓ DISCUSSION POINTS

1. What assumptions would you say many people in our society make about God and His attitude toward sin? In light of what we're seeing in the Genesis account of how God views "good and bad", give some examples of things you've heard people say that show they live with some very wrong assumptions.

2. Would you agree that in our society, most people feel that no one can fault us if we try our best, "give it our best shot". How does that assumption compare with what we are hearing in God's Word – that he rejects peoples' attempts – even their best attempts - to make themselves acceptable to Him and only accepts what He provides? Does that sound "fair" according to our cultural norms? If not, how are we to think about this correctly?

3. Briefly consider some of the implications of the fact that God is the giver of life. Does that truth contrast at all with some of the values we see lived out in our society?

➡ ACTIVITIES

1. Ask a minimum of 3 people (with at least one non-believer respondent) then record/summarize their answers to these questions;

    1. How would you describe evil?

    2. Where does it come from?

    3. Do you believe that God is the giver of life?

    4. What does that imply, if anything, for the way you make decisions, small or large? (Whether "yes" or "no" to #3)

1.18 Cain and Abel's offerings

 OBJECTIVES OF THIS TUTORIAL

Learners will continue to explore and discuss the themes and the truths presented in God's Narrative. The portions of Scripture referred to in this tutorial are: **Genesis 4:2-26**

Last time

Innocent animals died in order for God to make acceptable clothing to hide Adam and Eve's shame. Knowing the terrible prospects of them eating from the tree of life and living forever in their current state, God shut them out from the garden. Although they were far from what God intended for them, He gave them the gift of being able to reproduce their lives – two sons were born to them. Cain and Abel, like their parents, are born outside, cut off from the pure, innocent, free access to God He desired for them and all human beings.

God had given them a way to approach Him

God continues His Narrative by relating to us some events from which we can glean a great deal about Him and His intentions for man. Also, we see some of the terrible consequences of Adam and Eve's choice for them, and for us all, to become our own moral compass... to make our own choices, independent of God.

It is apparent from the way these events are described, that God had given Adam and Eve – and through them, Cain and Abel – a way to relate to Him in this new, fallen, cursed context that was now their lives. Of course, as we know, they had no way to restore the relationship they were responsible for fracturing. Their rebellion, their choices, their willing alignment with God's Enemy, the stench of death that clung about them, the evil in their hearts...all formed a barrier they could never overcome. And God has already shown graphically that any effort of theirs to make themselves presentable or to gloss over what they've done - who they now are - will be a pathetic failure. He simply will not, cannot, accept anything that is the fruit of their corrupted efforts, their tainted hearts. Or ours, for that matter. But because of this thing about Him that we see illuminated ever more brightly against the dark backdrop of human evil - His grace - He has provided a way for them to approach Him.

They were to kill an animal – a sheep – letting its blood flow out. This - and of course the animals dying to clothe Adam and Eve previously – sets a pattern which is to become very familiar in God's Narrative from here on. And the principle that emerges is that the only way that God's corrupted image-bearers can approach Him is after blood has flowed resulting in loss of life.

Cain and Abel approach God in different ways

The Narrative, as we've noted before, is sparse in detail but immeasurably full and rich in its implications. Cain and Abel approach God, seek perhaps His blessing, or even – we're not told exactly – to venerate Him. Clearly Adam's sons take God's existence and presence for granted... surely they've heard much from their parents over the years, and no doubt have been instructed in the appropriate way to come to Him in their fallen state.

Cain, a "cultivator of the ground" brings crops – no doubt burns them in oblation, in offering. Abel, a shepherd, on the other hand, brings lambs (Genesis 4:2-4) – and we can safely assume, presents them to God with their throats cut and the blood running out until they're dead... these too would be burnt. And the result? God accepted Abel's offering but not Cain's.

Why? Because any approach to God is only possible under these conditions: when it's made on His terms, i.e. only after there has been death – innocent blood has flowed; when the one approaching knows they, and not the innocent victim – is the one truly deserving of death; and the approach is made in faith, believing what God says about the whole thing. So, as the Narrative tells us here (Genesis 4:4,5), God accepted Abel's approach, but rejected Cain's. Cain had come on his own terms, there had been no death, no blood shed, no recognition that death was his just deserts, and unlike his brother, he'd not come in faith, believing what God said, what God offered, to be true.

This matter of coming in faith, or *by faith*, is of course going to be another major theme that God will regularly illustrate with real events in His Story. And we'll also see that human beings constantly get this wrong. By nature, by inclination, by choice, we try to figure it out for ourselves. People want to find acceptance, blessing, forgiveness etc. from God the way they want. They'll try to make Him look different, try to change what He says, to underplay their sin and exaggerate the good... anything at all to come on their own terms. That will come out more in the Narrative but it's something we see and hear around us – and in us – on a daily basis.

The first murder

Showing amazing patience, God tries to make Cain see reason. (Genesis 4:6,7) He warns him about where his pride and anger are taking him. God is under no obligation to do this at all... to reason with Cain, to reach out to him. This is Grace shining out again. But Cain is beyond listening. Wounded pride, jealousy, fury have taken hold. The blood is pounding in his head. He wants revenge. The Enemy rides him like a wild animal. Driving him on to the terrible conclusion. He invites his brother out to the fields and kills him. (Genesis 4:8)

The Enemy's hatred of God and His image-bearers (now fallen) knows no bounds. He loves to destroy life. To crush hope.

The aftermath

As with his parents before him, God gives Cain opportunity to respond in contrition and humility. Obviously not for information, but giving Cain a chance to come to his senses, He asks where his brother Abel is. Cain comes back with the infamous line (Genesis 4:9). "I don't know, am I my brother's keeper?" Abdicating all responsibility for the life of his fellow image-bearers. Denying any value for the life that God alone had given each of them. And then, also like his parents, he hears God utter a terrible curse in response to his rebellion and sin.

We see here the high value that God places on the life He gives to humans. He avenges evil done against others; punishes the murderous taking of life. The curse on Cain, again with similarities to his parents, is to be banished from that area and to wander, to be a nomad, without a home. (Genesis 4:10-15). Even now there's no sign of any kind of repentance with Cain. No recognition of God's perspective on him and what he's done... no acknowledgment that he deserves whatever is coming to him...that he desperately needs God's help.

The whole issue of repentance is going to emerge more out of the Narrative as God teaches us what it is, what it's meant to be. And it will become clear that God's definition goes a lot further and deeper than a dictionary, and common usage might say: "feel or express sincere regret or remorse about one's wrongdoing or sin".

So the Narrative concludes the tale of Cain's disastrous life with some details that paint a sad picture. Succeeding generations of his descendants increasingly focused on materialism and were indifferent to God their Creator. (Genesis 4:16-24)

Finally, the Narrative flashes back to Adam and Eve (Genesis 4:25,26) to whom God gives another son, "in place of Abel". He, Seth, founded a family line that understood their need for God in their lives. In fact, it says, they began to worship the Lord by name. Clearly, it's possible for the relationship, though fractured by the fall, to be restored when the approach to God is by faith, on His terms. That's really what the rest of the Narrative is about.

❓ DISCUSSION POINTS

1. Would you agree that our society highly values the intellect, the mind, being able to think things through and work them out for ourselves? Much of our education is built around that value. Okay, think about Cain and Abel... did God want them to reason things out for themselves? If not, then how does this relate to faith? Are faith and reason mutually exclusive? Do they function in completely separate categories as our society generally assumes?

2. Take a moment to consider the amazing fact that even though Adam and Eve had rejected so much that God had done for them and had listened to the lies of His Enemy, God was still willing to give them a way to relate to Him. What does that tell you about the importance he places on His relationship with these human beings, created in His image? How does thinking about His grace impact you on a personal level?

3. In everyday life, how much do you find yourself weighing up the things you consider to be good against others you're not so pleased with? How much does this whole "weighing up" process feature in your relationship with God as His child? Are there truths underlined by the story of Cain and Abel that shed any light on all of that?

➡ ACTIVITIES

1. Read the Wikipedia article on faith and rationality. In approximately half a page, comment on what you agree or disagree with in the article. Feel free to include any thoughts from what's been covered in the Biblical Narrative so far.

2. Write another half a page in response to the final Discussion point above.

1.19 God punishes the world, but saves Noah

 OBJECTIVES OF THIS TUTORIAL

Learners will continue to explore and discuss the themes and the truths presented in God's Narrative. The portions of Scripture referred to in this tutorial are: **Genesis 5:1-32, 6:1-22, 7:1-24**

Last time
We listened to God's account of the sad life of Cain, Adam and Eve's first son. God had provided a way for humans to approach Him in the post-fall context. When, having rejected Cain's self-styled approach, God accepted his brother Abel's offering made on God's terms and in faith. Cain murdered his brother in jealous rage. God avenged Abel's death with a curse on Cain. Adam and Eve had another son, and two human lines emerge on earth: Cain's, materialistic and indifferent to God; and Seth's, worshippers of the Lord.

10 generations come and go on earth
In Genesis 5 God continues the Story of His interaction with man by recording some details of the 10 generations from Adam, through Seth and on to Noah. The family line that came to God on His terms. The record of each generational head gives the number of years they lived, their sons, and concludes with the statement "and then he died". Death was now part of life on earth. The race of God's image-bearers were all now born with death and sin as part of their being, their lives…and their end. Now, left to himself, it would be separation… from God, from physical life and the body in death, and endless separation and punishment in eternity.

In the generational record, one man - the 7th after Adam – is singled out. (Genesis 5:21-24) Twice in the brief notes, it says that he "lived" or "walked in close fellowship with God." So not only is there the possibility of an approach to God He can accept – if by faith, on His terms – but even a close relationship is available. This is an exciting confirmation for us, who were created specifically for that! A later reference in God's

Narrative shed's more light on Enoch's life and his role of God's storyteller to the people of his time. He warns them - without effect - that God would punish them for the evil things they were saying and doing. A fascinating mention is made in the Narrative of the fact that Enoch did not physically die, simply stating that "one day he disappeared because God took him".

God decides to destroy a world that has become corrupted

We now come to a part of God's Story that is no doubt familiar to us – often extracted from the overall Narrative with the focus put on "Noah and the ark". But this is, indeed, God's Account of who He is, revealed against the backdrop of real-life events in His interaction with man. Already, only 10 generations after the turning away - the Fall - almost all the people had no interest in God or fear of His judgment. They are writing their own stories. A later reference in the Narrative sheds light and explains that - not at all unlike our culture - they were mainly interested in entertainment…the latest event, avoiding boredom, having fun. With God's Enemy working overtime to distract and deceive their already corrupted hearts and minds, they refused to respond to the truth that God's Spirit was offering to them; through their surroundings telling them God's Creative Narrative or through His messenger, His chosen storyteller, Noah.

Evil, it says, (Genesis 6:5 and 11) was rampant. People's hearts, their imaginations, the things that consumed their thoughts were "consistently and totally evil". It's a sobering fact that God knew their innermost thoughts and motivations. As we've noted, His understanding and insights are universal and exhaustive. Nothing escapes His observation, and therefore His just assessment. The text (Genesis 6:6,7) says that God was sorry he'd put these people on the earth. One English version of the Narrative puts it that "it broke his heart" to see what the race of His image-bearers had become. God is revealing to us the depth of feeling that leads to his decision that he's going to wipe this human race from the earth and destroy the lesser beings He had originally put under their (our) oversight and care.

God determines He'll save Noah and his family

As God looks at this hopeless, pathetic, evil race, there is one exception. One man and his family. A *righteous* man who is *blameless* and *walking in close fellowship* with God, the Narrative says (Genesis 6:8-10) And that's all it takes for God to determine that He'll make a way to save Noah and his family from the coming universal destruction. Not because Noah had somehow earned it. In fact, all he'd earned as a member of Adam's lost race and by his own sin, was destruction, separation. But God is always looking for an opportunity to do this amazing thing that is so unique to Him – He extends grace. ("extends" – an awkward verb) Noah has approached him in faith, on God's terms, humbly relating to God in real life ways, and so God gladly, eagerly, graciously puts His plan into place.

God's plan and their participation

He tells Noah that a boat is to be built. He gives him precise dimensions and specs. He explains that a devastating universal flood is coming, that will destroy life and cover the earth. (Genesis 6:13 -17) God wants Noah to engage his intellect, to understand, to participate. As we've noted before, God gives real responsibilities with genuine opportunities to be involved in what He's about. There's real work for Noah and, no doubt, for his sons. Any past experience will be valuable. Skills will be utilized. They will need to bring discipline and commitment to complete the enormous project.

But they'd be entirely out of their depth if they tried to design the boat that's needed. They can't begin to imagine the scale of the destruction coming. Nor can they picture the scope of God's plan to preserve them and other life. They need His guidance. He has to provide the plan for this boat, this rescue capsule made from cypress wood and tar, (traditionally called an "ark"). As we know, it's His Story, after all. There's to be only one door, one entry, one way to safety. God is demonstrating again that any approach to Him must be on His terms alone. Any hope that we, His lost human race, have is by the way that He alone provides for us. And Noah simply took God at His word, believed Him despite not having seen rain, much less a flood. Later in God's Narrative, this would be used to describe real faith. Faith like this goes against our human tendency to go our own way, to work things out for ourselves. It is not in conflict with reason, but neither does it rest on our reason, on tangible, empirical evidence. It is accepting that God knows. That He is always right, always righteous, always gracious.

God saves everyone in the boat from the destruction

So we know the story. Before it began to rain, a week before in fact, when God told them it was time, the family entered through the one door and took with the animals as God had said they should. (Genesis 7:4-10) Then – a small but incredibly significant detail is added: God says that He, the Lord, the personal caring Father, "closed the door behind them". He was ensuring their safety, personally. He was shutting out the destruction. And when it came, as it did, of course, those outside were shut out from safety. There was no negotiating, no further appeal, no ritual they could perform, no service they could give, no prayer they could offer, no sacrifice they could make, no approach they could attempt... The time when people could agree with God's assessment of them and their evil, acknowledge their need of Him and turn to Him for help – in other words, to *repent* - those days were done.

God's grace doesn't ever run out, but His righteousness means that He won't forever overlook sin. It has to be paid for. Justice has to be done. And it was done. God's indignant power was released in the form of water, from the sky, from the earth...flooding, swirling down in sheets and torrents, filling, consuming, drowning forests, digging canyons, changing the landscape forever, altering the crust of the planet, laying down layers of sediment, an entire fossil record to be read - or misread - millennia later. Until everything was covered. Only the still surface of the waterlogged planet to be seen with one small boat floating in all that great expanse. (Genesis 7:17-24) No one outside the boat left alive. No one inside the boat harmed.

❓ DISCUSSION POINTS

1. Describe some of the prevailing assumptions in our society about death. Also, think about any movies you know of over the last few years that relate to the after-life. What do you think might be the underlying purpose or message behind what is packaged as entertainment?

2. As you listen to the Biblical account of human history and the number of generations recorded since creation, how do you account for the commonly accepted and very different picture most of science sees in the fossil records? How important do you feel it is for believers to be informed with facts to respond to challenges or even genuine questions that might come? What part, if any, do you think a convincing short-earth argument has in someone coming to faith?

3. The lesson makes the point that God graciously warned people through Noah of their impending doom. With that picture in mind, consider briefly any varying levels of responsibility we might have today to people who have opportunity to hear, in contrast to those who have no way of knowing the terrible realities they face as a result of their sin.

➡ ACTIVITIES

1. Of the many theories about the origins of "Homo sapiens" the very shortest time span any of them posits is at least 50,000 years – about 9 times the Genesis account – and then only as a sub-branch of millions of years of primate evolution. Read the Wikipedia page about "Human Evolution."

1.20 God remembered Noah. God scatters at Babel

 OBJECTIVES OF THIS TUTORIAL

Learners will continue to explore and discuss the themes and the truths presented in God's Narrative. The portions of Scripture referred to in this tutorial are: **Genesis chapters 8, 9, 10 and 11:1-9**

Last time

In the Narrative of His interaction with man, God gave a brief record of the first 10 generations of Seth's line. Then His account of He, the Creator, disgusted and broken hearted at man's evil disregard for Him deciding He'll destroy the degenerate human race. The one exception, Noah, and his family, because of his faith, were to be saved and animal species preserved. The boat was built, they entered by the one door, they were securely shut in by God… then the unimaginable destruction by a catastrophic, global flood. Every human and much of the animal life outside was destroyed, only the living contents of the boat are saved.

God completes the rescue, making the flood recede

God didn't forget the boat floating along with its precious cargo. (Genesis 8:1-4) It says that He "remembered Noah" and all in the boat. He had them in mind, had His eye on them. His rescue of Noah and family from the global destruction was His plan from first to last and He made sure it was completed. He caused, or "sent", a wind to blow until the waters receded, mountain tops appeared like islands, and 5 months from the time the flood began, the boat came aground on the mountains of Ararat in modern day Turkey.

These events which can be so easily taken for granted are – or should be, to us - amazing examples of God's control over every part of His Creation. The record reflects this – it is stated simply, without fanfare or elaborate defense. It's His Story and He gives us the choice whether to believe it and then make appropriate efforts to understand how the physical (geological, chemical, socio-historical) record confirms it, OR to start with human pre-supposition and then contort, or even reject as unscientific myths, His account of how all these things took place. In light of that, it's worth considering the confusion and deception that God's Enemy specializes in, and his ability to use the most sophisticated packaging.

They left the boat and acknowledged God

As can be imagined, it took some time from their grounding on the mountaintop until the water had receded enough for them to leave the boat and begin their new lives. (Genesis 8:5-14)

Finally God gave the word and they climbed out and released the animals. (Genesis 8:15-19) We can only speculate about the range of emotions they experienced as the only humans left on the planet. One thing we do know is that they gratefully acknowledged that it was God who had rescued them. In fact, the first thing the Narrative records is Noah building an altar, a platform of stones, and killing specific animals and birds and then burning them there.

Think about it... these animals had been in the boat with Noah and family for just over a year. Now, the innocent animals that shared the safe haven of the boat, have lost their lives.

God took no pleasure (He later tells us) in the innocent deaths of creatures He'd created. But He was willing to pay that price, and much, much more, it turns out, in pursuit of a relationship with His image-bearers, even as degenerate as they now were/are. They had turned away as a race, chosen rebellion, evil, the side of the Enemy, but He would respond in grace and love to even one who would approach by faith, on His terms, with innocent animal blood shed and life taken, to represent the lot that was, rightly, theirs. And that's what happens here. (Genesis 8:20-22) God, He says, is pleased at the aroma coming from the sacrifice – in all it represents.

And as Noah stands there looking out from that mountain at the recently flooded landscape, God stretches a rainbow out in the sky and says that it symbolizes a firm promise He's making that he will not destroy the earth in that way again. Here's a perfect example of something that *can* be defined only in materialistic terms - sun-light being refracted from water particles in the air, usually after recent rain, OR that can be *first of all* seen as a part of God telling His story, writ large in the sky... only *then* to be described in the lesser, subservient and limited "story" of physics and science.

The descendants of Noah's three sons

The Narrative moves on from this point to describe the repopulating of the earth after the universal destruction of the Flood. Noah's three sons, Ham, Shem and Japheth, are identified (Genesis 9:18,19) as the forebears or progenitors of the entire population of the earth from the flood to now. God records some early generations (Genesis 10), giving many insights into the way nations developed. Again, the way that we resolve any apparent conflicts between God's Account (recorded here as the book of Beginnings – i.e. Genesis) and the *positivist* claims of *ethno-history* will depend on our pre-conceptions, faith level commitments, about who the primary Storyteller really is.

The tower

Now the Account moves forward to a time more than 3 generations after the Great Flood. A civilization that had settled in a plain of Babylonia, a part of the Middle East which would later be called Mesopotamia. (Genesis 11:1-4) And the picture is not a pretty one from God's perspective. Remember that the great-grandparents of these people had been eyewitnesses of the global destruction and had been in the boat God had used to preserve them and the animals. But already they had moved far away from an appropriate appreciation of Him as Creator. They had given up coming to Him in the way He had graciously given to humans after the fall – in faith, with the sacrifice of animals. They were telling their own stories; in fact, a concerted effort was made to have their story as a people, a civilization told in the form of a great tower or ziggurat for all to see. It was to reach to the sky. A monument to them. A means of physical protection and a way of preserving their reputation for history.

It is not difficult to see the hand of the Enemy in all of this. It reeks of his arrogant ambition to supplant God's rightful place. It's ironic then, that the name of the tower, Babel, is associated not with great success and unity, but with failure and dispersion.

The scattering

God, knowing their arrogant intentions, is unwilling to let them gather their strength and resources together in a concerted denial of their need for Him, their Creator. (Genesis 11:5-9) Over the centuries and millennia since, many other civilizations and countless individuals have literally or metaphorically shaken their fist in defiance at God. Sometimes the results are immediate, more often God graciously gives them opportunity to see their foolishness.

But in every case, the results have been, and always will be, the same. He will not let anyone else take over His role as the Writer and Teller of His Story.

Fascinatingly, God does something to the post-flood civilization that makes it impossible for them to tell their story to each other as a homogenous group. In tangible terms, it made cooperation on their audacious project impossible. He targeted something He'd gifted man with in the first place but which was now taken for granted – speech, the ability to communicate tangible facts as well as ideas and abstract concepts. His Narrative simply says that He confused their languages and this had the effect of scattering them over the world. This, of course, has enormous implications for the ethno-history of the earth, as extended family groups expanded and gradually moved out from the Mesopotamian plains, heading south into Africa, east into Asia and beyond. Also, it should be noted, it forced the fulfillment of His original intention for man, which was to populate the earth.

? DISCUSSION POINTS

1. If you were to ask people in the community if it was right for God to destroy almost all human life because of their rebellion against Him, their creator, what do you think they would say? (Of course this would be a purely hypothetical question for the many who don't believe in a creator God.) How would you lay out a compelling argument for the justice of God's actions?

2. How does it impact you personally to think about God providing a way of escape from His judgment on mankind for those who believed Him, and that in the middle of all the widespread chaos and destruction He was concerned about them personally?

3. What do you think about the idea that we are just as prone to idolatry in our cultural context as those who venerate actual physical representations of gods or God? Think of some of the less obvious things or ideas that people devote themselves to, or that they rely on, to the point that they are substitutes for God's proper place in their lives.

4. Without going beyond the truth established in these lessons so far, share any thoughts that come to mind about God scattering people through creating language divisions. Would you agree that on the surface it might seem to make more sense to have everyone in one place, speaking the same language? So how do you think this might serve His purpose of calling people to repent and trust only in Him for their needs?

→ ACTIVITIES

1. Do some personal research on current views of the Original Human Language, begin by reading the introduction to the Wikipedia article on "The Origin of Language."

2. Browse an Ethnologue map of the world's current living languages.

1.21 God chose Abram. Lot choses Sodom and Gomorrah

 OBJECTIVES OF THIS TUTORIAL

Learners will continue to explore and discuss the themes and the truths presented in God's Narrative. The portions of Scripture referred to in this tutorial are: **Genesis 11:27-32, Genesis 12, 13:1-13**

Last time
We followed the record of God completing His rescue of Noah and His family from the global destruction. Records were given of the three lines of the human race, coming from Noah's sons Ham, Shem and Japheth. The Narrative continues when, only 3 generations after the Flood, the population, settled in the Babylonian plain, is indifferent or actively defiant toward God. In pursuit of their humanistic goals they planned to build a great tower but God thwarted their plan by changing their languages, and thus beginning the process of scattering humans around the world.

God interacts with Abram, a descendant of Shem
The Account moves forward 10 generations (approx. 350 years) to now focus on someone that God is going to relate to in a very special way. (Genesis 11:27-30) This relationship will prove to have enormous consequences for the entire Story of God's interaction with human beings. The man, of course, is Abraham – at this point still called by his birth name, Abram. A descendant of Shem, Abram had grown up in Southern Mesopotamia (modern day Iraq).

Back when the languages were divided at the time of the failed Tower project, a group speaking an early form of *Aramaic* settled not far from the Babel area, founding the very important city of the time, Ur, on the lower Euphrates. By Abram's time, far from worshiping the true, Creator God, as a community, they had told their own, entirely different false story, which included gods created out of their own imaginations and from the natural world around.

This *idolatry*, would prove to be a common feature of human cultures everywhere, and at every point in history, including today. And, as we'll see in the Narrative, it is something of particular abhorrence to God because it formalizes and systematizes the human default away from Him, from the relationships with man He pursues, away from an appropriate faith-based approach to Him, away from His righteousness and grace. And, perversely, it puts into His rightful place things that He himself created.

Abram was clearly different to the majority culture of his community, including his own father, Terah, who we're told worshiped idols. We're not told all the details of how Abram came to know God, but the Narrative does describe his obedient response to God's revelation and communication. In the introduction to the extended family and its history, there is mention made of a fact that will prove to be significant to the Story. Sarai, Abram's wife, it says, is unable to have children.

The text here in the Genesis account (Genesis 11:31,32) goes on to describe Terah initiating a migration of the family to Canaan in the west, near the Mediterranean. We also know from other parts of God's Word that Abram's joining with his father on this move was prompted by God coming to him and telling him to go. So Abram, responsive to God's direction begins the move with his wife, father, and nephew Lot. To avoid the Arabian Desert they must make a large loop north and west, then eventually south to Canaan in the "Fertile Crescent." Heading up the Euphrates river valley, probably via Nineveh, they reach the city of Haran (near the modern Turkish city, Urfa), where Terah dies.

Abram is to have a significant role in God's plans

We don't know exactly how long Abram and his group stayed in Haran, but while there God again communicates with him directly... we're not told whether in direct, audible speech, but that was often the way God spoke back before His written Word became the primary means - as it is today - of His communicating with people. He tells Abram to start out again and travel with his extended family group to a particular area – a "land" the text says, that God will show him. (Genesis 12:1)

Along with the directive, God makes him some momentous promises. (Genesis 12:2-3) He's to become the father, the progenitor, of a great nation. God will cause him to prosper and protect him, he'll bless those who help Abram and curse those who oppose him. He will become a famous and important man and, most significant of all, through Abram, God declares, "all the families of the earth" will be blessed.

God has clearly not forgotten His plan to rescue His lost image-bearing race that was first intimated hundreds of year back now in the dark, terrible day of the Turning Away, the Fall. The One He said who would come to crush the head, to break the power of the

Enemy. Despite the ongoing rebellion before and after the Flood, despite the idolatry, the defiance, the sin, the indifference, the rebellion… God's grace was not diminished. Those things only have the effect of making it shine out all the brighter. So now, the Plan is to be moved forward a significant step. The pathway for the Deliverer is to be initiated. A man, a family, a people, is to be situated for the Promised One to come through.

The Narrative doesn't say, but we can safely assume that Abram knew about the Promised One and was waiting for Him to be revealed. Whether he understood the full implications of God's promise that through him the families of the earth would be blessed we can't be certain. Regardless, having God the Creator making these declarations must have filled him with a sense of excitement and anticipation. The fact that he simply believed God though is remarkable. Remember that he had no children, his wife being unable to conceive.

And yet Abram believes God, believes His promises. This faith, specifically Abram's (later Abraham) like Noah's would be used as a benchmark, a definitive mark of faith… believing something for which there is no evidence or even contrary indications, based entirely on God's assertions.

The family migration is completed

He and Lot, their families, servants, livestock, and all their possessions leave the trading city of Haran and begin the journey west and then south, paralleling the Mediterranean coast down to Canaan. (Genesis 12:4,5) Although having long ago given up their city culture for a nomadic lifestyle, Abram and Lot were by no means destitute wanderers. In fact, they would have been considered quite wealthy, with livestock numbering well into the hundreds, and mention of silver and gold. Later, when needed, Abram is able to muster over 300 men for battle so there must have been well over this number of people in his extensive household. Certainly they were able to occupy large tracts of grazing land without being driven off by any existing inhabitants.

Initially Abram and Lot's groups settle side by side, but eventually tensions between their staff over pasture allotments necessitate a separation. Lot chooses the well-watered lands of the Jordan Valley proper, near to the city of Sodom. In time this will prove to be a very poorly advised choice as it locates them near to the city of Sodom, a notoriously evil community that would become synonymous of course, with "life-style" choices that God would judge harshly. Abram, on the other hand, chose to settle for a time, possibly under God's guidance (though we're not told specifically) in the less fertile country to the west, near to Hebron… what is now called the Judean hills.

GOD CHOSE ABRAM. LOT CHOSES SODOM AND GOMORRAH

? DISCUSSION POINTS

1. The lesson highlights the fact that God spoke to Abram (Abraham). Think back over what we've covered so far of God's actions in history and try to remember all the different times God communicated. Also put that in the context of Him speaking to us now through His Word. Would you agree that this aspect of communication is something profoundly essential to who He is? Make any observations you'd like to about what this means to you personally, and also any wider implications.

2. Do you feel a kinship with Abram and his early life in Mesopotamia as a believer in a majority culture that rejects God? What challenges does this bring? Also comment on any parallels you see between God calling Abram to a journey of faith into a new land and your own journey with God into unknown areas (geographic or otherwise).

3. Consider the whole area of faith and trusting God. Describe the contrasts – if any – you see in the picture of faith that is developing in the Biblical narrative and the way it is often presented in popular Christian teaching and books. How do we avoid the trap of being self-seeking or trivial in the exercise of our faith?

➡ ACTIVITIES

1. In approximately half a page write a synopsis of the life of Abraham. Please include a map showing key places.

1.22 God's promises to Abram. God destroyed the twin cities

 OBJECTIVES OF THIS TUTORIAL

Learners will continue to explore and discuss the themes and the truths presented in God's Narrative. The portions of Scripture referred to in this tutorial are: **Genesis 13:14-16, 15:12-16, 17:5,6,15-17, 18:22-33, 19:1-26**

Last time
God recorded His interactions with a man, Abram, whose faith stood in stark contrast to the idolatrous worldview practices of his birth community. At God's urging, Abram left his home city of Ur with his father, Terah, and extended family group to migrate to Canaan. They reached Haran where Terah died. Here God again spoke to Abram, telling him to complete the journey and also making some amazing promises, most notably that through him all the families of the earth will be blessed. In Canaan, Abram and Lot settled in different areas.

God interacts again with Abram
After Lot leaves with his group to settle in the fertile Jordan Valley, God speaks again to Abram. (Genesis 13:14,15) He gives to him and his descendants, all the land around, for as far as he could see in every direction and much more…in fact, He later clarifies, from the Euphrates in the north to the Nile in the south.

God also promised that He would give Abram many descendants. As mentioned before, this was a startling and faith-stretching revelation given that he and his wife, Sarai had never had children. And now, they were well past an age when they could possibly expect to conceive anyway.

Proclaimed righteous
We should take note here of an enormously important theme that will emerge from God's ongoing Narrative and for which Abram is later used as a key example. Abram, of course, was part of Adam's lost, rebellious race and in his daily life, like all humans, he

constantly failed to live up to God's perfect standards. Left to himself, he would inevitably live here on earth separated from God and then experience the ultimate, eternal separation at death.

But because God had provided a way by which man could approach Him, and because Abram did so in faith, taking God at His word, believing His promises - however unlikely they might seem - because of this God accepted Abram, even, we're later told "counting him as righteous". The language and concept here is very much a legal or accounting one. Like all humans, Abram has a "sin-debt" he cannot repay. But Abram knows this, humbly recognizes his need, approaches on God's terms and believes what God says. Seeing this, God *graciously*, credits Abram's faith against his sin debt and proclaims him *righteous*. The *righteousness* is not his own, it is a free gift given from God's own unassailable and limitless righteousness.

Amazingly, God re-writes Abram's story, blending it with His own forever.

A prophecy and new names

We pick the Narrative up again (Genesis 15:12-16) with God foretelling that Abram's descendants will be "strangers in a foreign land where they'll be oppressed as slaves for 400 years". God goes on to say He'll punish the oppressing nation and bring Abram's descendants back to the land He's promised to Abram.

Some time later, as part of a covenant, a contract if you like, with Abram, God changes his name to Abraham (father of many) and Sarai's to the more familiar, Sarah, indicating that she will be the mother of many. God promises her a son, regardless of the seeming human impossibility. (Genesis 17:15-17) Obviously, as the one who wrote the laws of biology in the first place, the fact that Abraham is 100 and Sarah 90 years old and barren creates no obstacle to God fulfilling these promises. He is the Life-giver, the Creator.

Lot in a depraved community

The Narrative now gives us an account of events related to the twin cities of Sodom and Gomorrah…also to Lot, Abraham's cousin and his family who are now living in Sodom itself. The life-style of the inhabitants of these cities had become so flagrantly evil that God decides they cannot be allowed to continue. He will destroy them. The fact that God has allowed them to exist at all – for that matter, any member of Adam's rebellious race – is just another example of His grace. But these people have taken rebellion against God's standards to new levels. Their path is set. He will not continue to endlessly give opportunity for repentance to those who have determined they want no part of Him.

The Narrative (Genesis 18:22-33) records a fascinating exchange in which, Abraham, deferential but persistent - at one point calling himself "but dust and ashes" - gets the Lord to agree not to destroy Sodom if there are 50, 40 even as few as 10 people following Him there. This, of course proves not to be the case.

We're now given an account of incidents that show the depravity which had become commonplace in the two cities. (Genesis 19:1-9) Perhaps partly with the purpose of a final demonstration of just how corrupt the society was, God has two of His angels – His spirit messengers – take human form and come to Sodom. Lot, not knowing who they are but recognizing they are no ordinary people, respectfully invites them to stay at his family home. During the evening, men from all over Sodom surround the house demanding the two men (as they thought) be sent out so they can have their way with them. Lot argues, and, demonstrating at least the temporary absence of God-given moral judgment, offers to send out his two virgin daughters instead. But the men of Sodom will not be diverted from their evil lust for the male visitors that has consumed them. The text says that the angels blinded the eyes of the men so that they eventually gave up.

The homosexuality that was obviously taken for granted in these communities is not given as the direct reason for God destroying them. But it is certainly highlighted in the Narrative as a measure of how far they'd moved away from any concern about God's moral standards. The institution of marriage and the family back in Eden was linked closely with man's caretaking role of the earth as God's image-bearers. As we've seen already and will see throughout His Story, marriage and the family are intended by God to provide a place of mutual love and support, and a context in which His truth can be passed on from one generation to the next. Communities that are in the process of collectively rejecting God's values inevitably evidence that by a devaluing of marriage. Sex outside of marriage becomes the norm, homosexuality is tolerated, those relationships are seen as normal and even formalized legally as "marriage". At that point, not only have individuals made concrete choices that lead away from God, but entire communities, even cultures have utterly rejected Him and His right to tell their Stories. A dangerous place indeed, and one that our society is in today.

Lot and family are rescued as God destroys the cities

So the final act in this particular part of God's story plays out. (Genesis 19:10-25) God graciously decides to save Lot, having listened, we're told, to Abraham's request. The angels tell him to take his family and leave the city before they destroy it. Eventually, when Lot hesitates, the angels rush him, his wife and daughters out. Once they're safely away, the Narrative says that fire and burning sulfur come raining down. Is this part of a volcanic eruption, or an entirely supernatural event? We're not told and, in the final analysis, it really doesn't matter, does it?... God takes complete responsibility, however

He chose to do it. The cities are engulfed and anything remaining is burned. Both are obliterated along with all the inhabitants.

One disturbing cryptic footnote is added to Lot's rescue. The text says that as they are running away his wife looks back and is turned to a pillar of salt. We would no doubt like to know more about this incident, and it is tempting to speculate, but for His own reasons God has chosen not to give us further details. And after all, who are we to argue with how He chooses to tell His Story?

 DISCUSSION POINTS

1. Do you struggle with wondering if, like Abraham, God has accepted you as completely righteous? If so, describe the thought processes involved. What is the source of your concern? How do you try to resolve this? If not – if you're confident in God's view of you as righteous – what do you base this on? (In answering, draw as much as possible on the truth covered in the Biblical narrative so far.)

2. It is clear from the promises God made to Abram, as well as from many other parts of His word, that God can describe what, for us as humans, is still in the future. Describe any personal encouragement you find in knowing this. Also think about how you might try to answer someone who puts forward the argument that surely a loving God who knows the future would stop disasters and tragedies.

3. What do you believe should be our response to living in a culture that accepts homosexuality as nothing more than a personal choice? Should Christians have an active political stance towards issues such as gay marriage? Would you ever have a gay person as a friend? (Please flesh out your answers, using as much as possible any relevant truth from the Biblical narrative so far.)

1.23 God gave Isaac and delivered him from death

 OBJECTIVES OF THIS TUTORIAL

Learners will continue to explore and discuss the themes and the truths presented in God's Narrative. The portions of Scripture referred to in this tutorial are: **Genesis 21:1-3, 22:1-18**

Last time

God promised to give Abram and his many descendants the land of Canaan. Abram's faith, we note from information given later in the Narrative, was credited against his sin-debt, with God proclaiming him righteous in his eyes. Abram became Abraham and Sarai, Sarah. The Narrative describes the events surrounding the rescue of Lot and family from Sodom as God destroyed it along with the city of Gomorrah because of those communities' incessant, unrestrained evil life-styles.

God gives a son to Abraham and Sarah

God continues to tell us His Story (Genesis 21:1-3) with the record of the birth of a son to Abraham and Sarah at the ages of 100 and 90 respectively. God is honoring His promises to Abraham first given many years before. And the circumstances make it very clear that God was responsible. This demonstrates again something we've already seen highlighted in the Narrative so far… God always does what He says, always fulfills His promises – He always acts consistently with who He is. Unlike us, He is not affected by the passing of time, changing interests, new perspectives, different circumstances, trends or public opinion. He speaks and acts out of His own complete and perfect being.

And so having once promised a son to Abraham – with all the implications of that – He made sure that it happened. The time that had gone by, Abraham and Sarah's advanced years, her barrenness… none of these were obstacles or caused God the slightest concern in giving them the son He'd promised.

God tells Abraham to sacrifice Isaac

We pick up the story again after some years have passed. Abraham and Sarah's son, named Isaac, is now a young man. God, the text says, is going to test Abraham's faith. The test will be unimaginably tough. One day, quite suddenly, God tells Abraham to go with Isaac to a particular mountain and there to sacrifice his son.

The simple words of the Narrative provide the outer surface of something full of implications and meaning. Abraham has known the Lord for many years and believed the promises, reaffirmed a number of times over the years. God has said that this entire land of Canaan will be owned by Abraham's descendants, a line that will come through a son God will give to Abraham and Sarah. Through him, Abraham, all the families of the earth are to be blessed.

Now the long-promised, long-waited-for son is here. They've watched him grow…no doubt have been delighted at each stage of his development. We don't know, perhaps Abraham even thought this son was the fulfillment of the prophecy given so long ago to Adam… the Deliverer. Now, without warning, God wants him to build a platform of stones on a mountain top, to have Isaac lay there and to cut his throat until his life-blood runs out! And then to burn his body. To sacrifice him as he would a lamb.

But this is his and Sarah's son. Born against all the odds in their old age. What about the promises? The nation? The blessings to all people of the earth? How would that be fulfilled? No doubt the questions swirled around in Abraham's head. Was there turmoil, the temptation to ignore God's command as too much, too extreme, beyond reasonable expectation…? Hadn't he left his home years ago at God's urging? Hadn't he believed God's promises through the years? Didn't he need to set margins? Does he have no rights? OR, Did Abraham focus on the fact that he actually has no rights before God the Creator anyway. That as part of the lost, rebellious human race and himself a willing sinner, it was only through God's grace he hadn't already paid the ultimate penalty? Had he walked for so long with God that he didn't for one moment doubt, or consider that God would do anything but fulfill His promises? Was Abraham, although naturally as a father concerned for his son, convinced that God cared for and would look after Isaac no matter what? Did he trust God so completely that he was glad to allow Him to write the Story as He intended and as He knew it should be written? It seems so.

They travel to the mountain for the sacrifice

Whatever Abraham's exact thought processes, we do know for sure he believed God and that the belief translated into action. (Genesis 22:3-8) The Narrative says that the next morning Abraham makes preparation and sets out with two servants and Isaac. As would have been normal, given that they are going to a desert, mountainous area, they take firewood so the sacrifice can be burned. They travel for 3 days until, leaving the servants and the donkeys, Abraham and Isaac go alone, with Isaac carrying on his shoulders the firewood with which he will be sacrificed. As they climb the mountain, Isaac is curious about the fact that they have everything needed for the ritual except the usual sheep to be offered to God. Abraham's answer is full of significance. He says, "God will provide a sheep for the burnt offering, my son." This resonates with the faith that God desires to see in us, His image-bearers. This is the opposite of Adam and Eve choosing to work out right and wrong for themselves, to be like small gods in a universe of their own making.

It is acknowledging that He writes the Story of reality, including our lives, our circumstances, and that if we have any significance at all it's because He graciously allows us to be in His Narrative. This faith recognizes our absolute need for Him, in every way.

God provides a substitute to die in Isaac's place

The record, (Genesis 22:9-10) typically, describes in straightforward terms the proceedings that in reality must have involved deep emotion and drama for the players involved. God, as He sees His servant Abraham, obedient and trusting Him implicitly. Abraham, as we can only surmise, beginning to picture taking his own son's life. And Isaac: what emotions must he have experienced as he willingly allowed himself to be bound and laid down on the altar of stones with firewood around him? Then, the climax comes… Abraham picks up the knife; it is suspended above his son's throat. And, at the last possible moment, God relieves the terror and provides a way out. (Genesis 22:11-13) The Narrative says that the Lord – the personal relating One – calls out Abraham's name and tells him to stop. Abraham has proved beyond a shadow of a doubt that his devotion to God is greater even than his love for his son. But in God's economy, a sacrifice has to be made. The approach to Him has to involve death. What's to be done? God's grace again shines out when things seem darkest. He has already provided. A male sheep, a ram, is there caught in the bushes nearby. The ram is sacrificed in Isaac's place. We can only imagine the relief and joy for Abraham and Isaac.

What else is God telling us beneath the surface of these real events? For one thing, as we've already noted, He always follows through on His promises. Abraham's confidence that God would provide is well founded. He has protected the life of the son he'd promised then given to Abraham and Sarah, and He has shown His commitment to His rescue plan for mankind.

The family line, the nation that would come through Isaac, the avenue for the promised Deliverer, would be put in place.

Isaac's situation also provides us with a remarkable and powerful analogy for the plight of the human race. Bound by our sin and the deception of God's Enemy we helplessly wait for death, the ultimate separation. The only hope is God Himself. His grace. His provision. Fortunately for us, that's what He has chosen to make this true Story of His interactions with Adam's hopeless fallen race all about.

❓ DISCUSSION POINTS

1. Given our society's strong emphasis on personal rights and the need to protect our families against extremist religious views, how does it strike you that Abraham unquestioningly obeyed God's command to sacrifice his son? Are there any relevant truth principles you can identify from the narrative so far? Is there any way of applying all of this to today's realities?

2. Comment on the fact that, like Abraham, we are meant to love and respect God, more than anyone or anything on this earth. Reflect on what this means for you. What are the difficulties? What real life factors are involved? In what direction do you look for growth, progress in this area?

3. What is your personal reaction when you consider the fact that like Isaac, bound and about to die, the majority of people are condemned to eternal punishment for their sin? What is your response to the thought that many do not know about their imminent danger or that a perfect substitution has been made on their behalf?

➡ ACTIVITIES

1. Research Mount Moriah - the significant events that have taken place there throughout history as well as its importance today.

1.24 God chose Jacob to be the ancestor of the Deliverer

 OBJECTIVES OF THIS TUTORIAL

Learners will continue to explore and discuss the themes and the truths presented in God's Narrative. The portions of Scripture referred to in this tutorial are: **Genesis 25:1-11,19-34, 27:1-29,41-44, 28:10-16, Genesis 29-35**

Last time

Isaac, the son first promised to Abraham and Sarah long before, was born. God tested Abraham's faith by telling him to sacrifice Isaac, now a young man. Abraham believed and obeyed God. They set out on their journey eventually arriving at the mountain of Moriah where Isaac was bound and laid on the altar. With the knife about to descend, God called out, stopping Abraham and telling him that a ram had been provided as a sacrifice in Isaac's place.

Isaac's wife and sons

We pick up the thread of the Narrative when Isaac is 40 years old. (Genesis 25:19-20) He has just married a woman named Rebekah. Abraham, unwilling for Isaac to marry a local Canaanite woman, has sent back to his Mesopotamian homeland for a wife to be found among his extended family line.

The Account records Abraham's death and the fact that Isaac became the one to whom God entrusted His Promises for that generation. He was to receive the blessing – the special position given by God in those days to the patriarchal ancestor of His chosen people. The line through which the Promised One would come. This special place, originally held by Abraham and now Isaac, included with it assurances of God's special protection and favor. It also came with the right to a double portion of the inheritance and the head place in the family group.

Rebekah was unable to have children but after Isaac pleads with the Lord on her behalf, she becomes pregnant. We're given a few brief but fascinating details related to the pregnancy, which proves to be a difficult one. (Genesis 25:21-23) Concerned, Rebekah asks the Lord what is happening to her. He explains that she is to have twins and that what she's feeling is a prenatal rehearsal of the conflict that will exist between her two sons in life. They are to be the progenitors of two rival nations.

Once again God's straightforward Narrative of events reveals important underlying truths and offers tantalizing clues that draw us on to find out more. Although most of the human players so far have been men, we see the relationship Rebekah has with the Lord. It's also worth noting that God is entirely familiar with her two sons and their futures before they're born. In passing too, we should register the fact that already in the Narrative, God has placed great importance on nations, peoples, language groups and family lines. Clearly He relates to people as individuals, but He also deals with them collectively, as groups.

Jacob and Esau – siblings at odds

Rebekah gave birth to twins, but they were certainly not identical, either physically or in character. (Genesis 25:24-28). Esau, Isaac's favorite, the firstborn - and therefore with the rights to the blessing and inheritance that came with that position – would grow up to be a hairy, rough, impetuous individual, uncomfortable indoors, a hunter. His brother Jacob, is described in the text as having "a quiet temperament, preferring to stay at home." It also adds that his mother, Rebekah, particularly loved him.

An account is given of an event which would have enormous consequences: for them personally, but also in the wider scope of the Narrative. (Genesis 25:29-34) Esau arrives home one day, no doubt from a hunting trip. Tired and ravenously hungry, he demands some of the stew his brother has cooked. Jacob, seeing an opportunity, gets Esau to swear over his birthright to him in exchange for the food. The text comments that this showed Esau's "contempt for his rights as firstborn". Certainly the choice to swap his birthright seems silly and impetuous. And we can see that it was foolish in terms of the material inheritance he had jeopardized. But was this more than just a bad choice made in a moment of weakness? Later God's Word would describe him as "immoral" and "godless". But why? Was this reputation deserved?

As we've noted before, God graciously offers genuine responsibilities to human beings who walk humbly in dependence on Him. But Esau was indifferent to this amazing opportunity. He placed no value on the God-given role of guardian of the Promises as family head. And he was also demonstrating a complete lack of interest in the Promised One for whom God had chosen that family line, and eventual nation, through which He'd come. Like Cain and numerous others not identified in the Narrative, like millions of people today, he was preoccupied with his own felt needs and materialistic interests and was unaware or unwilling to acknowledge his desperate need to see his sin-debt paid for.

Jacob, it turns out, was completely different. We might question his tactics but clearly he hugely valued the firstborn birthrights. As comes out in the next parts of the Narrative, Jacob did recognize his need before God. He humbly approached God on God's terms, sacrificing innocent animals in recognition of the death-separation that his own sin deserved. And, we can safely assume, looking forward with keen anticipation for the arrival of the Promised Deliverer. There is certainly indication later in the Biblical Narrative that God, knowing what these two men would be like, had chosen Jacob for the special position of leading the family line in caretaking the Promises – and so for the enormous privilege of being an ancestor of the Promised Deliverer.

Jacob's journey when he runs away from Esau

Later, Jacob, with Rebekah's complicity, tricks the now aged and blind Isaac into thinking he is Esau. His father gives him the verbal blessing and binding confirmation that he will inherit the firstborn rights. Esau, who as we've noted was indifferent to the spiritual aspects of the position, was furious at the loss of inheritance this represented. The text says that from that time on Esau hated Jacob and decided he would find a way to kill him as soon as their father died. When their mother, Rebekah, hears about his plan she organizes for Jacob to escape and stay away until Esau's anger has time to cool off. (Genesis 27:41-44)

Isaac sets out on the journey of many days north and east from Canaan to Haran, the trade city where Abraham and his group had lived for a time on their family migration from Ur, and where his father Terah had died. It was also Rebekah's home area. Jacob has his famous dream while sleeping outside one night on the trip. (Genesis 28:10-16) A staircase reaches from earth to heaven, with God's messengers going up and down. By showing this to Jacob and having the incident recorded in His Narrative, God was giving a powerful illustration or metaphor for what the Deliverer would do. Through the rebellion of Adam – head of the human race – the relationship between God and man, between heaven and earth, as it were, had been severed. The way God had provided for people to approach Him through the sacrifices was always a stopgap measure.

Satan, death and sin still ruled the earth and its inhabitants. This had created an enormous obstacle to the permanent access between God and man He desired. The sacrifices provided a temporary way around but didn't deal with the problem. That's what He would send the Deliverer for - to provide a permanent avenue for free, unrestricted interchange between God and man, between Heaven and earth. God spoke to Jacob in the dream, reaffirming the promises He'd made to his grandfather Abraham and father, Isaac.

Jacob completes his journey to the lands of relatives in northern Mesopotamia where he lived, as it turns out, for some 20 years. During that time he marries two sisters,

Leah and Rachel. He has 11 sons, the last, Benjamin being born after their eventual return to Canaan. During the trip back God gave Jacob a new name, Israel. He settled in Canaan again, and in time the growing family, then later the nation (that did and continues to have such a large part in God's Story) would bear his name.

? DISCUSSION POINTS

1. Clearly Esau and Jacob were very different kinds of people. Make some observations about the whole "nature vs. nurture" debate. (If necessary, do some brief research on what modern psychology says about this issue). Was Esau somehow less responsible for his actions than Jacob because of predilections he was born with? Are you ever tempted to excuse your attitudes and actions because "that's just who you are"? How would you describe God's perspective on this issue based on this story and the rest of the narrative so far?

2. As highlighted in the lesson, Jacob's dream reinforces once again that salvation is all about God making a way for man. Reflect on anything you might have heard in "gospel messages" that seems to paint a different picture than this. Would you agree that often the focus is on what people have to do to receive salvation, or the results in their lives? If so, do you have any thoughts on why this so often ends up as the focus instead of it being on God and his response to our real need?

1.25 God promoted Joseph. God took Jacob's family into Egypt

 OBJECTIVES OF THIS TUTORIAL

Learners will continue to explore and discuss the themes and the truths presented in God's Narrative. The portions of Scripture referred to in this tutorial are: **Genesis 37:1-36, 39:1-23, Genesis 40, 41, 42**

Last time

Abraham died and Isaac inherited the blessings and the Promises as head of the family line. With his wife, Rebekah, he had two sons, Esau and Jacob who were vastly different in character. Although Esau was the firstborn, Jacob - God's chosen successor to Isaac - is able to get his brother to relinquish his rights as guardian of God's Promises and then to be blessed as principal heir by his father. While traveling to Haran to escape Esau's murderous anger, in a dream Jacob was shown a stairway from earth to heaven that symbolizes what the Deliverer will do. Later he has 12 sons and was renamed Israel, by God.

Joseph, loved by his father, hated by his brothers

God's story now focuses on Joseph - favorite son of his father Jacob, having been born to him later in life. (Genesis 37:1-4) Though obviously not distinguished by the special blessing and firstborn rights of his generation in the family line, Joseph nonetheless had a very real relationship with God. Later in God's Narrative he would be identified alongside other historical figures known for their faith.

The account of Joseph's life starts when he's 17 years old, working as a shepherd under his brothers as they tend the family flocks and fields. Joseph informs his father Jacob about some bad things the brothers are up to. Their resentment and criticism turns to hatred after their father gives Joseph a particularly fine robe, as a measure of his favoritism. Their hatred is fueled further when Joseph tells them a dream he's had in which they, represented by bundles of grain, bow down to him. (Genesis 37:5-11) As we see later, this dream was actually God pointing to events that will unfold later in the

Narrative... reminding us again that God, existing outside of the confines of time, has full knowledge of things that to us are still "future".

Later, in another predictive dream, his family, symbolized by planets, bow to him.

Sold as a slave and taken to Egypt

The resentment, jealousy and hatred of Joseph's brothers can be contained no longer. (Genesis 37:12-36) One day Jacob sends Joseph to check on his brothers who have taken the flocks to pastures a long way from the family home. The brothers seize the opportunity. Their first thought is to kill him, but when they see a caravan of Ishmaelite traders on their way down to Egypt, they sell Joseph to them as a slave. The brothers send the distinctive coat back to Jacob covered in goat's blood, and he believes that wild animals have killed Joseph. Meanwhile, Joseph is sold as a slave to Potiphar, an officer of the king (Pharaoh) of Egypt.

Promoted, falsely accused, imprisoned, promoted

Joseph's situation in Egypt proves not to be terrible, at least for a time. (Genesis 39:1-6) God says in His Narrative that He was with Joseph and helping him to succeed in the house of his master, the captain of the Pharaoh's guard. He becomes Potiphar's personal attendant and is put in charge of the entire household, eventually being made administrator of all his master's affairs.

But trouble is brewing. (Genesis 39:6-20) Potiphar's wife propositions the young, handsome Hebrew. He refuses her, being unwilling to betray the trust invested in him by her husband and, more importantly, to sin against God in this way. In resentment after repeated refusals, she maliciously accuses Joseph of trying to rape her. He is thrown into a prison which, the text says, is where the "king's prisoners are held". But here too, we're told, (Genesis 39:21-23) "the Lord was with Joseph... and showed him is faithful love." He is orchestrating events. Joseph becomes a favorite of the warden and is put in charge of all the prisoners and the running of the place.

Interpreting dreams, then governor of Egypt

The next part of the Narrative (Genesis 40) records an incident in which God gives Joseph the ability to interpret dreams for some former high-ranking fellow prisoners. It seems an isolated incident, but will prove important two years later when Pharaoh has two very disturbing, apparently predictive, dreams. (Genesis 41:1-13) It's worth noting here that God was perfectly able and willing to communicate in this way to the ruler of a culture, which had long ago turned away from God as their true Storyteller. As Pharaoh, he was given semi-divine status in a complex system of polytheistic beliefs with a multitude of deities (the Sun and the Nile river among many), creation myths and elaborate religious rituals. When the divination experts – the "magicians and wise men" – are unable to make sense of the dreams, it is remembered that a young Hebrew slave in the king's prison has abilities in this area. When sent for (Genesis 41:14-32), Joseph denies the ability to divine such things himself, but asserts that God is able to clarify the meaning for Pharaoh if He chooses to.

The Pharaoh recounts his dreams of 7 emaciated cows eating 7 well-nourished cows and 7 diseased heads of grain swallowing 7 healthy heads. Joseph explains to Pharaoh that God has revealed to him that this represents 7 years of prosperity He will bring to Egypt followed by 7 years of famine. Joseph suggests that someone be put in charge of Egypt to coordinate the collection and storage of crops during the plentiful years against the following time of want. (Genesis 41:33-36) This idea's merits are obvious and Joseph having impressed Pharaoh with his intelligence and wisdom is promoted to the position. In fact, he is given a rank in the nation of Egypt answerable only to Pharaoh himself. (Genesis 41:37-46)

Famine spreads and Joseph's family comes to Egypt

Events unfold just as God had said they would. (Genesis 41:47-57) Joseph, in his position of enormous influence, sees to it that the surplus is gathered and stored during 7 bumper years... then the famine hits. Egypt and the surrounding countries are gripped by drought and food becomes short.

Now Joseph's foresight pays off. The storehouses are opened and distribution begins. And people from neighboring countries are forced to buy grain from Egypt. To the north-east, Canaan is severely impacted by famine as well. Hearing that grain is available in Egypt, Jacob sends his ten sons – Joseph's older brothers – to buy some to tide them over. (Genesis 42)

They come before the governor overseeing sales of grain. They are unaware that it is Joseph but he recognizes them as they bow before him, in fulfillment of the predictive dreams he'd had from God so many years go. He accuses them of being spies, but they protest their innocence, stating they are 12 brothers, with one missing and one back home in Canaan.

Joseph sends them back to get their youngest brother as proof of their story, keeping one, Simeon, as hostage. With the famine worsening, the brothers return to Egypt to buy more food, this time with their youngest brother Benjamin. Joseph stage manages a number of events which put the brothers under a great deal of stress, but eventually reveals his identity as the brother they'd sold into slavery years before. Of course they are dumbfounded. Pharaoh and the palace are delighted that Joseph has renewed contact with his family. He insists that Joseph sends for his father to come to Egypt. In wagons provided by Pharaoh, Jacob (also known as Israel) and the entire extended family, along with all their possessions and their livestock come to Egypt. They settle there and, as a people group, come to be known as "The Children of Israel". And his 12 sons, of course, would be the patriarchs of twelve tribes.

For the human players in all of this, it would have played out as sequential experiences of life. They had no way to see all the immediate connections or future implications. But God was hands-on involved in working the events seamlessly together for His purposes. Remember the prophecy He had made to Abraham, Jacob's grandfather – that his descendants would go to a foreign land where they would be strangers. The Plan was on track. He was, and is, writing His Story of reality in and through the lives of people.

? DISCUSSION POINTS

1. Can you describe any personal parallels with Joseph's experience – a time when you felt that you had been sidelined or when a particular direction had been blocked? In retrospect, can you see how God was achieving something different - but better - than you had originally planned? Reflect in a broader sense on what this tells us about God and how He works in and through the lives of people.

2. The lesson makes the point that the giving of dreams to the Egyptian ruler is an example of God sovereignly using people to achieve His purposes. Think back through the Biblical narrative so far and identify any other such instances. Also note times when God gave very real choices to people, even holding them accountable for their decisions. Give your thoughts on how we can come to terms with this apparent contradiction in the way God deals with us.

→ ACTIVITIES

1. Research and write in less than a page a summary of the time in Egyptian history where this part of the Narrative takes place. Have a look at the culture and lifestyle plus the religion of Egypt around the time of Joseph (sometime between 2000 and 1600 BC).

1.26 God preserved the Israelites and protected Moses

 OBJECTIVES OF THIS TUTORIAL

Learners will continue to explore and discuss the themes and the truths presented in God's Narrative. The portions of Scripture referred to in this tutorial are: **Exodus 1, 2, 3, 4:1-17, 29-31**

Last time

God's Narrative focused on the life of Joseph, one of Isaac's 12 sons. Hated by his brothers for his father's very evident favoritism, they sold him into slavery in Egypt. He experienced some major ups and downs, but with God orchestrating the outcomes, he was eventually promoted to governor of Egypt. In time he was reunited with his family and, at the invitation of the Pharaoh, they came and settled in Egypt.

The Israelites are made slaves in Egypt

We pick up the Narrative again a few generations later. (Exodus 1:6-10) The descendants of Jacob or Israel, living still in Egypt, now number in the hundreds of thousands. They have not assimilated into Egyptian culture but have retained their own distinct ethnic identity and monotheistic religion, i.e. worship of the One true Creator God. As a people, they are wealthy and have become a powerful force in Egypt.

Of course the king or Pharaoh who knew Joseph is long gone and the one currently on the throne has no affection or loyalty toward the Israelites. They present a dilemma for him and the ruling elite. Their skills are needed for Egypt's economy (a growing "world" power) but militarily they represent a real threat. What if they side with an enemy during an attempted invasion?

The solution, Pharaoh decides, is to retain their skills and sheer manpower, but to take away the freedom they've had to pursue their own prosperity. (Exodus 1:11-22) They are made slaves, purposely mistreated and brutalized. Their lives, the text says, were "made bitter". But the oppression does not have the desired result, at least in terms of population. As the years go by, the Israelites continue to grow in numbers. Pharaoh's iron fist clenches tighter. In the first recorded instance of ethnic cleansing, it is decreed that newborn males are to be drowned in the Nile River.

It is not difficult to see God's arch-enemy, Satan, maliciously at work in these events – fanning the hatred and encouraging the attempt to suppress, even to utterly destroy, God's people. He would not have been pleased to see Jacob's descendants growing into a real ethnic force, a nation (although yet without a homeland). He did not want to see the line flourishing by which God had said One would come to crush him, to take away his power over the earth and its inhabitants. This must be stopped. And in the Egyptians, already trapped in his web of deceit, he had willing, if unknowing, servants. Ironic, isn't it, that they thought they were the slave masters?

Moses is born and brought up as an Egyptian prince

It goes without saying that none of this came as a surprise to God. He had, after all, foretold it centuries before to Abraham, saying that his descendants would be strangers in a land where they'd be oppressed as slaves. God was under no obligation to relieve their suffering or to rescue them from the fierce oppression. Of course He had made promises to Abraham, Isaac and Jacob, but it's not like He's just held, in some technical objective way, by His word…although of course He will never break it. But His motivations are also very *personal*, as He's already shown us in His Narrative. He is moved by human suffering. He loves to show mercy, to be kind. He reaches out and rescues people who know that they need Him. And so He sets in motion a plan to deliver the Israelites. (Exodus 2:1-10)

A couple from the tribe of Levi have a son. After 3 months of trying to keep him hidden from the Egyptian authorities, a long-term solution must be found. Placing him in a waterproofed basket among the reeds at the edge of the Nile, his mother has her daughter watch to see what will happen. She feels that he's a special child. Will he be killed like so many other baby boys or will God do something? Pharaoh's daughter, coming with her attendants to bathe, finds the child and though realizing he's Hebrew decides he's to live. She names him Moses and later adopts him as her own child. He receives an Egyptian education, probably the most advanced of any in the world at the time.

God, we'll see, was equipping and positioning Moses to contribute in His plans to rescue the Israelites. As we've noted a number of times, God gives real responsibilities to humans and we'll see as the Narrative continues, that He equips His people and draws them into efforts to rescue others in need.

Moses' years of exile

As an adult, Moses starts to feel empathy for the oppressed Hebrew people with whom he shares a common ethnicity. (Exodus 2:11-22) He visits the areas where they live and work. At one point he kills an Egyptian after he's seen him beating a Hebrew. Burying the body, Moses thinks he's in the clear, but when the news gets out, even reaching Pharaoh's ears, Moses is forced to run away…the text says to "Midian", probably somewhere to the north-east.

Moses married and settled in the area, isolated for many years from both his Hebrew birth community and the Egyptian one in which he grew up.

The Narrative tells us (Exodus 2:23-25) that although Pharaoh died – to be succeeded of course by another – the misery of the Israelites did not lessen. God says that He heard their cry for help. He remembered His covenant promise to Abraham, Isaac and Jacob and the, text says, He "knew it was time to act".

God is reminding us in His Story of things we've already noted before: He is compassionate and merciful and eager to help those who recognize their need for Him. He is also faithful and absolutely committed to the things He's said He'll do. Like Isaac on the altar, the situation of the Israelites provides us with a powerful analogy of the plight of the human race as a whole. Held in bondage by Satan's deception and in servitude to sin - the merciless taskmaster - there's no escape, no hope…except for God, unless He has a Plan, unless he sends Someone.

So God listened and began to act, but typically, it's not in a way we'd expect. One day Moses leads the flocks he's tending into the wilderness area on a mountain that will prove significant in the future – Mt Sinai (also called Horeb).

"I AM", recruits Moses for His rescue plan

There he sees an extraordinary sight, a bush engulfed in flames, but without being burned up. He's awestruck when his name is called from out of the burning bush, especially when the speaker identifies Himself as no less than the God of Abraham, Isaac and Jacob. (Exodus 3:1- 4:17) The Lord says that He has seen the oppression of his people and heard their cries of distress. Now He intends to rescue them and lead them out, back to the land of Canaan, currently inhabited by a number of other people groups.

But this is not just information, the Lord tells Moses that He's sending him to Pharaoh, and that He's chosen Moses to lead the people out of Egypt. Moses is horrified. He doesn't feel qualified. He has no authority, no position. God reassures Moses that He is with him and, as a sign, tells him that one day he, Moses, will lead the Israelites to this very mountain to worship God there.

But Moses remains dubious. If he goes to the Israelites saying the God of their ancestors has sent him, they're going to want to know who it is, what's His name. Who should he say? In reply God says something linguistically simple but immeasurably deep in its implications. He says, "I AM WHO I AM" tell them "I AM" has sent you, and adds that this is His "eternal name" one to be remembered for all generations.

This name – which He'll use again under very different circumstances in His Narrative – is the most profound utterance possible in human language. We glimpse its infinite depths, but know we're never getting very far below the surface. It is God declaring verbally, in words, in a single name, His own eternal, absolute being…and, by extension, the complete ontological dependence on Him of everything, including us as humans.

Remarkably perhaps, despite this name, despite other signs and undertakings from God, Moses is still a reluctant. He pleads his lack of speaking ability. The interaction between them is wonderfully real and personal. God's patience finally wears thin. He asks Moses who made his mouth, whose decision was it to have humans speak or hear or see anyway? When Moses still asks for someone else to go, God agrees to allow Aaron, Moses' brother to be the spokesman.

Eventually the two of them go to the leaders of the Israelite community and tell them what God has said to Moses about rescuing them from bondage. (Exodus 4:29,30) After they see the miraculous signs from God they are convinced. The text says, "When they heard that the LORD was concerned about them and had seen their misery, they bowed down and worshiped." (Exodus 4:31)

? DISCUSSION POINTS

1. This lesson concludes that Satan was using the Egyptian ruler to destroy the lineage through which God had promised that the Deliverer would come. How does this strike you? Comment on how much the idea of Satan actively scheming against God's purposes comes into the normal course of your daily life. How would you try to talk about the existence of malevolent spirit beings to someone in our society, brought up with a scientific, materialistic worldview? (If necessary, do some brief research on materialism).

2. Make any observations you care to about the way that God prepared and then related to Moses. Do you think that the humility Moses displayed and his recognition of his own weakness was a necessary factor in being able to contribute to God's purposes? Can you identify a possible principle here: a connection between our posture and attitudes on the one hand, and God involving us in what He's about on the other?

➡ ACTIVITIES

1. The lesson touches on some of the incredible implications of God calling Himself "I AM". Contrast this with the worldview assumptions of existentialism (If necessary do some brief research on existentialism). What do you think of the idea that even we, who believe in a Creator God, often default to the view that it is our existence that is most important? Write or record some notes on your thoughts about this subject.

1.27 The Lord sent plagues on the Egyptians

 OBJECTIVES OF THIS TUTORIAL

Learners will continue to explore and discuss the themes and the truths presented in God's Narrative. The portions of Scripture referred to in this tutorial are: **Exodus 5:1-18, 6:1-8, Exodus 7-12**

Last time

The Egyptian Pharaoh had become concerned about the Israelite ethnic community which had grown dramatically in numbers, wealth and influence. They were enslaved, mistreated terribly and their firstborn sons were killed. One baby was saved by Pharaoh's daughter and raised as her son, Moses. As an adult he fled possible retribution after he'd killed an Egyptian. Many years later, God appeared to him in the burning bush and sent Moses and Aaron, his brother, to Egypt to lead His people out of their bondage.

Pharaoh flatly denies a request

Having first of all convinced the Israelite community that God has appointed them, Moses and Aaron now go to speak to Pharaoh. (Exodus 5:1-4) They pass on a message from the God of Israel, "Let my people go so they can hold a festival in my honor in the wilderness." The King is dismissive, "Oh yeah, sure! I don't know this Lord, why should I listen to Him. There's no way I'm going to let the Israelite people go." Moses and Aaron persist, but their request is flatly denied. In fact, Pharaoh's response is to make life even tougher for the Israelites…now they were still expected to reach their work quotas, but they had to find their own raw materials.

This arrogant ruler had no interest in knowing about, much less submitting to, the God of the subjugated Hebrew people. Revered as a deity in life, as he would be in death, head of the civil administration, supreme warlord and chief priest of the kingdom, he lived at the very pinnacle of his world. He presided over a society that had long before turned away from God's true Story and accepted a range of creation myths of their own invention. Sadly, none of their truly amazing architectural and artistic achievements were done with the guidance, or in honor, of God. Their assurance in their own abilities, their confidence in their own versions of how to cope with life and death, and their disinterest in God's truth even when it was readily accessible to them, are all startlingly similar to our own culture.

God achieves His purposes regardless of human response

Because of who He is, because He's always looking for opportunities to show grace and mercy, God would have gladly responded to Pharaoh and his people if they'd been willing to listen and recognize their need for Him. But when that's not the case, like here when the Egyptian ruler responds with arrogant dismissiveness, God isn't perplexed or caught off guard. In fact, it is clear from the Narrative – Exodus 7:4-5 and 9:16 point this out – that God knew full well, at every juncture, what Pharaoh's responses were going to be. So He doesn't manipulate or force peoples' reactions – remember that creating humans in His image involved giving us real freedom to make choices – but whatever the response (humble & repentant or proud and rebellious), He is always well prepared to use it as an opportunity to reveal himself.

So now God tells Moses that by the time He's done with Pharaoh he'll not only let the people go, he will actually "force them to leave his land." (Exodus 6:1-8) God is going to use this arrogant, stubborn king to demonstrate His power and to prove to His chosen people, the Israelites, that He is their God. He doesn't want their knowledge of Him to be a purely factual account of His interaction with Abraham, Isaac and Jacob…nor for their relationship to be reduced to dry religious activities. He wants this generation of his chosen people to know him *themselves*. Yes, to be familiar with the history of His interaction with their forefathers, but He wants to show who He is in the cut and thrust of real life events, as He frees *them* from bondage, responds to *their* very pressing needs, and provides what He knows they need most.

God demonstrates His power through 9 plagues

The Narrative (Exodus Ch. 7-10) now details 9 plagues that God inflicted on the Egyptian people. The impact of what some have dismissed as "natural" disasters, each coming on the heels of the other in quick succession, is difficult to imagine. It must have been completely devastating as the Nile river turned to blood, quickly to be followed by a plague of frogs, then swarms of gnats and biting flies. Next a disease wiped out Egyptian livestock in great numbers. After this came an epidemic of boils, then an enormously destructive hailstorm, a plague of locusts and finally 3 days of total darkness.

God was demonstrating His power in contrast to the impotence of the gods of Egyptian belief... the Nile and all the river deities, Akhor god of the earth, Apis the sacred bull god, Ra the sun-god, and numerous others were clearly unable to protect the Egyptians against the devastating power of the God of the Israelites, the One true Creator. This message was highlighted by the fact that the Israelite community was spared from the plagues. God was showing His love and mercy to them, and reaffirming that they were truly His chosen people. As each new plague or traumatic event gripped the Egyptian communities, Pharaoh would agree to let the Israelites go. When the situation would begin to ease, he'd become defiant and reverse his decision. Finally, after the last plague of intense darkness, Pharaoh says he'll kill Moses if he comes again to ask for the release of the Israelites. Something has to give.

God brings death while providing a way of escape

The Lord tells Moses He's going to strike one final blow against Egypt, after which Pharaoh will be eager for the Israelites to leave the country. The firstborn son of every Egyptian family, God says, from the throne down to the lowest peasants, will die. (Exodus 11:1-7) But this time, rather than automatically shielding the Israelites, God gives instructions they are to follow precisely if they're to avoid calamity. As always, His intention was to communicate, to reveal, to instruct... for them in their time but also for all who would hear and read this Narrative in the future.

They were to choose a flawless lamb or young goat, without deformity or injury – a reflection of God's own perfect, righteous standards. (Exodus Ch. 12) Then, at a designated date they were to kill the lamb... as usual, its life-blood was to flow completely out – a striking picture of the death their sin-debt had incurred and so that animal could die in place of their firstborn children. The parallel with Isaac and the substitute ram provided by God is obvious. An instruction is added by God that, on the surface, seems of little importance but which will prove to have real significance later in the Narrative – He says that the bones of the animal are not to be broken as it's killed or later eaten.

The Israelite families were to smear some of the blood on the sides and top of the doorframes of that house. Then, having eaten a meal that included the meat of the lamb or goat, they were to stay inside the house with the blood marks on the doorframe. God promises (Exodus 12:12-13) that when He's going through the land of Egypt taking the life of the firstborn children and animals, demonstrating that He, not the Egyptian false gods are in control... during this night of terrible death, He will take no life in the houses where He sees the blood on the doorposts. The blood would serve as a mark, as evidence, that death had already come. As always, the way of escape was only by His provision, according to His specifications, aligned with who He is. Any efforts of their own, no matter how sincere, devout, even painful or costly, will not suffice. They are in no position to argue or attempt some other means of escape. The situation is urgent, desperate. It's life or death. And the Israelites the realities of the situation. They believed God and followed His instructions implicitly. And they were able to hide, as it were, behind the safety of the blood with all it represented. (Exodus 12:28-30)

The Egyptians of course were defenseless. Their arrogant defiance, the stories they'd told themselves, the belief system they'd developed, the gods they'd imagined…none of it protected them against God's righteous judgment. On the doors of their houses there was no blood, nothing to indicate that substitutionary death had taken place. And so at midnight, the Narrative says God struck down the firstborn sons of Egypt, from the Pharaoh's household, right down to the sons of prisoners in the dungeons. As each family discovered their dead the sound of dreadful mourning could be heard rising up from one house and then another throughout their community.

Pharaoh tells the Israelites to go

Pharaoh has finally had enough. (Exodus 12:31-33) He sends for Aaron and Moses and tells them to take their fellow Israelites and leave his country. And the Egyptians were so eager to have them leave that they gladly handed over large amounts of their wealth, including silver and gold. God had fulfilled His promises, to Moses and His people. And His prophecy to Abraham hundreds of years before had proved to be entirely true as well… even in the details that His people would come away with great wealth after the enslaving nation had been punished.

❓ DISCUSSION POINTS

1. As the lesson notes, ancient Egypt had rejected the true Creator God. In light of that, draw any parallels you can between that civilization and our own, keeping in mind the remarkable achievements of both. Are there observations to be made from this about what it means for humans to have been created in God's image despite our fallen condition?

2. As the lesson explains, God used the plagues to reveal Himself and demonstrate His total superiority over the gods of the Egyptians' beliefs. Describe briefly what you can of a worldview system significantly different from that of our majority culture (do some study if necessary). Then, in outline form, describe how you would attempt to share about God with someone who held those beliefs.

3. What is your personal response to the fact that God protected the Israelites from the terrible results of the plagues? Note some other instances in the Biblical narrative so far that stand out as examples of God's grace. Think of some ways that the word or idea of grace is used in our society that falls short or is entirely different from the grace we see in God's dealings with people.

1.28 God delivered the Israelites & continued to provide for them

 OBJECTIVES OF THIS TUTORIAL

Learners will continue to explore and discuss the themes and the truths presented in God's Narrative. The portions of Scripture referred to in this tutorial are: **Exodus 13: 17-22, Exodus 14, 16,17**

Last time
Pharaoh arrogantly dismissed Moses' request from God to let the Israelites go. God, already aware of all the outcomes, inflicted a series of 9 plagues on the Egyptian community, but protected His own people. When Pharaoh remained defiant, God brought one final calamitous judgment. He instructed the Israelites to smear the blood of the animals they'd killed on their doorframes and then to stay inside. That night, God took the life of every Egyptian firstborn son, but seeing the blood on the Israelite houses, he spared them. Pharaoh ordered the Israelites to leave the country.

God led the Israelites to the Red Sea
So God had achieved what He said He would... after the years of bondage, His chosen people were finally free to leave Egypt. He had amply demonstrated His power in the process and was keeping His promises to Abraham, Isaac and Jacob about their descendants. He was also preserving Abraham's family line, now an embryonic nation, through which the promised Deliverer was to come.

Finally, as we'll see in the Narrative, by protecting the Israelites, God was putting in place a people group who would be His human storytellers for the next 1500 years. This would be through individuals - prophets - whose words spoken at God's instigation would be recorded in what we call the Old Testament.

God also tasked the people group as a whole with preserving and telling His Story, for the benefit of all humanity. In part, the telling of his Story, revealing who He is...was also to be told in the narrative of their lives - as they showed the other people groups what it was like to live in a relationship with the true and living God.

GOD DELIVERED THE ISRAELITES & CONTINUED TO PROVIDE FOR THEM

Moses was God's chosen storyteller for the first part of the written record of His Narrative. His contribution comprises the first 5 books in what would eventually be called the Old Testament.

So now, Moses, an eyewitness of course to these events, continues the account, as God wanted it told, of the escape of the Israelites from Egypt. From Goshen, the location of the Israelite community in Egypt on the south-east edge of the Nile delta, the shortest and most obvious way out of Egypt, and especially toward Canaan, would have been the caravan route that followed the Mediterranean coast around. Instead, God leads them out into the desert in a south-easterly direction away from a potentially demoralizing encounter with the hostile Philistines. A warlike seafaring people, they had by now established themselves along the Mediterranean with a line of garrisons that dominated the coastal trade route. But how exactly did God lead the Israelites? Remember this would have been an immense group strung out for kilometers – perhaps over 2 million adults and children, with all their livestock and belongings. (Exodus 13:17-22) The text says that God was then leading them by a pillar of cloud that stayed with them throughout the entire journey.

God had now taken up a very visible role of leading them as a community. Moses was His human mouthpiece, but it would be God showing the way. He leads them to the shore of the Red Sea where they camp. (Exodus 14:1-4) But why are they here? What now? The people were no doubt perplexed. And their consternation was going to get a lot worse. But God was completely in control. They still had much to learn about Him and He was, as always, committed to teaching and revealing who He is.

Trapped! Only God can rescue them

Pharaoh and his ruling elite have been having second thoughts about the Israelites' departure. Now he gets word that they are camped at the shore of the Red Sea, apparently without any clear plan of where to go or what to do. He sees a chance to get them back. (Exodus 14:5-9) Undoubtedly urged on unknowingly by his slave master, Satan, Pharaoh is still defiant. After everything that has taken place, he still hasn't learned anything.

Access to truth is clearly not the only prerequisite to wisdom; it also involves humility in the stance that people take before God. There's no one so profoundly blind as a person who refuses to see what's right in their face. So Pharaoh decides to recapture the Israelites. The troops are mobilized and Pharaoh leads them in the pursuit until they're almost within striking distance of their former slaves. When the Israelites see them coming, they panic: (Exodus 14;10-14) They call out to God, but not in faith. Suddenly they've forgotten all the things God has done to get them out of Egypt. They turn on Moses, "Why didn't you leave us alone in slavery? We said this would happen. Better to be a slave in Egypt than a corpse in the wilderness." He tells them to just wait and see what God will do. Certainly, without God in the picture, their situation was a desperate one. They were trapped. Pressed against the Red Sea with the revengeful king and his army bearing down on them.

These real events provide us with yet another powerful analogy for the plight of the human race. Like the Israelites, we have no way of escape. No direction in which to escape what it means to be part of Adam's lost race. No way to be free from the sin that we are willingly enslaved by. No chance of avoiding the ultimate separation of death, and the punishment that we deserve. Without God providing a way of escape we truly have no way.

God rescues His people and destroys the Egyptian army

The Narrative here is familiar to us, but the contempt that comes with familiarity itself is no doubt one of the Enemy's objectives. To reduce God's Narrative to a series of nice Sunday school stories, the well-trodden territory of 3-point sermons or even the plot of old blockbuster Hollywood movies. But as we've reminded ourselves before, these events were truly God in action, revealing who He is then and now, as we follow His Narrative.

So the Israelites have no other option and the Egyptians think they're going to round them up and take them back to slavery…perhaps killing some as a lesson not to even think of leaving again… At this critical moment God acts. He has not turned His back on His people even though they don't deserve His mercy at all. (Exodus 14:15-31) He has Moses raise his staff – his all-purpose shepherd's crook and walking stick – and God, the creator of oceans, seas, rivers, lakes, water, hydrogen, oxygen and sodium molecules…makes a dry path in the sea bed. And the whole 2 million plus Israelites with all their animals and all their stuff walk through, "with walls of water on each side".

The Egyptians coming behind don't hesitate. They don't stop to wonder how this is happening, or how long it will last. Down they go with their chariots, into the path God has made. They're intent on their mission, to bring back their slaves on whose backs so much of their prosperity has been built. It's night, but they push hard. Suddenly, just as dawn is breaking, there's confusion, their wheels are bogging, they can't steer, the cry goes up to turn back, turn back. The Lord is fighting for the Israelites. But it's too late. The walls of water come crashing in. As the sun comes up God's people see the bodies washed up on the shore. And they were filled with awe at this God, the God of their fathers, now *their* God.

Awe is an apt response when God reveals himself to us through his actions…a mixture of reverence, respect, fear and wonder. Securing the Israelites' release from Egypt, followed by the dramatic rescue at the Red Sea, serve in God's Narrative as a landmark. His actions there have been remembered down through history as the unmistakable evidence of His faithfulness, His power, and His mercy. And the events continue to provide us with powerful analogies and metaphors for how He rescues and redeems people in bondage who turn to Him for help.

God provides in the wilderness

It's a month after the dramatic departure from Egypt, with the sea to their right, the 12 tribes have traveled down the Sinai Peninsula. They're now deep into the wilderness. The euphoria of their Red Sea escape has evaporated in the dry desert...along with the gratitude to God for their escape, and their confidence in Aaron and Moses. (Exodus Ch 16 and 17) They're questioning again whether they weren't better off in Egypt. "Did you just bring us out here to starve to death?"

God, graciously and patiently overlooking their ingratitude and lack of faith, provides food – flocks of birds, quail, for meat and a fine, almost flour-like substance that's left on the ground each morning... called manna - "what is it?" - in memory of their first astonishment. Later, when water is short, they return to their complaining. God again graciously provides. They deserve no less than to be left to die of thirst in the wilderness, but God, the provider, gives them the water that they need. Moses is instructed to strike a particular rock. When he does, water comes gushing out... more than enough for the people and their livestock.

For better or worse, God's Story has now also become the Story of a particular people. Complaining, frustrating, lacking in faith, argumentative... but His people. He chooses to join His great Narrative with the smaller stories of individuals and the story of a Group of People who He calls his own... through no merit of their own, entirely because of His grace.

❓ DISCUSSION POINTS

1. The lesson makes the point that God chose Israel as an avenue for His communication to the world at that time. Focusing just on the Old Testament narrative for now, consider the enormous consequences of His Story being written down and preserved. What does this tell us about God? What are some of the historical results: for the world, for the Jewish people, for us as believers?

2. By taking the Israelites to the Red Sea where they had no escape, God created a situation in which only He could save them. Describe how this is consistent with one of the most important themes emerging from the Biblical narrative. Do you believe this is a message that many people in our society, or any other welcome?

3. Make any observations you care to about the fact that although the Israelites saw many events which could only be explained by God's intervention, this did not seem to produce lasting faith. Reflect on your own experience in relating to God: are you ever tempted to think that your faith would be stronger if God did more tangible things on your behalf? How does He reveal Himself, and do you have thoughts on why this would be the very best way?

➡ ACTIVITIES

1. Research the geography/terrain of the Sinai Peninsula and the shores of the Red Sea. (Map on the following page)

GOD DELIVERED THE ISRAELITES & CONTINUED TO PROVIDE FOR THEM

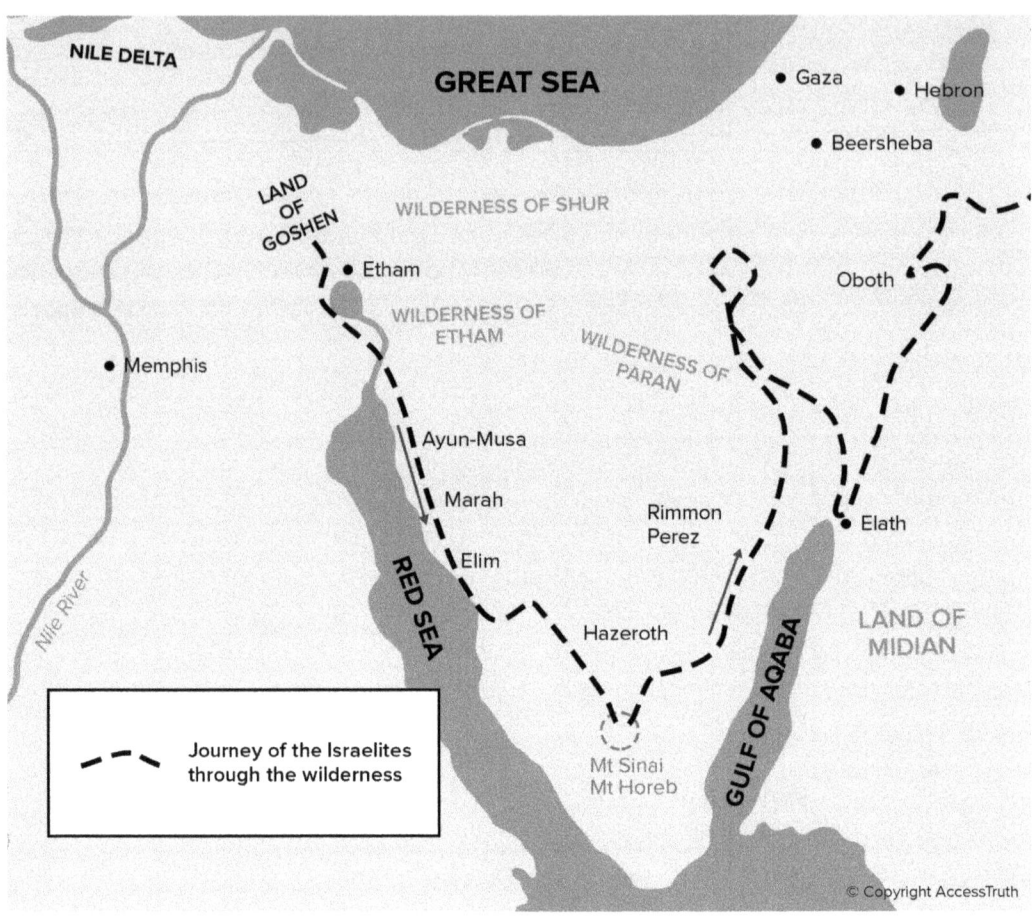

1.29 God's agreement to bless the Israelites if they obey Him

 OBJECTIVES OF THIS TUTORIAL

Learners will continue to explore and discuss the themes and the truths presented in God's Narrative. The portions of Scripture referred to in this tutorial are: **Exodus 19:1-8**

Last time

God led the Israelites out of the inhabited communities of Egypt toward the Red Sea. When Pharaoh heard they seemed directionless, he set out with his army to recapture them. Trapped with their backs to the sea and their enemies thundering toward them in chariots, the Israelites had no escape unless God rescued them. God opened up the sea and, once they were safely through, allowed the water to crash back down, drowning the pursuing Egyptian army.

He provided food and water for the Israelites as they pushed on into the wilderness.

God leads the Israelites to Mount Sinai

Continuing to lead the Israelites by day and night, God brings them to the foot of Mount Sinai. (Exodus 19:1,2) They set up camp there in the wilderness with the mountain looming over them. God's "sign" to Moses way back during the burning bush conversation – that He would bring him and the Israelites back to this mountain to worship Him – has indeed come true. What takes place at Sinai is going to have massive implications for the Israelites and for the human race as a whole. The things God was to reveal about Himself there would echo down through history and have an enormous influence on many societies and cultures, including our own. But here in the immediate time frame of the Narrative, God had brought the Israelites there, as we'll see, to make an agreement with them as a people.

Another term for this agreement in English is *covenant*, which, correctly, gives the sense of it being more formal, and binding, contractual... the older English word that has fallen out of general use is *testament*. The fact that the first two thirds of the written record of God's Narrative is called the Old Testament reflects the pivotal role this covenant had in God's interaction with His people in particular, and humans in general.

God puts forward a proposal to the people

Leaving the people camped below, Moses climbs the mountain to speak to God. (Exodus 19:3-8) The personal, relating Father, the Lord, speaks of having carried the Israelites out of their bondage in Egypt on eagles' wings and having brought them to *Himself*. In light of all He's done for them and the mercy He's shown when they were so needy, He makes a proposal... He paints a picture for them to consider. On his part, He says, He will value them as His special, highly valued people on this planet, this earth that is all His. They will have access to Him and be understood to be set aside for Him, to be part of His purposes. For their part, they will need to obey Him implicitly in all that He's going to lay out for them. Moses takes this proposal, this agreement or covenant, to the people and puts it before them. What do they think? How will they respond to God?

The Narrative does not give the impression that this proposal was met with a lot of soul searching or careful consideration. It seems that with no hesitation at all the people unanimously give their confident response, "Whatever God commands we'll do it." In light of how quickly they had forgotten God's mercy after the Red Sea rescue, and given how shallow their faith in God had proved to be in the wilderness, their confidence in their ability to obey implicitly was clearly misplaced. Even without knowing all the specifics of His commandments, their consciences should have told them that they were not equal to the task. They should have remembered that even when not doing overt evil, their attitudes, values, thoughts, words and actions were always tainted by sin. An appropriate response would have been to humbly acknowledge the hold that sin and Satan had on their lives and to ask God to send the promised Deliverer to rescue them from their spiritual bondage...in much the same way He had already rescued them from their physical slavery in Egypt. But they had a lot yet to learn about God's perfect standards and about their own inability to live up to them.

The Israelites prepare to receive God's Law

This is not going to be a light-hearted wilderness retreat. God is not going to throw out some mild suggestions about what the Israelites could possibly do to uphold their end of the covenant they'd so confidently agreed to. There will be no casual exchange with everyone offering opinions. Only Moses will be allowed to speak with God and function as His designated mouthpiece, His human storyteller to the people.

The people are to prepare themselves... the text uses the word "consecrate", to physically and mentally dedicate themselves to this one purpose of receiving God's laws. A boundary is to be set around the foot of the mountain. No one, not even their livestock, is to set foot beyond that. Anyone who does so is to be put to death. God is declaring this His holy place for this law-giving event. He wants them – and all who would hear His Narrative – to get a glimpse of His unapproachable holiness and righteousness. They are sinners, with no inherent right to approach Him. The physical boundary and the terrain rising beyond it to the summit and God's presence represented death for them. This was the one with whom they were entering into a covenant. And then, on the morning of the third day, a dense cloud covers the upper parts of the peak. They can hear thunder crashing and see lightning flashing. The whole thing is smoking and the ground is shaking. Moses leads the terrified people right up to the boundary at the foot of the mountain, and then at God's command disappears up into the smoke and fire.

He will come back down with God's Law. He will tell the people what is involved in holding up their side of the bargain, the Covenant. And, it will be impossible! They will not be able to even come close to obeying. And that's the point God was making. It's the point He'd been making in every interaction with humans after the Fall. They were unable to please Him with their own efforts. Adam and Eve could do nothing to make themselves presentable in their shameful nakedness. Cain could not come with his own ideas about how to approach God. Noah and his family had only one door through which they could enter the safety of the boat God had told them to build. Isaac, bound and with the knife about to plunge had no hope except for God providing a substitute sacrifice. And the Israelites had no way to escape at the Red Sea without God providing them a way.

So now God is ramping up this message. A whole people group wants His blessing and protection. They are saying they want a special relationship with Him, and they're happy to sign the contract, as it were. But they still don't get it. They think they'll have no trouble earning His acceptance. God has graciously chosen them to be His people. They are to be the nation through which the promised Deliverer will come, through which all the families of the earth are to be blessed. But His holiness and righteousness is such that it cannot tolerate the sin-cursed efforts of Adam's race, no matter how devout or well intentioned.

So now, from out of the shaking, smoking, holy mountain they're going to receive His Commandments. This too is part of His Story to them and to mankind. And his purpose is that as they, as anyone, grasps the full import… the full impossibility of His Law, they'll realize their hopelessness, their total inability to completely fulfill even one of the commandments, much less the whole Law. And as they do, they'll turn to Him in humility, they'll agree with His view of them, they'll recognize their sinfulness and guilt and they'll throw themselves on His mercy, believing in the way that He alone provides for anyone to be acceptable and to have the relationship with Him they were created for.

GOD'S AGREEMENT TO BLESS THE ISRAELITES IF THEY OBEY HIM

? DISCUSSION POINTS

1. God's Word paints a picture of Him leading and providing for His chosen people in the wilderness. What does this tell us about the relationship He desires to have with human beings, made in His image? Think of other instances in the Biblical narrative so far that highlight this intention. Reflect on how far the human race is in general from having this kind of relationship with its Creator today.

2. What has been your experience of how God's law has been presented? Have you heard direct teaching, or perhaps an underlying assumption, that we should try to obey God's law? Or, has it not come through clearly and consistently: i.e. why the law was given, and how it relates to us as believers? Give a brief synopsis of your current view of this issue.

3. Describe in your own words why you feel God chose to accompany the giving of His Law with thunder, lightning and with the threat of death hanging in the air? Do you think He was trying to intimidate them into obeying the commandments? What do you feel was His purpose?

1.30 God gave the Ten Commandments

 OBJECTIVES OF THIS TUTORIAL

Learners will continue to explore and discuss the themes and the truths presented in God's Narrative. The portions of Scripture referred to in this tutorial are: **Exodus 20:1-17**

Last time
God led the Israelites into the wilderness to the foot of Mount Sinai. He proposed a covenant in which He would bless them as a people if they'd obey His commandments. They readily agreed to this. They were told to prepare themselves for what was coming. A boundary was placed around the foot of the mountain, and anyone going beyond this was to die.

On the third day Moses had the people gather at the base of the mountain, and then walked up the slopes that were trembling with earthquakes, into the billowing smoke and lightning flashes above.

Ten overarching commandments
Moses eventually comes back down and presents to the Israelite tribes God's law that would govern their lives now as a community. In a great deal of detail, the law paints a picture of how they are to behave, and many specific things that are prohibited. But in a preface to the main body of the law, God gives 10 overarching commandments, which provide the premise or paradigm by which the long list of regulations and instructions can be understood. (Exodus 20:1-17) Before beginning the list of 10 God reminds them first that He is Yahweh, the Sovereign One, who rescued them out of slavery in Egypt. His right to be their Law Maker is based on being the Creator, but also their personal Rescuer and Provider.

The 1st commandment is also the most fundamental. Under the covenant He is to be their God... exclusively. They are to have no other god, but Him. So as a community and as individuals, nothing, no person, no object, no desire, no ambition or idea is to take His rightful place in their lives. He is their Story Writer and Teller. There can be no other voices that are louder than His, no forces that shape their individual character or their corporate culture that are not orchestrated by Him. There's to be no reliance on anything or anyone in His place as provider, no turning for help elsewhere first in a crisis. And, critically, at no point are they to function as though they, themselves, are the center of their universe… in effect, their own god.

For things to be any other way, whether intentionally or not, even for a moment, is to have broken this first law, and therefore the whole covenant.

The 2nd commandment makes further application of the first. They are not to make idols – manufactured things that are then revered as having divine qualities. This is the universal practice of the cultures around them. God knew it would be a great temptation, a stumbling block to the Israelites… as the Narrative will show. He tells them that He is a jealous God. He won't tolerate His place being given to another, even the figment of their imaginations.

On a deeper and broader level, this addresses the universal tendency of fallen humans to focus on and be enamored by the material, tangible world. To assume that what can be perceived with the senses is the most important… and particularly those things that humans have made. To worship what's created, even to fail in any way to constantly observe and acknowledge the Creator God's role, is to break this and all commandments.

The 3rd commandment says they are not to misuse His name. The Egyptians who the Israelites had lived next to for so many generations, and the communities they will soon have contact with, used the names of their divinities in chants and incantations to entreat or invoke against harm. This commandment very clearly condemns blasphemy and profanity. But mindless repetitions of His name in religious ritual or treating it as a lucky charm are also misuses of His name. God is painting a picture in which, unlike the relationship of the people groups around them to their false gods, the Israelites would always show Him complete respect and honor as a real Person… yes, as sovereign King, but also as their merciful, gracious Rescuer, Provider, Guide and Father. The way they spoke to and about Him must always fully reflect a perfect reverence for His position and appreciation of the relationship He desired.

The 4th commandment tells them that they were to keep one day in the week holy… set aside for Him. The Sabbath (*Sabat* in Hebrew – rest). God refers to Himself "resting" after the 6 days of creation. Stopping for a day from the normal work activities, would be an acknowledgment of His place in Creation and in their lives… also recognition of God's rights over the earth in the face of Satan's false claim on it. God knows that their human tendency will be to go about their lives and forget about Him. But He wanted to be central in their lives as individuals, as families and as a community, bound to Him by the covenant. So the commandment is about one day in the week, but in its essence it would be broken if even for a moment they forgot about God, didn't recognize His hand in creation or even once relied on themselves rather than on Him.

The 5th commandment is the first of the laws that refers to their relationships as a community. It says that they are to honor their father and mother. The family unit is a vital part of the picture God is presenting to them of the perfect covenant community with Him at its Head. Parents, as will be stressed in the ongoing Narrative, are to teach their children about God. His intention is for each generation to equip the next with truth. If there is no honor and respect for parents then this breaks down…and ultimately there will be no honor and respect for God in the community. Any personal or communal failure in this area of filial respect and recognition of God's intention for the family would be a violation of His covenant law.

The 6th commandment prohibits the taking of human life. God places enormous value on the life He has given to His image-bearers, even corrupted by the Fall. His Law embodies the expectation that the Israelite – and, by extension all humans and their societies – will hold with the same high regard, the lives of others as they do their own… to see them as God's gift.

Later parts of God's Narrative demonstrate that the underlying essence of this law goes far beyond physical murder. It also covers actions that put another person's life at risk through carelessness or neglect of duty. But even beyond this, to the very attitudes of heart. To despise someone as worthless, to hold bitterness in one's heart toward them or to hate them, in God's perfect economy is to be guilty of their murder; and is to have violated God's righteous standards that are codified in His Law.

The 7th commandment again focuses on the high value God places on marriage and the family unit. It prohibits adultery – and by extension all sex outside of marriage. Marriage, with its companionship, mutual support and its intimacy was a gift given to humans at the very beginning of God's Story. Adultery – in fact, *any* sexual intimacy outside of marriage - violates this gift and steals from God the glory that He should get as a result. It also harms the entire community by eroding values and creating tensions and divisions. Later, God's Word clarifies that this law is not only violated by physical acts, but also by entertaining desires and lustful thoughts.

The 8th commandment says that they are not to steal. On the surface, this might seem a straightforward injunction against taking someone's possessions or money, and that is certainly the case. But in its essence this law reaches much further. It covers any situation in which someone puts their own needs, desires, comfort and fulfillment above someone else's. It is the ever-present default of humans to assume a place at the center of their world. Viewed in this light, stealing includes a million subtle things like inappropriately taking someone's time, energy and attention…or dominating a conversation, or taking credit for something we don't deserve.

And it also includes taking for ourselves glory that is rightfully God's.

The 9th commandment forbids speaking falsely about others. But the wider paradigmatic concerns have to do with honesty in general. As the Storyteller, Communicator and Revealer of all that's true and real, God detests falsehood and deception. Right from the beginning Satan has utilized half-truths and straight out lies to create a web of deceit with which to trap human beings. God knows the devastating results that deceit, innuendo, false accusations etc., would have on the Israelite community and He wants them to avoid this. But in the bigger picture of his Law, He wants them and all humans to realize they can never function consistently and fully in Truth like He does.

The 10th commandment deals with another area that God knew would be problematic for the Israelites and for all humans – wanting what they don't have. The underlying principle here has elements that would violate their relationship with God, with other individuals and the community as a whole. To covet what is someone else's is to be ungrateful and dissatisfied with what God has given us. It is to assume that we are more important than someone else and that our needs and desires should be given a higher priority than theirs. Often envy is not just directed at material things, but also intangibles: relationships, status, popularity, influence, appearance and many others. Like the other nine, to fail in this one area even in what might seem to us the mildest way, is to violate it completely and therefore to break His perfect Law in its entirety.

❓ DISCUSSION POINTS

1. Comment on any differences you see between the way that most people view the law and the judicial system of our country, and the way we should view God's law. Do you think the well-documented corruption and obvious weaknesses of the whole legal system would be a factor in how someone would also view God's law? How would you try to introduce the subject of God's law to someone from our culture? What would be the misconceptions you'd try to avoid?

2. Describe the pluralism and relativism that is so common in our society (do some research if necessary) and comment on how these concepts conflict with the exclusivist nature of the commandments (e.g. "You must not have any other god but me."). Do you sense any danger of evangelical Christianity adopting pluralistic attitudes at odds with God's (Yahweh's) exclusivist claims?

3. The third commandment (Exodus 20:7) is usually related to blasphemy. This is certainly true, but dig deeper into the essence of what God is saying here. What is contained in the concept of God's name? How might a person treat this idly, or with disrespect? Describe how, even if someone never uses God's name "in vain", they constantly fall short of obeying this command.

4. On the surface, the seventh commandment (Exodus 20:14) is strictly about faithfulness within a marriage. But consider the wider paradigmatic application (the "spirit") of this command and all of God's law. In light of that, reflect on how it is appropriate to say that everyone (whether they have never married or are "faithfully married") has failed to live up to this command? Give concrete examples of how God's righteous, holy standard for marriage is impossible for humans to attain to.

➡ ACTIVITIES

1. Find three people you know - a mixture of believers and unbelievers if possible, and ask them the questions - "What are the Ten Commandments?" and "How do you think they are relevant today?"

1.31 God told the Israelites to build the Tabernacle

 OBJECTIVES OF THIS TUTORIAL

Learners will continue to explore and discuss the themes and the truths presented in God's Narrative. The portions of Scripture referred to in this tutorial are: Exodus 24:3, 12, Exodus Ch 25 - 29, 32, Leviticus 16

Last time
God gave His Law to the Israelites to describe His expectations for them under the Covenant. The substance of the Law was summarized in 10 overarching Commandments as a preface. Viewed against the backdrop of God's holy and righteous character, it soon became obvious that as individuals and a community the Israelites were not able to perfectly fulfill even one commandment, much less the entire Law. What was true for them is also true for all human beings.

The commandments in stone
We noted before how readily the Israelites agreed to the concept of a contract with God. Now, when Moses comes back with the Law, the terms of the contract, they again unanimously concur that they'll do everything God has commanded. At God's direction, Moses goes up the mountain once again and this time God gives him a copy of the commandments engraved on panels or – the traditional way it's expressed in English - "tablets" of stone… a permanent record of His perfect standards. (Exodus 24:12)

God was graciously going to live among His people
During this time on the mountain, God also gave some astonishing news. Though the sovereign Spirit God, Creator of the universe, He was graciously going to live among the Israelites. They were bound to Him now by the Covenant and He was going to be part of their community. Because at this point – and in the foreseeable future - they were a nomadic people, His place, like theirs, would be transportable. In essence a large meeting tent – traditionally translated "tabernacle" in English.

This would not just be some community center with people idly coming and going or hanging about waiting to talk to Him. It would be a special place that in every detail of its construction and furnishing would speak of His holiness - unapproachable by sinful humans. As we've come to expect from His Narrative, God was not going to ask anyone else to come up with the design of the Tabernacle, its furnishing, or the objects it would contain. He would describe what He wanted in very specific detail to Moses who was to carefully pass on His instructions. (Exodus Ch 25 – 27)

God knew that the Israelites' self-confidence in their ability to follow His Law and fulfill their side of the Covenant was misplaced. Despite being God's chosen people, like all humans since the Fall, they were sinners – it's who they were. They would also choose to sin constantly – it's what they did. And they would consistently fail to live up to God's holy character and standards (as the Law shows) – it's what they were unable to do.

As the Narrative records, God had given sinful humans a way to approach Him. Previously this was done as individuals or family groups. Now that He's relating to them as a nation under the Covenant with a more permanent, special presence among them, the tabernacle would provide a formalized way for them to approach Him. It would serve the needs of the 2 million plus people to sacrifice animals in recognition of sins and shortcomings. It would also provide a central focus for their corporate worship of Him as their God and Divine Ruler.

God gave specific instructions for the Tabernacle

As mentioned, the construction had to be such that the Tabernacle could be erected, dismantled, moved considerable distances and assembled again. The materials God told them to use for the outer surfaces were basically the same as their own tents – fabricated from animal skins and hair. The layout would be simple…an outer courtyard (46m x 23m) surrounding the main tent or pavilion (about 14m x 4.5m). This was made up of two rooms, separated by a thick curtain that would serve as a reminder of the impenetrable barrier of sin that separates people from God's presence.

The first room, the larger, was called the Holy Place. It gave access to a second, inner room, half its size - the Most Holy Place. This was the most important place in the Tabernacle, indeed in the entire community. It was God's sacred place, set apart for Him. Of course God is Spirit, and unlimited by physical confines of space, but because of His grace He was willing to come and have a personal presence among His people. A special wooden chest covered in gold was to stand inside the Most Holy Place. Traditionally translated "ark" – relating to protection of contents…hence the ark of the flood and the ark the infant Moses was floating in. This golden chest would contain the Law – the terms of the Covenant, so it was called the ark of the covenant. Then above that, covering the law – the lid of the chest – was the atonement covering, or place of mercy – where wrongs are made right. This was where God's presence, the bright light of His glory, would be focused. The symbolic and very real implications are enormous.

God had chosen them as His people. He had been willing to draw up contractual terms under which He would be with them and bless them as a community. But He knew full well they would be unable to fulfill the terms of the Law. They would offend His righteous standards continually. No attempt of theirs to atone - to pay - for their offences would be acceptable. But His grace and commitment to them was such that He would make a way of atonement, He would specify how an appropriate, humble approach would allow Him to show mercy to His people, rather than annihilating them as they deserved. The Law was there, carved in stone, unchanging, definitive, implacable. But His grace and mercy would make a way to cover over the sins of the people, temporarily holding off God's righteous anger and judgment...until the promised Deliverer, in fact, would come and provide a permanent solution.

The ark of the covenant was the only object in the Most Holy Place. The other objects God specified for the Tabernacle and outer courtyard facilitated the individual and communal approach to God for the atonement – the covering – of sins. A large altar - a place for burning offerings – made of brass, stood in the outer courtyard. Here a person, aware of their sin and need for forgiveness, would bring specified animals to be sacrificed. Before it was killed and burned, the individual would be required to place their hand on the head of the innocent animal, humbly asking God to accept its death in place of their own.

Other decorations, furnishings and objects functioned as practical and symbolic reminders of God's holiness and grace. They also provided powerful analogies of things which would only be fully appreciated later, in the unfolding of God's Narrative.

A priestly line was instituted

God told Moses that a line of priests was to be instituted to serve God and the community. They would oversee the Tabernacle and officiate in the sacrificial system. Aaron, Moses' brother, was to be the first of the high priests with his sons functioning under him. The office would be passed down through succeeding generations of the family. (Exodus Ch 28, Leviticus Ch 16) One of the high priest's exclusive and most important functions would be to enter the Most Holy Place one day each year - the day of atonement. He would take the blood of an animal into God's special sanctuary and sprinkle it on the atonement covering - the lid of the Ark of the Covenant. If God's instructions were carried out precisely, He promised to withhold the punishment of the sins of the Israelite community for that year.

GOD TOLD THE ISRAELITES TO BUILD THE TABERNACLE

The people made a golden calf

It was immediately evident that these extensive measures for atoning for individual and communal sin would be desperately needed. (Exodus Ch 32) While Moses was still on the mountain receiving all the specific instructions for the Tabernacle and the priestly system, the Israelites had already violated the conditions of the Covenant, and in the most grievous way.

When Moses took much longer than expected, a golden calf had been made as an idol or cult image, and was being venerated as the god that had brought them out of Egypt.

Clearly, it was going to be totally impossible for them to fulfill God's law and satisfy His perfect standards. Any confidence they had in themselves to carry out their side of the Covenant was entirely misplaced.

? DISCUSSION POINTS

1. How do you feel about the fact that God, the holy and all-powerful Creator, was willing to come and live in the middle of the nomadic Israelite community? Would you agree that the evangelical tradition most of us come from is very focused on personal applications and how God relates to us as individuals? In light of that, make any observations you care to about the picture here of God relating to His people as a community.

2. The Biblical narrative describes God giving very detailed instructions about every aspect of the Tabernacle's construction. Does this seem to be at odds with a view of God as eager to have a genuine relationship with humans? Is God, after all, rather hung up on the trappings of religious form? Describe in your own words why you think He gave all those precise specifications. What bearing does any of this have on your relationship with Him?

3. How does it make you feel to think about God's commitment to these people despite Him knowing very clearly that they would not fulfill their side of the bargain. And His willingness to provide for the atonement - the covering over - of the people's failures and shortcomings... their sins? Share anything you care to about how this adds to what you've observed from the Narrative so far of God's grace.

1.32 The Israelites did not believe God would give them Canaan

 OBJECTIVES OF THIS TUTORIAL

Learners will continue to explore and discuss the themes and the truths presented in God's Narrative. The portions of Scripture referred to in this tutorial are: Exodus 40:36-38, Numbers 10:11, 13:21-30, Ch 20, 21:4-9

Last time

God gave Moses a copy of the Law engraved on panels (tablets) of stone. He also gave specific, detailed instructions for the construction of a large tent or pavilion – a Tabernacle. This would provide a center for community worship and the sacrifices to atone for their sins – failures to live up to God's standard. In an inner room, the Most Holy Place, God's glory would rest on the atonement covering, the lid of the golden chest containing the Law. Aaron would be the first High Priest, and patriarch of a line of priests.

God brought them to the edge of Canaan

We pick up the Narrative at a point when the Israelites begin their journey again. Since the dramatic events of the Law being given, the Tabernacle has been completed. And because it had been done according to His instructions, God has come to live with them. His glory has settled in the Tabernacle. The entire community of Israel can see the evidence of God's presence in the form of a cloud covering the tabernacle. (Exodus 40:36-38)

Then one day, 10 or 11 months after they first came to the foot of Sinai, the cloud rises up, indicating that the entire community should get ready to move. With God leading them, they journey through the wilderness until they eventually come to the border area of Canaan, the land God had promised centuries before to Abraham. A place called Kadesh Barnea.

THE ISRAELITES DID NOT BELIEVE GOD WOULD GIVE THEM CANAAN

Corresponding roughly to modern-day Israel, the Palestinian territories, Lebanon, and the western parts of Jordan and Syria, the land God had promised for Israel's homeland as a nation is by no means uninhabited.

A number of tribes - Semitic peoples – i.e. descendants of Shem and mostly speaking languages related to Hebrew, exist in city states throughout the area. A number are aggressively trying to expand their territory, wealth and influence through warfare. It seems that without exception, as communities, they had long ago turned away from God's Story and worship of Him as Creator, to pursue cult practices and local stories.

Centuries before, in reference to one of these groups, God told Abraham that his descendants would return to Canaan at a point when the sins of the Amorites would warrant their destruction. God had graciously given them opportunity to turn to Him in repentance, but that opportunity was now at an end. He would use events to achieve His dual purpose: providing the promised homeland for the nation of Israel, while also meting out judgment on the existing inhabitants who refused to acknowledge Him as Creator God.

The Israelites didn't trust God to give them the land

A number of events take place while the Israelites are camped at Kadesh Barnea, but we pick up the Narrative with God telling Moses to choose 12 men – one from each of the ancestral Israelite tribes - to go into Canaan and come back with a report of what they found. (Numbers 13:1,2, 21-29)

After nearly 6 weeks of traveling to different areas they bring back news and even physical evidence of a rich, fertile country. But they also relate disturbing accounts of heavily fortified towns and inhabitants of huge stature – giants. Two of the group of 12 spies, while not denying the realities of the challenge before them, encourage the people not to be dismayed...to believe that God would enable them to conquer all the territory He'd promised. (Numbers 13:30) These two individuals, Caleb and Joshua, will have notable roles in the ongoing Narrative. Their encouragement falls on deaf ears. The people listen instead to the negative, fearful counsel of the other 10 spies and, true to form, begin to ask through their tears why Moses and Aaron didn't leave them to die in Egypt or the wilderness. Becoming increasingly agitated, they consider stoning Caleb and Joshua and overthrowing the leadership of Moses and Aaron. In the stark context of the Narrative, the lack of faith and gratitude toward God of these people can seem incredible. But the reality is, in that sense they are much more typical than exceptional. Despite all the evidence, people do not readily acknowledge who God is, what He has done, or take Him at His word.

As in every other such case, before and since, lack of faith and rebellion against God has dire consequences for the Israelite community. God declares that this generation will not be the ones to enter in and inhabit the promised territory. They will wander for 40 years, a day for each year the spies explored the land. Eventually they'll die in the wilderness and it will be their children's generation that will inhabit the land that God has promised for the nation.

Water from another rock

God continues to give an account in His Story of events, and His interaction with the Israelites while they are wandering in the semi-arid wilderness, probably of the Sinai peninsula. An account is given (Numbers Ch 20) of a time when the nomadic community runs out of water. Just like another time, years before, when God had recently brought them out of Egypt and through the Red Sea, they did not turn in faith to God for help. Instead they complain and blame Moses and Aaron for leading them out to die here in the wastelands. This time God tells Moses that water will be provided if he will speak to a nearby rock. But Moses, frustrated with the people, strikes the rock with his staff. Although God does bring water out for the Israelite community and their livestock, He is displeased with Aaron and Moses over their disobedience to His instructions. In time Aaron would die without entering the promised land and then, later, Moses would also.

The bronze snake

It isn't long until the Israelites, weary and frustrated by the long journey, begin again to complain against God and His designated mouthpiece, Moses. They complain about the lack of good food and drink in the wilderness, expressing hatred for "this horrible manna". This time God's punishment comes in the form of poisonous snakes whose bite is lethal. When the people acknowledge their sin and ask Moses to pray for the Lord's help, He tells Moses to make a replica of a snake and put it on a pole. People having been bitten by a poisonous snake who look at the bronze replica will be healed.

This provides us with yet another powerful analogy for understanding God's perspectives and intentions. Like the Israelites and the snakes, the human race has no way of escaping the lethal "bite" of sin. Death is a very appropriate result for us as a rebellious, ungrateful people. But, for no reason other than His grace and mercy, God promised to send a Deliverer who would destroy the power of Satan and provide a solution to the dilemma of our sin. The symbolic connections between God's response to Israel's physical predicament here, and how through the Deliverer He would deal with the much larger dilemma facing the entire human race, are of course explicated later in the Narrative.

THE ISRAELITES DID NOT BELIEVE GOD WOULD GIVE THEM CANAAN

? DISCUSSION POINTS

1. Consider the way God was directing every movement of the traveling Israelite community. How do you feel about this picture of a very "hands-on" God, directly involved with His people, wanting them to be dependent on Him for every aspect of their daily lives? What would you say has been the picture built up throughout your Christian experience of the kind of relationship God is seeking to have with His children?

2. Territorial sovereignty and land rights are obviously highly controversial issues about which wars continue to be fought today. What foundations of truth then should help us correctly view the Biblical account of God giving the land of the Canaanite nations to the Israelites? How would you try to explain this to someone from our society given the wide-spread influence the media has on popular opinion and the perspectives that many people unthinkingly hold?

3. What is your personal response to the account of God, first of all, sending the snakes to punish the Israelite's unbelief, and then providing the remedy in the form of the brass serpent. Without going beyond truths covered in the Biblical narrative so far, put in your own words what this powerful story tells us about God and how He relates to human beings.

➡ ACTIVITIES

1. Research the tribal situation that existed in Canaan when the Israelites spied out the land and do a short write-up of your findings. Find out a little about the tribes who occupied the land, where they were located and a little about their languages, cultures and religions.

1.33 God took the Israelites into Canaan and chose their king

 OBJECTIVES OF THIS TUTORIAL

Learners will continue to explore and discuss the themes and the truths presented in God's Narrative. The portions of Scripture referred to in this tutorial are: **Numbers 27:18-23, Deuteronomy 34:1-8, Judges 2:7-13,16-19, 1 Samuel 8:1-7, 13:13,14, 2 Samuel 7:1-17, 2 Chronicles 2:5,6**

Last time

God brought the entire Israelite community right to the border of Canaan, the land He'd promised to them. But when they chose to fearfully listen to the negative reports of their spies rather than trust God to help them occupy the land, He declared that they would never enter - it would be the next generation who would go in. Later, when the community was plagued by lethal snakes, God graciously provided a solution (and a powerful metaphor for sin and salvation) - a brass serpent was put on a pole so that when someone was bitten, they could look at it and be cured.

Joshua is appointed as Moses' successor

As God had declared, the adult generation who'd come out of Egypt never entered into the promised national homeland of Canaan. Because of their unbelief back in the border area of Kadesh Barnea, they all eventually died during the years the 12 tribes were moving from place to place in the inhospitable wilderness. Their unbelief and its dire consequences provides us with an instructive analogy of the result of all unbelief.

The only exceptions were Joshua and Caleb, the two spies who'd insisted that, although the obstacles were great, they should trust God and move in to occupy the promised territories. Only they, from the original generation, would have the privilege of entering the land. In fact, God now tells Moses to appoint Joshua as his successor to lead the Israelites. Joshua had proved his faithfulness over many years as Moses' assistant, and had demonstrated his faith in God. (Numbers 27:18-23)

Not long after, God has Moses go to the top of a mountain overlooking Canaan, reminding him that this is the land He'd long ago promised to Abraham, Isaac and Jacob.

Moses dies there on the mountain with no witnesses but God Himself.

They possess the land but problems persist

Time and space force us to condense a great many events of God's Story at this point as He assists the Israelite nation to move in and occupy Canaan. Joshua leads them in the ensuing battles as they displace many of the communities previously occupying the territories God has promised them. At times they act in obedience and faith and see God's power displayed through their victories. But their frequent failures to believe and follow His instructions implicitly mean that the occupation and eradication of their enemies takes much longer and is less complete than He desires. As a result, for generations, the 12 tribes deal with hostile enemies living on their doorstep, seeking to reconquer their lands and expel the Israelites.

But the more insidious danger is spiritual, as God's people are repeatedly seduced by the cultish practices and idol worship of these communities living on their doorstep, or even among them. The results of this will echo down through history. The Narrative records (Judges 2:7-13) how after the death of Joshua and his generation, "who had seen all the great things the Lord had done for Israel", those who come next abandon God in favor of false gods.

We're reminded of the tireless efforts of Satan to deceive and turn God's image-bearers away from the light of truth to the darkness of deception. Behind everything – apart from God - that humans ultimately look to for their answers, rely on for their needs, or elevate as primary in their lives, we find evidence of Satan's involvement. He's there in the shadows, ably assisting, encouraging evil desires and willing people on to their destruction. The unfaithfulness of the Israelites, the text says, makes the Lord "burn with anger" against the nation and He allows enemy raiding parties to inflict heavy defeats and carry off their possessions.

The time of the "judges" or "rescuers"

A cycle emerges which repeats itself many times over the next few hundred years. Periodically, the Israelite communities turn away from God and indulge in the cultic practices of neighboring peoples. God allows their enemies to wreak havoc and even conquer large sections of their territory. In their desperation they finally turn back to the Lord and repent – agreeing with His perspective and acknowledging their treacherous sin. At this point God brings to prominence an individual who unites the tribes in effective military action against the oppressive, occupying enemy forces. (Judges 2:16-19)

The traditional English translation "judges" does not do justice to the role of these various individuals who surface to lead the fledgling nation in periods of military conflict and then in the ensuing peace. Another term, occasionally used, "Deliverer" or "Rescuer", carries an echo of the one, great, promised Deliverer who would come through this nation. Despite the Israelites' repeated unfaithfulness – God often characterizes it as spiritual *adultery* – He remains faithful, graciously ready to rescue them when they turn back in humble repentance to Him. In doing this He also demonstrates His commitment to the promise, first made long ago in the dark day of the Fall, to send one who will destroy the strangle-hold of Satan, sin and death.

At the nation's insistence, a human monarchy is instituted

The last of the judges, Samuel, was God's mouthpiece to Israel for many years. However, with Samuel growing older and with no obvious successor, the nation demands that a monarchy be established. (1 Samuel 8:1-7) This was, in effect, a rejection of God's divine rule over them as a people, the role He'd willingly and graciously assumed since Egypt. Now, despite God's warnings through Samuel of the consequences, they insist on a tangible human kingship like the ethnic groups around them.

The first king, Saul, starts out well but gradually moves away from reliance on God and becomes increasingly belligerent towards the Lord's instructions that come through Samuel. No royal dynasty will be established through Saul. In response to his defiance, God appoints a successor, David. (1 Samuel 13:13,14) In time, after many fascinating and instructive events recorded in the Narrative, and Saul's eventual death, David is crowned. He goes on to become Israel's greatest and most famous king. David, of course, like all human beings, was part of Adam's lost race and a sinner by choice. But he continually acknowledged his failings and wrongdoings; his approach to God was on God's terms. In the Narrative, in all of history, David stands out as a human being who truly desired a close relationship with the Lord.

He was not only appointed by God as king of His people, but also one of His storytellers... a prophet, specially enabled by God to speak His Word.

As we know, David wrote many of the Psalms - heartfelt, often painfully real, cries to God for mercy, and also songs of joy and praise for who He is. They form a unique part of the Narrative: a remarkable, very personal record of God's relationship with a human being He loves dearly.

A permanent dwelling for God – a temple – is built

As king, David consolidates Israel's borders and leads the nation into a time of peace and prosperity. With the nation's nomadic years long in the past, and conscious of the splendor of his own palace, David wants to build a permanent and more fitting dwelling place for God – a temple. God is pleased, but through His prophet, Nathan, says it will be David's son who will undertake the building of the temple. (2 Samuel 7:1-17) God also gives an undertaking that David's lineage will hold the throne forever. As the Narrative unfolds, this will prove to be a promise about the coming Deliverer who will be a direct descendant of David. The second king of Israel has become the recipient and guardian of the messianic promises given to Abraham, Isaac and Jacob.

King David sets about accumulating the gold, silver, special timber and other materials for the building of God's permanent dwelling place in the community. It is his son, Solomon - the third king of Israel – however, who undertakes the huge task of building the Temple. (2 Chronicles 2:5,6) At its completion, the Temple is dedicated to God with the offering of many animal sacrifices. As God enters the Temple, intense, bright light is seen by the people as visual evidence of His glorious presence. In grace, He has come to the Most Holy Place in the Temple - as He had in the Tabernacle - to have a direct, tangible presence with His people.

As always, it is His desire to be at the center of the individual and communal lives of human beings who approach Him humbly, in repentance and faith. He never wavers in His commitment to be the one Storyteller for His people and to graciously write their stories into His true Narrative.

The nation of Israel would never again know a time of peace and prosperity as it did under David and Solomon. In time it would split over rival succession claims into separate northern and southern kingdoms. Of their respective kings - some 20 for each - all but a few would fall to the seduction of the cultish practices and idolatry of the surrounding nations. Remarkably though, although repeatedly grieved and angered by the nation's unfaithfulness, God never gives up on them. He pleads, rebukes and punishes, but He at every point in their often tragic history as a people, He gladly receives them back when they turn to Him in humble repentance and faith.

? DISCUSSION POINTS

1. What would be your response to someone who thought it unreasonable of God not to allow that generation of Israelites into the promised land of Canaan? What does this tell us about God's view of unbelief? Describe any difference you see between the unbelief God apparently views so harshly, and doubts that might be considered "normal".

2. The lesson makes the point that God is the one who determines when someone will die – that life, and death, are in His hands. How does this reality contrast with the generally accepted view in our society? Would you agree that for most people science and medicine have filled the slot that is rightfully God's? What are some of the ethical dilemmas this creates for a society?

3. In the short history of the Israelite people covered so far we've already seen them turn to idolatry on more than one occasion. Trace out what you believe are the reasons for people's readiness to turn away from the true, living God to worshiping other tangible things, including "gods" of their own creation. What are some of the ways you can identify that this human disposition plays out in today's society?

➡ ACTIVITIES

1. List the Judges of Israel and in just a few summary sentences, in your own words describe: (a) their background, (b) Israel's situation that brought them to prominence, (c) the part they played (e.g. as military leaders etc.).

2. Go through the Chronology of King David's Life. Note any events that are unfamiliar to you and read the relevant Biblical accounts.

1.34 God sent His prophets to the Israelites, they are refused

 OBJECTIVES OF THIS TUTORIAL

Learners will continue to explore and discuss the themes and the truths presented in God's Narrative. The portions of Scripture referred to in this tutorial are: **Isaiah 29:13, Jeremiah 6:13,14, 2 Kings 25:1-12**

Last time

Joshua, Moses' successor, led the Israelites' push to occupy Canaan. The following centuries saw a pattern repeated; first *apostasy*, then *judgment* in the form of military defeat and occupation, eventual *repentance*, then finally *deliverance*, when a "judge" or "rescuer" was raised up to lead the nation. In time the people demanded that a human monarchy be established. Saul was crowned the first king, but when he proved disobedient to God he was replaced by David, who became Israel's most famous monarch. After the reign of Solomon – builder of the first Temple in Jerusalem – the nation split into a northern and southern kingdom. With only a few exceptions, the kings of the respective kingdoms did not acknowledge God's sovereign rule.

God's commitment is unwavering despite Israel's unfaithfulness

God continues, in His Narrative, to describe many key events from the ensuing 500 years of Israel's history. Much of the account is dominated by the nation's repeated violations of the terms of their covenant relationship with God. Again, the predominant metaphor is that of marriage, with one partner being unfaithful while the other waits patiently for the eventual return, repentance and restoration. Of course God, although grieved, does not play a passive, victim's role. He vigorously seeks out His faithless chosen nation in many ways, and often allows harsh punishment to come in order to get their attention. Their national spiritual philandering has many tragic consequences for them as individuals and as kingdoms – now known respectively as Israel and Judah.

The truly remarkable theme that continues to emerge throughout this often sad history is God's unwavering commitment to communication, to revelation. The predominant way that He communicates to Israel and Judah during this period is through His appointed storytellers, His prophets. Some of the most well known prophets of these centuries are Isaiah, Jeremiah, Ezekiel and Daniel. Often their message is polemic – powerful, confronting condemnations of the communities' tolerance of and involvement in godless practices…along with warnings about looming judgment. Some, like Jonah – famous for being swallowed by an enormous fish – are sent to warn the surrounding nations about the terrible results ahead if they continue to ignore the true Creator God. Throughout this period, there are always some individuals from both Israel and Judah, who respond to God's revelation and approach Him humbly and in faith, on His terms rather than their own. Occasionally one or the other of the two kingdoms, in dire circumstances or under the direction of a rare reforming monarch, undertakes a public return to God. These, however, are exceptions rather than the rule. In general, God's exhortations and warnings through His prophets go unheeded.

It should be noted that for much of this period, the sacrificial system officiated by priests at the Jerusalem Temple continues. But for the most part this has become a meaningless ritual that God condemns. Through the prophet Isaiah (29:13) he says *"These people say they are mine, they honor me with their lips, but their hearts are far from me. And their worship of me is nothing but man-made rules learned by rote."*

God's priority has always been genuine relationships with human beings on his terms. Religious forms are valid if, and only if, they serve this purpose. As empty rituals, they are a mockery of true, heartfelt repentance and worship. Throughout its history, Israel is dogged by false prophets, claiming to speak for God. They often have populist appeal with a message that dismisses fears about God's judgment and offers temporal prosperity. Speaking as God's mouthpiece, Jeremiah says (6:13, 14) *"From the least to the greatest their lives are ruled by greed. From prophets to priests they are all frauds. They offer superficial treatments for my people's mortal wound. They give assurances of peace when there is no peace."* This kind of poisonous mix of truth and lies – at times dazzling and dramatic, at others soothing and seductive – continues to be one of Satan's favorite stratagems for confusing those who know something of God's Story.

God judges the two kingdoms
Eventually the time of God's patient, gracious appeal to His people comes to its tragic conclusion. As we've noted before in the Narrative, His grace never runs out, but when people finally and completely reject His efforts to rescue them, they then face the inevitable punishment His righteousness demands. Isaiah prophecies to Israel, the northern kingdom, that the Assyrians – an ascendant super-power in the region – will defeat them in war if they do not repent. When they refuse to listen, Assyrian forces do indeed

lay siege to the northern capital, Samaria, for 3 years. It finally falls around 722 BC and Israel comes under Assyrian control.

Thousands are taken as captive slaves. Then, consistent with Assyrian practice for their occupied lands, they bring people from other subjugated nations to settle the northern areas of Canaan. Inevitably, these people do not know the true, living God, but have their own cult deities and practices. Over the ensuing decades and centuries, there is extensive intermarriage between the remaining Israelites and the new settlers. Their descendants become known as Samaritans. As a people, they claim to worship Yahweh, but they assert that only the Pentateuch – the first five books of the Old Testament written by Moses - is God's Word. They build a rival to the Jerusalem Temple on Mt. Gerizim in their own territory of Samaria.

Isaiah's counterpart to the south, Jeremiah, along with other prophets, repeatedly warns the kingdom of Judah that they are in imminent peril if they do not repent and return to the proper covenant relationship with God. Their indifference results in the fulfillment of his prophecy that Babylon, the other super-power of the region, will destroy them. The Babylonian forces, when they do come and over-run the kingdom, are ruthless, tearing down the Temple and even the stone walls of Jerusalem. Like with Israel, a large percentage of Judah's population is taken away into exile in Babylon. (2 Kings 25:1-12)

Back from exile, then domination by the Greeks and Romans

In exile, many of God's people return to the truth, finding ways to engage with His Word while cut off from the Temple with its sacrificial and *Levitical* – or priestly - system. After a generation some of the exiled Hebrew people in Assyria and Babylon begin to make their way back to Canaan. In time, the city of Jerusalem, its walls and Temple are rebuilt. As a people they become widely known as Jews, probably a contraction of Judah, the predominant Israelite tribe to the south, in the area of Jerusalem.

Sadly, the return to their homelands does not result in a permanent and sincere relationship with God as divine Guide and focus of the community. As a nation they do not provide – as the Lord always intended – an example of a living, vibrant Theocracy in contrast to the dark polytheism around them. Instead, a religious system becomes increasingly entrenched - a slavish adherence to the letter of the Law, with more and more additional regulations… based on the faulty assumption that this is the way to please God, to avoid punishment and to receive His blessing.

Around 400 BC Canaan is overwhelmed and occupied by the military might of Alexander the Great. Although his reign is short-lived, Hellenisation – the spread of Greek culture – impacts the entire Mediterranean basin and well beyond. Greek becomes the language of wider communication throughout the entire area, including Canaan.

After Alexander's death, the wars between his generals over how his empire will be divided sweep through the territories of the Samaritans and the Jews. Forming a strategic land bridge between the Seleucid Empire based in Syria to the north and the Ptolemaic Kingdom of Egypt to the south, the Hebrew territory is a hotly contested military prize for the next century and a half. Partial Jewish rule over Palestine is reinstated after the Maccabean revolt around 164 BC but in 60 BC, the iron military machine that is Rome rolls through and Israel becomes a vassal state. The people are heavily taxed to pay the imposed tribute to Rome.

? DISCUSSION POINTS

1. What is your response to the picture of God as the great Communicator, doing everything possible to rescue the lost race of people He created? Also of history as the story of this rescue effort? Do you see any parallel between the responsibility of the prophets to speak God's message and our responsibility to share His Word, particularly with those who are cut off from its reach?

2. Without taking for ourselves what is God's role as Judge, can we draw a valid parallel between the many Israelites going through the form of the sacrifices etc. and similarly religious people in our society? Why do you think that many people now, as then, are vulnerable to the message of false prophets? Trace out the basic worldview and "heart" issues you feel might be involved in causing people to follow something that is close to the truth but is, in fact, a lie?

→ ACTIVITIES

1. Read the book of the prophet Micah and these other related Old Testament passages that give some historical background: 2 Kings 15:32–20:21; 2 Chronicles 27–32; Isaiah 7; 20; 36–39.

2. In a few sentences, describe the impact each of these had on Israel's history in the centuries before Christ:

- Assyria
- Babylon
- Alexander the Great
- The Hasmoneans
- Julius Caesar

3. For some extra background, do some research into the Samaritan people.

1.35 God foretold the birth of John and fulfilled His promises

 OBJECTIVES OF THIS TUTORIAL

Learners will continue to explore and discuss the themes and the truths presented in God's Narrative. The portions of Scripture referred to in this tutorial are: Luke 1:5-25, 67-79

Last time

We noted how God's commitment to Israel, to communicating with them, and through them to the other nations, did not waiver despite their repeated unfaithfulness. Eventually, after many warnings through His prophets, God judged the two kingdoms through military defeat and exile. After a generation, many Hebrews returned to Palestine. Their territory was occupied by others a number of times over the following centuries, culminating with the Romans around 60 BC.

A prophet is to come to prepare Israel for the Deliverer

Around 340 years before the Romans, God equips and sends one of His storytellers, His prophets, to the Jews. His name is Malachi, the last prophet recorded in the first of the two major divisions of God's Word, the Old Testament. Malachi reminds the Jewish people of God's promise – first given in the dark time of the Fall – that He would send a Deliverer. He says that this long-promised one will come soon. But just before he does, another prophet will come bringing a message from God designed to prepare them for the arrival of the Deliverer.

After Malachi's death, God does not send another prophet for 400 years. It is as though God is silent, waiting to send the promised one. In fact, those 400 years are traditionally called the "silent years" for that reason. However, as we look back on this period of history, we are able to see how God is using events and individuals to prepare for what is coming.

Through the process of Hellenisation, the Greek language has become widely used throughout the entire region. Many people groups formerly isolated are now able to communicate with each other. Later, to further Rome's military ambitions and then serve the needs of the Empire, a vast network of roads is built. Cities throughout the provinces are linked in ways that has never happened before. During this time, Hebrew people spread and settle throughout much of the Mediterranean basin, bringing monotheism and a knowledge of God's Word with them. Synagogues are built in far-flung communities and for the first time, God's Narrative with its promises about the Deliverer becomes widely accessible.

John "the Baptist" prepares the way for the Deliverer

We pick up the Narrative at a time when Palestine has been under Roman dominance for some decades. Among the Jews eagerly waiting for the arrival of the Messiah - God's specially chosen one - is an elderly, childless couple, Zechariah and Elizabeth. (Luke 1:5-25)

One day, while Zechariah, a priest, is carrying out his duties in the Temple, one of God's spirit messengers – an angel – appears in physical form. Zechariah is told that, although aged, he and Elizabeth are to have a son. They are to call him John – in Hebrew or Aramaic form, "God has shown grace". As the angel goes on to describe John's role, it's clear that he is the prophet Malachi predicted would come immediately before the Deliverer. His message would be designed to prepare people's hearts for the Promised One. But most startling and exciting of all, was the news that the Deliverer would be the Lord Himself. Somehow God would be coming among His people in a special way. What could this mean?

So John is born to this couple in their old age. As we've noted before, God is not restricted by the laws of nature which are, of course, His design anyway. A few days after the birth, God the Spirit gives Zechariah the special ability to speak for God – to prophecy. (Luke 1:67-79) He declares that the promises passed on by God's prophets down through history about the Messiah are about to come true. And God is going to come good on the promise He made to Abraham... the promise that through him, through his family line, all the families of the earth would be blessed.

John, when he grows up, is to prepare the way by telling the people about their sins and how they can be saved from them. The one whose way John is to prepare will be the Lord Himself. Zechariah says that because of God's mercy the morning light of heaven is about to break upon them. And light will come to those who sit in darkness and in the shadow of death.

Since Adam and Eve willingly listened to the lies of Satan, in many ways darkness had ruled the earth and its human inhabitants.

Of course God's creation continued to speak day after day, to tell His Story. And He had revealed Himself to human beings numerous times. He had made a covenant, given His Law and lived among his people, the Israelites. He'd sent His prophets, and their words had been recorded. But Satan had seen to it that people continued to be confused. And the people themselves, the Narrative says, on the whole prefer darkness because they feel it allows them to do what they want without accountability.

So God is now going to come into the darkness Himself. And by doing so, He's going to bring light, truth. To expose things for what they really are. To reveal the lies. And above all, to demonstrate who He really is in a way that has never happened before. He's going to come and find those who'll listen. Those who through John's work, through His written Word, through His Spirit, are ready to listen. And He's going to tell His Story directly to them, in an unprecedented way. This event, God coming into the world in this way, is going to be the most momentous event in all history. It will prove to be the thing which ties together and makes sense of everything in God's Narrative… the past, the present and the future.

GOD FORETOLD THE BIRTH OF JOHN AND FULFILLED HIS PROMISES

❓ DISCUSSION POINTS

1. The lesson makes the point that during the 400 years between the Old and New Testament narratives, God was preparing the way for the Deliverer. Do some research as necessary and describe the context in the Mediterranean area by the end of that period. Include some thoughts on the geo-political situation, the cultural and linguistic changes, and the technological advances that would later allow the Message about the Messiah to spread rapidly.

2. Picture yourself as a believing Israelite in the house of Zechariah and Elizabeth that day when he was prophesying about the coming Deliverer. How do you think you'd feel to hear that the long-awaited Messiah was about to come? Describe in your own words the emotions, the excitement, you'd feel. What do you think might be some wrong assumptions you could make about what His role would be and how He was going to deliver His people?

1.36 God was about to fulfill His promises concerning the Deliverer

 OBJECTIVES OF THIS TUTORIAL

Learners will continue to explore and discuss the themes and the truths presented in God's Narrative. The portions of Scripture referred to in this tutorial are: Luke 1: 26-31, Matthew 1:1, Deuteronomy 18:15-18, Psalm 110:4, Isaiah 9:7

Last time

One of God's messengers, Malachi, described another prophet who would come just before the long-promised Deliverer. 400 years followed in which God seemed silent, but during which - we can now see – He was creating favorable conditions for the arrival of the Deliverer throughout that entire region of the world. In time, a child called John was born to a Jewish couple. His life-task, it was foretold, would be to bring a message that would prepare Israel for the arrival of the Messiah. Incredibly, this coming one would be the Lord Himself.

A woman called Mary is to be the mother of the Messiah

In a small town in northern Palestine, a young woman has become engaged to a man who, like her, can trace his lineage back to King David. Mary, like all descendants of Adam, is a sinner, but she is one of those Jews who is earnestly waiting for the arrival of the Deliverer. Now, God sends an angel to inform her that God has chosen her to be the mother of the Deliverer. (Luke 1:26-31) The Narrative will show that she is someone who humbly recognizes her sin and approaches God on His terms, conscious of her need for forgiveness. But she has not *earned* the wonderful privilege of being the Messiah's mother. God's choice to involve her in His plans is yet another instance of His grace. The angel goes on to tell Mary that when her son is born, she is to give him the name Jesus, English for the Hebrew Yeshua, meaning *Yahweh saves*. Jesus will, the Angel says, be the Son of the Most High.

Jesus will be completely God and completely man

The second person of the three-in-one God is to become a man. God, a spirit, unrestricted by time or space, the all-powerful Creator, is to be born as a human baby. He will now restrict Himself to a human form with its limitations and frailties. Completely human, he will also be completely God. This is how God will bring about the rescue effort He'd promised back in the special garden, when man first turned away from Him…when sin and death entered. The angel also tells Mary that her son will reign as King forever. Some 6 centuries before, God had foretold these things through His prophet Isaiah. He wrote that a child would be born, a son given. He would be called things like Wonderful Counselor, Mighty God, Everlasting Father and Prince of Peace. He would inherit the throne of King David, but His fair and just reign would never end.

Mary, of course, has questions. How can this happen? How can she give birth to a son? She has kept herself pure. She's a virgin. The angel reassures her that this is something that God will bring about. God who initiated life, the life-creator and giver, will simply see that a child grows in her womb and is born in the normal way. At the same time, He will most definitely *not* be a normal human child in some immensely significant ways. Having no human father, He will not inherit Adam's sin. He will be the one exception to the hard and fast rule that all humans are moving in a trajectory *away* from God. He will not, like other humans, assume a self-centered position in the world, even though He created it. He will not attempt to be His own storyteller, as people invariably do, even though He is God's greatest Storyteller. He will always take a humble place, always put His Father's wishes above His own, always eagerly point people to the Father and not to Himself. The Narrative will demonstrate these characteristics in dramatic ways.

Mary, with straightforward faith accepts that God can and will do everything the angel has told her will happen.

Matthew says that Jesus will be *the Christ*

One of God's appointed storytellers for Jesus, Matthew, would also be one of His companions on earth. At the beginning of his account (Matthew 1:1) in introducing a record of Jesus' lineage, he calls Him *Jesus the Messiah*.

Messiah is our English version of the Hebrew word Moshiach. In Greek, this term for *the anointed one* was translated Kristos, which became our English, Christ. So what does it mean when the Narrative calls Jesus "the Messiah" or "Christ"? We've already noted that it means anointed, but what is the significance of this? Anointing was an ancient ritual which involved pouring oil over someone's head to indicate they were chosen, set apart, for a particular task or purpose.

So when Matthew refers to Him as Jesus the Messiah, or the Christ, it alludes to the fact that He is God's chosen or anointed one.

Fifteen centuries before, Moses had passed on a message to the Israelites from God that He would one day raise up a **Prophet** from among the Israelites. God said that He would put His words in the mouth of this Great Prophet and that He would tell the people everything He commanded Him to say (Deuteronomy 18:15). Jesus was the fulfillment of this prophecy – he was anointed, specially chosen by God as the greatest of his Storytellers, the ultimate Prophet.

David, Israel's greatest human king and also one of God's prophets had written in a Messianic song, or Psalm, that the Promised One would be an eternal High Priest. (Psalm 110:4) The High Priests in the Levitical system came with the blood of animals to sprinkle on the atonement covering. But they, of course, had to do this year after year, generation after generation.

Jesus, as we'll see in the Narrative, was to be God's chosen **Priest** who would bring a one-time offering that would never have to be repeated.

As we already read, the prophet Isaiah – some 700 years before – had said that a descendant of David's would come and rule with justice and fairness forever. (Isaiah 9:7) Jesus was God's appointed **King** to rule all of creation. So the Messiah, the Christ, had been anointed or set apart by God to be His ultimate Prophet, Priest and King.

These instances from 3 of God's prophets - Moses, David and Isaiah - are just a few of many prophecies about the Deliverer. With God existing outside of the limitations of time, He was able to effortlessly weave into His Story threads which would re-appear in full clarity later in the Narrative. So throughout the record of His interactions with humans before the Messiah came – the Old Testament – numerous prophecies were made about the lineage, birth, life, character, death and resurrection of Jesus.

The Narrative, which is now picked up by 4 of Jesus' companions and contemporaries, eyewitnesses to these events, will demonstrate God's commitment to completing even the smallest details of what He says He'll do.

GOD WAS ABOUT TO FULFILL HIS PROMISES CONCERNING THE DELIVERER

? DISCUSSION POINTS

1. Without going beyond what has been covered so far in the Biblical narrative, explain in your own words why the long-promised Deliverer had to be both God and man.

2. The Biblical narrative has repeatedly highlighted the fact that God communicates – that this is an essential part of who He is. With that as a backdrop, reflect on the Incarnation and the fact that, as the Christ, Jesus was God's ultimate Prophet to man. What do you think this actually means? Does it really have any relevance to our society in the 21st century?

➡ ACTIVITIES

1. Find 3 different instances in the Old Testament where something or someone is anointed. Briefly describe the circumstances and the purpose of the anointing.

2. Choose one of the names for the Messiah mentioned in Isaiah 9:6 (Wonderful Counselor, Mighty God, Everlasting Father, Prince of Peace). Describe what you think might have come to mind for an 8th century BC Israelite when they heard that name. Then briefly describe your own thoughts and response to that name.

1.37 The Deliverer was born and grew into manhood

 OBJECTIVES OF THIS TUTORIAL

Learners will continue to explore and discuss the themes and the truths presented in God's Narrative. The portions of Scripture referred to in this tutorial are: **Matthew 1: 18-25, 2:1-18, Isaiah 7:14, Luke 2:41-52**

Last time
An angel came and told a godly young Jewish woman, Mary, that God had chosen her to be the mother of the Deliverer. His name was to be Jesus and He would be completely God and completely man. Having no human father, He would not be part of Adam's lineage and so would not inherit his sin. He was the long-promised Messiah, the Christ – God's chosen and ultimate Prophet, Priest and King.

An angel explains things to Joseph
We continue with Matthew's account of the Messiah's birth. It is, of course, a familiar story to everyone from our culture. It's regular repetition in one form or another at Christmas time does potentially take away from our appreciation of what a truly remarkable event it was. Here though we follow the account, not as an isolated story but as part of God's one, entire Narrative. And these events of Jesus' birth are the truly remarkable beginnings of the climax, the culmination, of God's Story of His interactions with man.

As we noted, Mary is engaged to a man called Joseph. According to the Jewish law and custom of the day, this engagement or betrothal is just as binding as marriage. So the betrothal ceremony has happened, but Mary is still living in her family home until the actual wedding, at which time she will move to Joseph's house and the legal tie will be consummated. (Matt. 1:18-25) When Joseph finds out that Mary is pregnant and knowing they have not slept together, he comes to the natural conclusion. At this point he has open to him the option of divorcing her and even bringing her before the authorities to have her stoned for adultery. Instead, the text says, being a good man and not wanting to disgrace Mary before the community, he decides just to quietly break off the engagement. Knowing Joseph's character and that he'll care for Mary and her special child, God explains things and draws him into His plans. In a dream, one of God's angels tells Joseph clearly that Mary has not broken her vows. She's pregnant because God has decided she will be. The same God who spoke all things into existence has now determined that a pure, virgin young woman, will be the mother of the Messiah.

His name, *Yeshua* (Jesus) "Yahweh saves", describes perfectly what He'll do - save His people from their sins. In addition, the angel says, He'll be called *Immanuel*, a name which joins the two Hebrew words for "God" and "with us". All of this perfectly fulfills Isaiah's prophecy, some 700 years before, that a virgin would conceive a child and call Him Immanuel (Isaiah 7:14). Joseph's response demonstrates faith, humility and obedience. Having understood the situation he proceeds to marry Mary, and when the baby is born, he calls Him *Jesus*, as instructed.

Jesus' birth, the wise men, and Herod

Matthew goes on to describe the circumstances of Jesus' birth. (Matthew 2:1-18) Events, well documented elsewhere, dictate that Joseph and Mary are away from their home town of Nazareth when the baby is due. Instead, the birth takes place in Bethlehem, today a city in the Palestinian-controlled West Bank.

Wise men from the east of Palestine – perhaps ancient Persia – following a star they'd observed in the sky, come to Jerusalem asking after "the newborn king of the Jews". The Roman-appointed king over much of the Jewish lands, Herod, when he hears of this, is shaken by the thought of a potential rival to his throne. He passes on to the wise men what the Jewish religious experts tell him – there are Old Testament prophecies about a ruler and shepherd of Israel being born in Bethlehem. Pretending that he too wants to worship the new king, he requests that they come back with a location, once they've found him in Bethlehem. They follow the star to the house where Jesus is with His mother. There they give gifts worthy of royalty and offer worship to the child. Of course this was perfectly appropriate as it was actually God himself who they were exulting. Heeding a warning from God, they head home without going back to Herod.

Meanwhile, an angel warns Joseph that he should escape immediately with Mary and Jesus to Egypt because Herod is looking for Him. They get away, just in time. Herod, furious and willing to stop at nothing to protect his throne and dynasty, has all boys two years old and under in Bethlehem killed. This brutal action by Herod is hauntingly reminiscent of the edict made by the Egyptian Pharaoh that all the newborn Israelite males were to be killed. It is not difficult to see here, as back then, the hand of Satan who would like nothing more than to destroy once and for all God's plan to send the Deliverer. It's worth remembering that even though he failed in both those attempts, not for a moment in the intervening years since has he given up the fight. He and his angel followers are just as determined as always to use every tactic available to deceive people and to stop them from hearing God's Story.

Jesus' formative years in Nazareth

Matthew records that after an unspecified period, God sends an angel to tell Joseph that it's time to leave Egyptian territory and return to Israel with Jesus and His mother. Notably, more than 7 centuries before, the prophet Hosea had foretold this return after the escape to Egypt... yet another instance of God embedding evidence of His authorship for those with the eyes and ears to recognize it in the unfolding Narrative of these true events.

The family returns to Nazareth, and this is Jesus' home town for His formative years – something also foretold by the prophets centuries before. Luke, the other of Jesus' biographers we've already heard from, comments succinctly about these Nazareth years, "There the child grew up healthy and strong. He was filled with wisdom, and God's favor was on Him." Jesus' physical and mental development is typical in many regards. But His growing up is also exceptional in terms of the relationship He enjoyed with God, His Father. For the first time, with the exception perhaps of the pre-Fall days in Eden, God enjoys the kind of relationship with a human being He's always intended.

Jesus visits the temple as a young man

Luke recounts a very instructive incident from the life of the young Jesus. (Luke 2:41-52) At 12 years of age, He goes with Joseph and Mary on their annual pilgrimage to Jerusalem to celebrate the Passover festival. This of course was the yearly remembrance of the time when God had brought death to every Egyptian household but had graciously given the Israelites a way of escape.

After the festival in Jerusalem is over, Joseph and Mary set out for Nazareth. Traveling for safety on the road with a large group of festival pilgrims, they don't realize until the end of the day that the young Jesus is not with them. Not finding Him among their relatives and friends they go back to Jerusalem and eventually track Him down. To their surprise, He's sitting in the Temple dialoguing with the Jewish religious leaders. Joseph and Mary, and everyone else for that matter, are amazed - Luke records - "at His understanding and his answers". How can a kid know the Scriptures like this? Where do these insights come from?

Of course it's perfectly understandable when we remember that this 12 year old boy has an intimate relationship with God the Father, and is in fact God as well. Later, His mother remonstrates with Him, describing their frantic search. She asks Him why He's done this. His answer is fascinating and rather puzzling to them. He asks rhetorically why they would search for Him, surely they should know that He'd be in His Father's house. Nothing trite or disrespectful should be read into these comments. It seems obvious that He was encouraging them to recognize who He truly is...perhaps a reminder too of the angels' messages around the time of His birth.

We see clear evidence here of God's character. John, someone who would become a close companion and one of the 4 authors of Jesus' authorized biographies, starts out famously by calling Him "The Word" - the expression or communication of God. As the promised Messiah, He is God's greatest and, in some senses, His final, Storyteller. His revelation of Himself in human form. As we'll see in the ongoing Narrative, He constantly encourages people to consider their assumptions about God, about themselves, about others... about Him. How much of God's Story He then goes on to tell them at that point depends on how prepared they are to hear it.

This is the case here with the religious leaders, and even with Joseph and Mary.

❓ DISCUSSION POINTS

1. What do you think is the image that comes to mind for many people in our society if they hear the term "angel"? Think about the way angels have been portrayed in movies, TV shows, Christmas cards, Nativity plays etc. Do you think this has made it difficult for people, including ourselves, to have anything like the correct picture of the angels who played such a significant role in the events around Christ's birth? Do some brief Bible study and describe what kind of beings these would have been.

2. The lesson makes the point that Jesus is the "center" of history. Apart from the BC/AD dating convention, what other observations would you make about Him being the focal point of history? How would you support this claim to someone from our society who was not a believer?

3. Do the necessary research to briefly describe one or two of the main extra-Biblical theories and traditions about who the wise men were, where they came from etc.

➡ ACTIVITIES

1. Study some maps from around the time of Christ. Make sure you're familiar with a map of Palestine so you have a picture in your mind where different places are (Jerusalem, Bethlehem, Jericho, Nazareth, Samaria, the route to Egypt, etc.) Then without other reference, place them on the following blank map provided.

THE DELIVERER WAS BORN AND GREW INTO MANHOOD

1.38 God sent John to teach & to baptize. John baptized Jesus

 OBJECTIVES OF THIS TUTORIAL

Learners will continue to explore and discuss the themes and the truths presented in God's Narrative. The portions of Scripture referred to in this tutorial are: **Matthew 3:1-17, John 1:29**

Last time

Joseph married Mary after an angel explained that the child she was expecting was the Messiah, God's Son. After Jesus' birth, wise men from the east arrived to worship Him.

King Herod failed in a vicious attempt to kill the young Deliverer. Growing up in Nazareth, in many ways as a normal boy, Jesus was also exceptional: He was fully God and enjoyed a wonderful relationship with God His Father. At age 12 He amazed the Jewish religious leaders and His parents with His depth of understanding and insights into God's Word.

John tells the people to repent

We pick up the Narrative with Matthew, who tells us more about the message of John, specially appointed by God to prepare the way for the Messiah. John has now based himself in the wilderness area east and north of Jerusalem, down to the Jordan river. (Matthew 3:1-6) He gradually gains a reputation and people start coming in increasing numbers to hear him. In some ways his message is similar to many of the Old Testament prophets. It is polemic, a fearless indictment of people's sin and self-righteousness, particularly the religious leaders.

And it is a call to *repentance*. In other words, a call for them as individuals and even as a community to see themselves as God does. To recognize that their piety and good works cloaks a terrible depravity of heart.

Repentance would mean abandoning their useless efforts to follow God's law and make themselves acceptable before Him… to forsake their pride in being God's chosen people and recognize their true identity as part of Adam's lost, rebellious, condemned race... to acknowledge their desperate condition and need for salvation. John and his message had been clearly foretold by Isaiah in words that Matthew quotes, "He is a voice shouting in the wilderness, prepare the way for the LORD's coming! Clear the road for Him!" John's lifestyle, like his message, is reminiscent of the prophets from the past. He dresses roughly, for the wilderness, in felt clothing made from camel's hair. He eats locusts and honey, the simple food of the rural poor. His entire life is devoted to his work, his message of preparation for the Messiah.

More and more people come from Jerusalem and southern Palestine... from all over the Jordan Valley, the text says, to see and hear this rather enigmatic character. Many are moved by what he has to say. His no-compromise, straightforward, tell-it-like-it-is message gets through to them. It resonates as the truth. They're sinners before God. They need His mercy.

This inward faith and repentance is acknowledged outwardly by having John baptize them. Of course, like anything humans *do*, having John submerge them in the river does not somehow wash their sin away or influence God's view of them. It is merely a public, symbolic action that they've now aligned their thinking to God's view of them and that they are trusting Him to save them, that they are ready and waiting for the arrival of the Messiah.

John lays it on the line with the religious leaders

Not everyone who comes to hear John does so humbly and ready to admit their sin. (Matt. 3:7-10) Members of the two leading Jewish religious factions have come from Jerusalem. Usually at odds with each other, they seem to have formed an uneasy alliance to check out what this radical is preaching in the wilderness, and why the people are flocking to him. Some are the ultra-conservative Pharisees, committed to rigorous observance of the law. The others, the Sadducees, are politically motivated and liberal in their interpretation of Scripture. They are dominant in the priestly and temple hierarchy.

John sees them standing among the crowd watching the baptisms and he denounces them for their spiritual arrogance. He depicts them as snakes trying to slither away from the fire of God's anger. But there's no humble repentance and turning to God for mercy. If so, there'd be a change in the way they live and relate to others. But no, their spiritual arrogance remains intact for all to see. They pride themselves on being Abraham's descendants and think that will keep them safe from judgment. But God is not impressed by that. He looks at reality, at what's in a person's heart, in how they approach Him... whether it's on their terms or His. They're like fruit trees that get cut down right at the roots, and are chopped up and burned because they don't produce anything worthwhile. All their following of laws and regulations and trying to keep themselves ceremonially pure is worse than useless. Their religious zeal is worthless. No matter how hard they try, there's no escaping their sin – it's who they are, it's who all humans are. They need God's mercy, to be saved. They need the Deliverer.

John's message about the Messiah, and Jesus' baptism

John is keen to keep the focus off himself. There's someone far, far greater coming after him and John isn't after any reflected glory. In fact, he says, he's not even worthy to be the servant who carries His sandals. (Matthew 3:11-16) Sure, John has baptized people physically in the Jordan, but the Promised one will eclipse this by seeing that those who believe in Him, will be "baptized" – submersed in and controlled by – the Spirit of God Himself. John has to accept people's responses as genuine, but the coming one will be able to right look into hearts and minds and see who's genuine and who's not. John has a mandate to give a general warning to people about the results of their sin, but the Messiah will have the authority to pass sentence and send unbelievers to eternal punishment.

Matthew now describes an incident that on the surface might seem puzzling. Jesus comes to John to be baptized. Why would He do this? Isn't John's message and baptism all about repentance from sin? But Jesus never does anything to offend God's perfect standards. In every way He's completely aligned to God's divine character. In fact He shares it entirely. He fulfills perfectly God's will and purposes. So why does He come to be baptized? John wonders this same thing and, in fact, tries to talk Jesus out of it. Jesus' response is simply that it has to happen because it's what God wants. A large percentage of the Jews – with the notable exception of the religious hierarchy – have accepted John's message and submitted to his baptism. Even though Jesus has nothing for which to repent, no changes in perspective and life needed, He humbly identifies with this group of the faithful. Not to do so may well have appeared as a refusal to obey God or perhaps would be seen as questioning the validity of John's prophetic message. So John does go ahead and baptizes Him.

Now Matthew records in his Narrative a remarkable and significant incident that takes place. As Jesus is coming out of the water God's Spirit comes down and "settles" on Him, the text says. Despite being God Himself, in His physical life on earth Jesus is taking a stance of complete reliance on His Father and the Spirit for the wisdom and strength to do the things they intend. In complete contrast to Adam, who rebelliously chose to tell his own Story, Jesus willingly, gladly, chooses God to write and tell His Story here on earth. He then makes Himself available to share that Story with others as directed by God's Spirit. The Father, knowing all of this, and seeing the humility and obedience of Jesus makes an incredible declaration that will go on to impact all of history. He says, "This is my dearly loved Son, who brings me great joy." God is delighted and completely satisfied in what He observes in Jesus. This is the kind of human being and the kind of relationship He has been seeking. And it thrills His heart.

Jesus is the Lamb of God who deals with sin

Another of Jesus' biographers, authorized by God, is also called John. In his account of this event, he records that when John – the other, baptizing one - sees Jesus coming toward him, he announces, "Look! The Lamb of God who takes away the sin of the world!" (John 1:29)

It's hard to see how the significance of this can be lost on the Jews, but we only later hear of two individuals who respond and follow Jesus as a direct result.

The sacrifice of lambs and other animals has, of course, played a prominent role in Israel's history. Lambs are sacrificed daily at the temple. The blood of lambs is annually taken into the Most Holy Place and sprinkled on the Mercy Covering. John is now stating clearly that Jesus will be sacrificed and that this will deal with the problem of sin, once and for all. All the blood that has run out as numerous animals have been killed down through the centuries cannot pay for sin. It was only ever intended to indicate that the person involved is conscious of their sin and their need for God to withhold His righteous judgment until a final payment can be made.

Now, John says, that final payment is going to be made. And it will be with the life of Jesus, God's own Son, who brings Him nothing but delight. The climactic chapter – if not the final one – in God's Story is unfolding.

❓ DISCUSSION POINTS

1. In light of the truth we've covered in the Narrative so far consider what God means when He tells people to repent.

- Look up the Hebrew and Greek words that are translated in English as repent.
- In what ways, if any, do you think normal English usage ("sincere regret or remorse") falls short?
- How, in your experience of being taught the Bible, has repentance been described? Is it accurate and adequate?
- Do you think that in essence repentance is the same for believers and unbelievers, or should a distinction be made?

2. Consider John's declaration that Jesus is the Lamb of God. How important do you think that would have been for Jews in that day? How about for our culture today? Think of a personal friend or acquaintance: in terms of them coming to faith in Christ, what value (1 to 10) would you put on them understanding John's statement? Please explain.

➡ ACTIVITIES

1. Put together a short Power Point presentation that you would use for teaching this particular part of God's Narrative to a small group. Include images, maps, text etc. Around 8 slides.

1.39 Jesus resisted Satan's temptations

 OBJECTIVES OF THIS TUTORIAL

Learners will continue to explore and discuss the themes and the truths presented in God's Narrative. The portions of Scripture referred to in this tutorial are: **Matthew 4:1-11, Deuteronomy 6:13, 8:3, Psalm 91:11,12**

Last time

People from Jerusalem and all over Palestine came to where John was living and preaching in an uninhabited area by the Jordan river. He was preparing the way for the coming Messiah by pointing out people's sin and true standing before God. Many accepted his message, repented and were baptized by John. A notable exception were the religious elite, and John was brutally honest in exposing their hypocrisy. After Jesus was baptized by John, God's Spirit came to Him, demonstrating that He was to be the dominant, guiding force in Jesus' life and ministry. God declared that Jesus is his Son and that He is entirely pleased with Him.

Jesus' encounter with Satan in the wilderness

Matthew's account now moves on to another amazing incident from Jesus' life that reveals a great deal about who He is; who God is. (Matthew 4:1-11) After His baptism, Jesus is directed by God's Spirit to go off on His own into an uninhabited area. After 40 days - nearly 6 weeks - without food there He's naturally very hungry.

No doubt hoping Jesus will be made spiritually vulnerable through physical weakness, Satan takes the opportunity to try to lure Him into saying or doing something that is against God's will. (Actually, Matthew uses the other common name for this fallen powerful Spirit being, the Devil). The special relationship between the Father and Son that God has recently testified to on the bank of the Jordan river is going to be put to the test. We're reminded of another such test of a man's willingness for God to be his absolute guide, rather than himself. In that case, of course, Adam failed; and the results for the human race were catastrophic. What will happen now? The stakes are just as high as they were then, in fact more so. If Jesus falls for Satan's deception, if in any way He resists God's guiding hand, or if He fails to live up to God's perfection, the entire plan to rescue the human race will fail. Like Adam, He will have given allegiance to God's Enemy. Only a perfect man can be God's special, chosen Prophet, Priest and King. Mankind will be lost, forever slaves to Satan, sin and death.

Test 1: Will He prioritize His own needs above God's will?

So Jesus is hungry, and alone in the wilderness – at least in terms of human companions. We don't know in what form exactly, but Satan begins to communicate with Him. Not only do we learn about God's character in this encounter, but we also gain insights into how His Enemy works. He prods and pushes in subtle, devious ways… looking for points of vulnerability, to twist and destroy. Clearly he would love nothing more than to drive a wedge between the Son and His Father. He starts out with something seemingly benign, neutral: food.

Jesus is obviously very hungry. Well, there's nothing wrong with food, is there? As the Son of the Creator it would certainly be easy to turn some of these stones lying around into bread. Where's the harm in that? Surely God wouldn't be unreasonable enough to not want His Son to eat? But Jesus sees the rotten core at the heart of this suggestion. There are more important things at stake here then His hunger, His needs. He won't be tempted to use His creative power to fulfill His own desires, no matter how real they are. Certainly He won't be guided by God's Enemy. He quotes from Scripture where Moses recalls how God took the Israelites into the wilderness for 40 years. (Deuteronomy 8:3) One of the important lessons they were supposed to learn there was that life is not ultimately sustained by food. Physical needs are transient, secondary. The important thing is Truth. It is allowing God to be our Story Writer and Teller. To put His will above our own concerns. That is the purpose and the essence of life.

Test 2: Will He try to force God to prove His faithfulness?

Next Satan insidiously brings into question how much God the Father really cares for His Son, and whether Jesus will manipulate God to find out. Okay, say you're standing at the highest point of the Temple in Jerusalem (and there they are, Jesus and Satan, on a ledge or rooftop, looking down into the void)… Then with incredible insolence, Satan quotes God's Word to Jesus but, typically, he tries to make it serve his own devious purposes. God says He'll protect people who trust Him for refuge, even sending His angels to make sure they don't come to harm, right? (Psalm 91:11,12) Well then, Satan implies, given this special relationship you're supposed to have as His Son, what have you got to worry about? Go ahead, jump. Find out if God really does care for you… see if the relationship is what God says it is.

But Jesus is having none of it. His confidence in God's care and faithfulness is rock solid. He has no intention of trying to force the Father to prove it. He quotes again from Moses' review of the Israelites' 40 years in the wilderness… when they demanded that God provide water for them. It's wrong to put God to the test like that, to try to dictate what He does. The mantra of many people in modern society is that they'd believe in God if He'd do this or that… But they insist on setting the terms for belief in Him. This is a reversal of the order of things. He is God. He's the one who sets the terms. He reveals Himself to us in the ways that He knows are best. Humans are in no position to force God's hand. The only appropriate posture is one of humble dependence and trust. And Jesus, the sinless Son of God, Himself the Creator of all things, chooses to take that very posture.

Test 3: Will He be seduced by a thirst for power?

Satan plays his final card. They are standing together looking at all the earth's kingdoms, thrones, and empires. The sum total of human power and glory, perhaps for all of history.

Satan, the great usurper, the counterfeit ruler of earth since man's fall, offers it to Jesus. He can have it all, right now. All the power, all the adulation. Even be a benevolent, humane ruler if He chooses. He could do some good. And best of all, there's no cost, no sacrifice, no pain. What was it again that God is offering? Being a sacrificial Lamb? Saving people from their sin? No, no, no. There's an easier road than that. Much less extreme, more reasonable, and realistic in a human sense. And only one small requirement. All He has to do is kneel down and worship Satan. What harm can there be in that?

Jesus is dismissive. He's had enough. He's not seduced by the power without sacrifice, the authority without cost, that Satan offers. That's not the road He's on. Not what He came to earth for. He concludes the conversation with a curt dismissal of Satan and one final quote from the same part of the Old Testament Narrative as before. "You must worship the LORD your God and serve only Him" (Deuteronomy 6:13) This of course is what Satan rebelled against, wanting for Himself the worship and servitude of everyone else. It is also what Adam and all his race fail to do, preferring on the whole to tell their own story and serve themselves first. But putting God first and serving only Him is what Jesus has chosen to do, no matter what the cost. And this is the very thing that qualifies Him, and only Him, to be God's Lamb, to save people from their sins, to be the Great Deliverer of mankind.

God's battle with His Enemy Satan, the battle with evil in fact, is not a struggle for supremacy between two well-matched opponents. Nor is it anything like the dualism of some religions - two sides that make up a whole: light/darkness, good/evil. Satan's

JESUS RESISTED SATAN'S TEMPTATIONS

power is real enough. As humans *we* are no match for his cunning. But God is in no way threatened by him. His supremacy is never in doubt. He writes the Story of reality from beginning to end, including, ultimately, Satan's destiny.

Matthew's narrative records that Satan leaves. Jesus has triumphed. His weapons have been truth, faith and obedience to God. A final intriguing footnote from Matthew adds that God's messengers, His angels, come and take care of Jesus.

? DISCUSSION POINTS

1. Taking each of the 3 temptations in turn, consider the following:

- Do you see any parallel here with Satan's original temptation of Adam and Eve?
- Is the underlying essence of the temptation something that our culture struggles with?
- As God's children, are we vulnerable to this area of temptation as well? If so, how does it potentially damage our relationship with Him?

1.40 Jesus began His ministry

 OBJECTIVES OF THIS TUTORIAL

Learners will continue to explore and discuss the themes and the truths presented in God's Narrative. The portions of Scripture referred to in this tutorial are: **Mark 1:14-42**

Last time
After Jesus' baptism, God's Spirit led Him into the uninhabited wilderness where He went without food for 40 days. Satan came and tested Jesus' relationship with God His Father, trying from a few different angles to tempt Him to sin. First he tried to entice Him into prioritizing His own personal concerns and needs, then to doubt and test God's faithfulness, and finally, to pursue power for its own sake. Each time Jesus was unmoved and responded by quoting from God's Word. Eventually He dismissed Satan who left, defeated.

John's work finished as Jesus' began
We now hear from Mark, another of Jesus' four contemporaries who recorded accounts that God included in the Bible, His written Narrative. Their inclusion was, of course, not based on popularity or random choice. The authors were specially equipped and positioned by God's Spirit for the task, and the things they wrote were exactly what He wanted them to say. Each of these 4 narratives, or books, was directed at a slightly different audience and has unique elements of style and focus. Together they form a composite and cohesive picture of the life and work of Jesus Christ, the Deliverer of mankind.

Mark records (Mark 1:14,15) that Jesus now starts to preach God's good news, which is that He is the long-awaited Messiah. Mark notes that this begins after the arrest of John… the one who prepared the way for Jesus and baptized Him. As we've heard, John is not someone to hold back the truth about someone's actions or attitudes, no matter who they are. He's arrested after a very open and scathing critique of the morals of King Herod (son of Herod the Great).

He's imprisoned for a time, and then Herod has him executed – beheaded.

Given that John's mandate from God was to prepare the way for the Messiah, it is appropriate that it concludes as Jesus - now about 30 years old - begins to emerge as a Teacher; initially in the northern Palestine region of Galilee. His message picks up on John's theme that people should repent: should recognize the reality that they cannot do anything to escape their sin or to deal with the debt it has incurred before God. But Jesus is able to add good news to the bad – a way of escape and the possibility of their debt being permanently dealt with is now here. Satan has ruled the earth since the human race turned from God, but his hold is to be broken. What God promised back then and repeatedly down through history has now become a reality. No longer do humans have to be God's enemies, helpless captives of Satan and sin and death. A new day in history has dawned in which it's possible for God to have the relationship with humans He's always intended... for Him be their Leader, their King, and for them to know the joy and privilege of freely following Him. And all of this is possible because Jesus has come. He urges them to accept and believe His message, to believe in Him. The essence of the message that Jesus preached remains unchanged today, some 2000 years later. The only way for people to escape Satan's control and to have their sin dealt with is to believe in Him: God's Son, Jesus the Christ, the Messiah.

Jesus began to choose some men to follow and help Him

Mark next records how Jesus invites some men to follow Him, to be His disciples. (Mark 1:16-20) This term is applied broadly at times to anyone who responds positively to His teaching. But more commonly, of course, it is a designation for the handful of individuals who accept Him as the Messiah, and who are His constant traveling companions and pupils.

The first men He approaches are brothers, Simon (or Peter) and Andrew. They are busy making an honest living as fisherman. But His invitation is compelling: He'll teach them, He says, how to "fish for people"; in other words, how to capture people's hearts with Truth, how to bring people to God, to him, the Deliverer. Of course they cannot see at that moment the scope of His purposes and the pivotal roles He plans for them, but the invitation does what He intends. It draws them to Him and to what He's about. They leave their work and follow Him.

Further along the shore, another two brothers, James and John are repairing nets, a never-ending job for fishermen. When He approaches them their response is also immediate – they follow Him as well. Part of the Jesus' work for the next three years or so will be to teach and mold these men and a few other companions into the kind of individuals to whom He can entrust the huge task that He has now begun.

Jesus demonstrates the authority of what He says

Jesus begins to demonstrate His authority as God's Son, the promised Messiah. (Mark 1:21-39) In Capernaum, a fishing village on the northern shore of the sea of Galilee, and home to Peter, Andrew, James and John, Jesus teaches in the Jewish meeting house – the synagogue. The Sabbath congregation are amazed at how confidently He explains what Moses and the other prophets had written…how he ties things together and makes them relevant to their lives. This is in stark contrast to those who usually teach – the so-called experts in religious law. They are always rambling and ranting on, but it's clearly just their own opinions and most of it is about the religious traditions, not what God's Word itself says. Whereas this young man speaks humbly and sincerely, but with incredible authority and clarity. Where is He from? How did He gain this kind of wisdom? Who is He? But He *has* been - by an evil spirit, one of Satan's fallen angel followers. And this one is living in or "possessing" a man who's in the synagogue that day.

From the Narrative we know that since the Fall, Satan has usurped God's place on the earth and has dominated the human race with his deception. He also very successfully traps whole communities, societies, cultures, entire people groups and nations, in his web of deceit. It is also clear that under certain circumstances when individuals make themselves vulnerable, one or even more of the evil spirit beings can take possession of them, so that the person is no longer in control of what they think or do or say. Now, one of these demons who has been controlling a man there is obviously terrified of Jesus. No doubt wondering if the time has come for them all to be sent to eternal punishment he asks, "Have you come to destroy us?" and He identifies Jesus as "the Holy One of God". But Jesus won't have his identity made public by an evil spirit. He'll demonstrate that he's the Messiah in God's time and in the way He intends. He orders the spirit to be quiet and to leave the man. This happens immediately with some obvious physical trauma to the man.

The people are even more amazed now. They've never come across anyone whose words carry such authority: in teaching Scriptures and even over the forces of darkness! And the news about Jesus quickly spreads.

Jesus has authority over sickness

Mark continues in his Narrative to record different incidents that highlight Jesus' compassion for people along with His authority as God's Son. He is showing that He is more powerful than any of the results of the Fall. He travels with His disciples from one community to another, at times speaking to crowds and at others interacting with individuals.

And His heart goes out to these people he encounters…He heals many of different sicknesses, and he cast out demons – orders them to leave the people who they control. Mark relates one incident where Jesus heals a leper (Mark 1:40 – 42) To contract leprosy is a terrible thing in these days, and in this society. Fearing contagion and with no cure available, lepers are shunned, outcast and despised by the community, forced to live in caves or wherever they can find outside the towns. But when a man with leprosy comes and begs to be healed, Jesus is "moved with compassion" the text says. Against all the conventions of the society He reaches out and touches this diseased man…and immediately he is healed. While Jesus is moved by the physical needs of people, His greater concern, as we'll see in the Narrative, is always for their deeper, spiritual need.

Leprosy is a powerful analogy of the human state that results from sin. With no cure then, the victim has no escape from this condition which gradually disfigures, cripples and eventually kills them. As Jesus spends time with people, He observes up close how sin has deformed and corrupted His image-bearing race, almost beyond recognition. Like being a leper then, their sin defines them. It is an identity they cannot escape, and a curse they cannot remove.

This is the great Cause that has brought Him to the world…to provide a way of escape for those who will come to Him, like the leper in Galilee, knowing their condition and turning to Him as their only possible answer.

His compassion today is no less than it was then. He is still seeking those who know they are lost and drawing them to Himself to find salvation.

DISCUSSION POINTS

1. What has been your understanding of "spiritual warfare"? Describe any systematic teaching or doctrinal standpoint that you've been exposed to. Are you seeing this line up, or contrast in any way, with what you're seeing from the Biblical Narrative as we trace it together? What are the primary weapons that you believe God's Enemy uses in his attempts to fight against God? How should we think about demon possession? Do you feel it is likely that there are people in our community who are demon possessed in the same way they were in Jesus' time?

2. Based on what we've seen in the Narrative so far about God's character and purposes, why do you believe that Jesus healed people during His time on earth? As a living embodiment of God's Narrative, what was God communicating then and now through Jesus healing the sick, casting out demons etc.?

ACTIVITIES

1. Review the Narrative we've covered so far and list as many of the embedded metaphors and analogies you can identify for the helpless situation of the human race because of sin.

2. Come up with 2 other possible illustrations from "modern" culture that would resonate with someone from our society. Include the explanation and application you would use when talking to them.

1.41 Jesus taught the necessity of the "new birth"

 OBJECTIVES OF THIS TUTORIAL

Learners will continue to explore and discuss the themes and the truths presented in God's Narrative. The portions of Scripture referred to in this tutorial are: **John 3:1-21**

Last time

Jesus began to emerge as a teacher in northern Palestine at the same time that John's role was concluding. His message, like John's, called for repentance from sin. But Jesus was also telling the people the good news that He had come to make it possible for them to live with God as their true Ruler, instead of being led by Satan and sin. Jesus began to choose some men to be His followers, His disciples. He traveled to different communities, initially in the region of Galilee, demonstrating His authority by His teaching, by the way evil spirits obeyed His commands, and by healing many sick people.

The religious leaders are threatened by Jesus & His teaching

We continue the Narrative with an incident that John records – not John the baptizer, of course, who by now is in prison or already executed – this is John, the brother of James, one of the fisherman Jesus invited to follow Him. He describes a conversation that Jesus has one night with a Jewish religious leader, Nicodemus. (John 3:1-21) Indications later in the Narrative are that he is wealthy. He is also a member of the Sanhedrin, the council of 71 leaders with ultimate authority on Jewish civil and religious law. They have extensive judicial powers, although with some restrictions under Roman rule. But anyone like John the baptizer, or now this Galilean teacher Jesus, who is drawing crowds through His teaching and healing, poses a potential threat to the status quo...and to the delicate political balancing act that is needed under the Roman occupation. He's beginning to make radical claims about who He is, and the role God has given Him in providing a way back to God.

And His teaching is threatening the basis of the leaders' influence over the people. He's saying that everyone is equally sinners... that no one can be made acceptable through following the oral or written traditions… that no one can even come close to fulfilling the Law of Moses. This was intolerable. Their hold on the people was maintained through their intricate knowledge of those very laws and traditions, and by their claim to fulfill them to the letter. And they were willing to go to incredible lengths to be seen publicly to do exactly that. If the people began to believe that those things did not produce righteousness and that they, their religious leaders, were just as guilty in God's eyes as prostitutes or even Samaritans… well, something must be done to stop this! They'd tried to discredit Jesus, claimed that if He was actually healing people and throwing demons out then it was through the power of Satan. But that had backfired, they'd been made to appear ridiculous. They'd sent delegations to try to trip Him up on finer points of the law, to get Him to say something heretical, but His knowledge of God's Word was amazing. People were contrasting their Scriptural acumen unfavorably with His.

Nicodemus is confused about being born again

So when one of their number, Nicodemus, a Pharisee, wants to talk with Jesus, it's not surprising he does so under the cover of darkness. His opening statements make it clear he doesn't share his colleagues' perspective of Jesus. He calls him "Rabbi", Teacher, and acknowledges that the miracles Jesus has done show that He's been sent by God.

Jesus' response is unsettling, confronting, confusing. He says that for Nicodemus to be one of God's people, under His rule, he has to be born again. But what can He mean? Yes, that's something you say about an outcast Gentile wanting to become a Jew… certainly, *they* need to be reborn. But he's one of God's chosen people. He and his fellow Pharisees have always prided themselves on being descendants of Abraham. God's family. Jesus must be talking about some physical thing, it's ludicrous, impossible. But Jesus is adamant that the only way to escape the rule of Satan and sin and death, and to be one of God's people, under His rule, takes a particular kind of birth. No, it's not a physical birth. Being born the first time is how Nicodemus and all humans inherited the sin and death that mark them as Adam's lost race. Everyone who has only been born once like that is under the rule of God's Enemy, the usurper who has set up a false kingdom on earth. Everyone is born with that identity and also makes the same rebellious choices as their ancestors.

And that is the same for Abraham's descendants, the same for the most religious, the most devout and sincere people like Nicodemus. In that sense, being an expert in religious traditions, acquiring a lot of knowledge about the Scriptures, knowing it off by heart… doesn't achieve anything. Even acknowledging that Jesus comes from God doesn't deal with the essential problem of birth. It doesn't take care of the issue of sin. So how does this mysterious second birth take place? It is the work of God's Spirit. It's not visible or perceived by humans, much less something they have power over. It's a miracle of the highest order. He doesn't force it on people, but when they are humbly willing to listen, to believe Him, then He uses His Word, His wonderful Narrative about Himself and all that's true. He helps them to understand and apply it in their hearts, in their spirits, and like some amazing water, clean beyond anything we can imagine, it changes them – they're washed and made new. A new person.

Jesus lays out clearly why He came to the earth

When Nicodemus is still confused, Jesus wonders out loud how a respected Jewish teacher can be ignorant about these things. But of course, in contrast, Jesus notes, *He* can speak with total eye-witness authority and certainty. He's not trying to work these things out from a limited, earth-bound perspective. He comes directly from God, and so the things He says should be believed for that reason. He uses a favorite term of reference for Himself, the Son of Man. He's the Son of God who has become a man. And He tells Nicodemus that He will be lifted up in a very similar way to the bronze snake Moses lifted up when the Israelites were bitten during their wilderness wandering. Of course this story from the Old Testament Narrative was very familiar to Nicodemus, but what was all this talk of Jesus being lifted up like that?

Jesus continues making spiritual applications from physical metaphors. When He is lifted up, those who believe in Him will have eternal life. Like the Israelites who had no way to save themselves from physical death, all human beings, religious or not, descendants of Abraham or not, have no way of escaping the spiritual separation from God that is the result of their sin.

But those who believe in Him, in Jesus, God's Son who became a man, will be born again into God's family and given eternal life.

Jesus went on to make a statement that would become one of the most famous in the entire Bible – what we identify as the 16th verse in the 3rd chapter of John's account. God, He tells Nicodemus, loved the entire world – all of His lost race of corrupted image-bearers. Because of His love He sent His Son as the Messiah, the Deliverer – Jesus. He did this so that anyone who would believe in Him would not suffer the destruction that was the just payment for their sins.

In fact, incredibly, they will be saved, rescued, and be given eternal life.

Although Jesus, like John, is teaching clearly about people's sin and their true condition before God, He didn't come as judge and executioner. The fact that everyone has sinned means that their sentence has already been passed. God doesn't want people to pay that horrendous sentence, but if they refuse to believe in His Son who He sent, then there's no escape for them.

JESUS TAUGHT THE NECESSITY OF THE "NEW BIRTH"

Tragically, even though God has shone light into this dark world marred and torn up by sin, many choose to scurry away from that light back to the darkness. They don't want to have their lives exposed. They don't want to have to give up what they wrongly think of as their freedom, their rights. God graciously sent the light, His Son Jesus, and He continues to shine that light today. Some, a few, are drawn to it: glimpsing what a wonderful gift and incredible opportunity this represents, they believe in God's Son and are restored to the relationship He always intended for His image-bearers. They become His people. His born-again children.

 DISCUSSION POINTS

1. What factors do you think make it possible for religious experts like the Pharisees to be extremely familiar with the written record of God's Story and yet fail to understand the most important things He is communicating? What kind of presuppositions and worldview commitments do you suspect were involved?

2. What is your personal response to Jesus' statement about the lengths God was willing to go because of His love for the world? Based on the Narrative so far consider: (a) what did He mean by the term "world", (b) do you have any responsibilities toward that "world"?

3. What exactly is the "Good News", the Gospel, that comes out in this portion of the Narrative? Is Jesus statement to Nicodemus that he must be born again the Gospel, or not?

 ACTIVITIES

1. Do some research about the Jewish Sanhedrin and write a half-page description in your own words. Try to find out its composition, the extent and limits of its powers under Roman rule, its relationship to the Herodian monarchy etc.

1.42 Jesus had power to heal & forgive. Jewish leaders plotted

 OBJECTIVES OF THIS TUTORIAL

Learners will continue to explore and discuss the themes and the truths presented in God's Narrative. The portions of Scripture referred to in this tutorial are: **Mark 2:1-17, 3:1-19**

Last time
A religious leader called Nicodemus visited Jesus under the cover of darkness. Jesus declared that for someone to be one of God's people they have to be born again. When Nicodemus was confused, Jesus explained that this is something the Holy Spirit does, using God's Word in the heart of a person who believes. He stated that God had sent Him into the world because of His love for all people. He wants them to believe in His Son and receive eternal life rather than face the destruction they deserve for their sin.

A paralyzed man is let down to Jesus through the roof
Let's continue with God's Narrative of the remarkable life and work of Jesus, God's Son, this time some incidents recorded in Mark's account. After traveling to a number of different communities in the area, Jesus returns to the town of Capernaum, which will be something of a base for Him and His followers for the next couple of years. (Mark 2:1-12) The news quickly spreads around the town. Jesus is back again. A few people come to the house where He's staying. He sits and talks with them, probably in a room off the inner courtyard. Soon there are far too many people for casual conversation. He speaks to the whole group, explaining the teachings of the prophets, making it clear. And like when he was here before, in the synagogue, it's done with such quiet authority. No one else comes even close to explaining God's Word like this. Certainly not the religious leaders who are here checking things out. They're not looking happy. By now the house is absolutely crammed full. Even the doorway and entrance to the house is crowded.

There's a commotion outside but no one gets up to see what it is. They're captivated by His words. But what is going on up there, on the roof? That loud thumping and cracking noise? Oh, they're making a hole. Sunlight is coming in. Dust and powdered plaster are falling on everyone. "Jesus, don't stop, finish what you were saying. We're still listening". Hands make the hole bigger, breaking the sticks and thorn-bush, the mortar and earth the roof is made of. They're letting something down through the hole with ropes. It's that paralyzed man. Now he's right in front of Jesus. His friends' faces looking down, dirty and covered in plaster but expectant, "Please Master, heal him. We know you can".

Jesus looks up at them, then down at the paralyzed man. But He doesn't heal him, at least not yet. He says, "My child, your sins are forgiven". The teachers of religious law appear outraged and from what Jesus says he obviously knows they're thinking, "This is blasphemy, only God can forgive sins." Jesus doesn't contradict this, but He asserts that He does have the authority to forgive sins. Why? Because He is God's Son. And now He demonstrates that He is God, the Creator. He turns back to the man and tells him to get up. Which the man promptly does. He grabs the mat he's laid on for so many years and walks out. People's jaws are literally hanging open. Then everyone is talking at once. "Praise the name of Yahweh." "Did you see that?" "He hasn't walked for years!" "Incredible!" "Could this be the One?"

Jesus goes to the house of a tax collector who becomes his follower

Later, near the lake, Jesus sees a tax collector sitting in his booth alongside the road, ready to collect duties from farmers, merchants and caravans. Like others who've chosen this way of making money, he is a despised figure in the community… a collaborator with the enemy, dishonestly adding to people's already heavy tax burden, and regularly coming into contact with unclean Gentiles. No one concerned with his popularity, of building a reputation and following as a Rabbi, would have anything to do with a man like this. Incredibly, Jesus invites him to become one of His disciples. (Mark 2:13-17) The tax collector, Levi, walks away from his secure, lucrative business and follows Jesus.

Whether through previous encounters with Jesus we don't know, but Levi has understood and agreed with God's true perspective that he is a sinner and that his only hope is to trust in Jesus as the promised Messiah, the Deliverer. Later to be known as Matthew, he would write an account – a Gospel or Good News - about the life of Jesus. We have, of course, already followed some of his account.

That evening Jesus and His close followers are eating dinner at Levi's house along with other tax collectors and what the text calls "disreputable sinners". The Jewish religious leaders, Pharisees, are incredulous and outraged. How can He eat with people like that? The scum of the earth! They, of course, are meticulous in observing the rules and traditions, many of which have been added to God's Law given to Moses. They wouldn't dream of eating a meal with those kinds of people...for one thing, according to their own nitpicking dogma, that would make them ceremonially unclean.

Jesus' response challenges their proud assumptions: the only people who go to the doctor are those who know they're sick. Similarly, it's only people who know they're sinners who can recognize Him, the Deliverer, as the only possible way their sin-debt can be dealt with. Those who think they're acceptable to God because of their own efforts are not interested in being saved. For them He doesn't represent Good News.

The religious leaders become actively hostile toward Jesus

As Jesus' teaching exposes their hypocrisy and lack of real insights into God's Word, and as people flock to Him in ever larger crowds, the religious leaders' antagonism toward Him grows. They're hoping He'll violate their religious law so that they can accuse Him. (Mark 3:1-6) It's the Sabbath. Jesus is at the synagogue. There's also a man there with a deformed hand. The religious leaders are watching like hawks because if Jesus heals him they're going to claim that it's *work*, a violation of the Sabbath. They'll have Him. They can accuse Him of breaking God's Law.

Jesus knows what they're thinking but He's not going to be deterred from doing God's will by their oral traditions and legalistic interpretation of the Law – their obsession with the letter of the law while completely missing God's intent. Standing with the handicapped man in front of them He poses questions to them about the actual purpose for the Sabbath in the Mosaic Law. In essence, is it about doing good, saving life - for example, healing this man's hand? Or, did God intend the day to be about doing evil, like letting someone suffer? Or perhaps plotting to kill Jesus on the Sabbath....? They don't respond. Jesus is angered the text says and, "deeply saddened by their hard hearts". Although knowing the details of God's Story, these religious leaders are unwilling for God to be their Storyteller.

Their hearts are hard in the sense that they are entirely committed to their own assumptions about God and themselves. Even though God's Son is standing there before them, they won't humble themselves enough to recognize Him. They are set in their opposition. Even when the man's hand is healed at one word from Jesus, they aren't willing to see this evidence that He comes from God, that He *is* God's Son. They miss the fact that His Word is just as powerful to heal as it was to speak the entire universe into existence. Far from being humbled, Mark reports that the Pharisees immediately go and conspire with supporters of King Herod about how they can kill Jesus. The religious elitist Pharisees normally despise these politically pragmatic advocates for a Herodian kingship. But in this case their growing concern about Jesus' populist appeal and their resentment at his teaching joins them in an unholy alliance.

Crowds of people come to Jesus; he chooses 12 apostles

And indeed they have cause to be insecure about their hold on the masses. Mark records how people are now coming to see Jesus from all over Palestine and from surrounding areas as far north as modern day Lebanon. They crowd around Him, in ever increasing numbers. Everyone wants to see these miracles they've heard about. The sick want to be healed. In every way He demonstrates God's character: by the truth that He speaks, the patient compassion that He shows for the needy and, of course, through the powerful miracles he performs. The evil spirits recognize Him - they shriek out that He is the Son of God. But He won't have His identity made known by the forces of darkness. He forbids them to say who He is. (Mark 3:11-19)

From among His many followers, Jesus chooses 12 men to be His close companions, His special disciples. He intends to equip them and delegate His authority to them. They are not particularly well-educated, wealthy or influential men that He now calls His *apostles*. In the same way that He was sent by God, these apostles, or messengers, would be His *sent ones*.

Jesus has come into the world to defeat God's Enemy and He has already begun the conquest. He is preparing to deliver the *coup de grâce* – the finishing blow. But He also graciously allows His true followers to fight with Him in the battle. This is consistent with the character of God we've seen in the Narrative many times, beginning with Adam's caretaking role in the newly created earth. He equips those who trust His leadership, he gives them genuine responsibility, and He *sends* them out to play a significant role in His purposes. It's worth noting that one of the 12 apostles is Judas Iscariot. The other men who'll be Judas' companions for the next couple of years don't know what he is really like. Jesus, who of course knows everyone's hearts, can see everything going on with Judas, and knows that he'll eventually betray Him. But, humbly submitting to God's guidance, He includes Judas now as one of His close companions.

 **DISCUSSION POINTS**

1. One dictionary definition for forgive is "to stop feeling angry or resentful toward someone for an offense, flaw, or mistake." Based on what we've learned so far about the character of God, how is this consistent or inconsistent with His forgiveness of sins? In light of that, explain the basis on which Jesus declared the crippled man's sins forgiven.

2. Mark describes Jesus being angered by the attitudes of the Jewish religious leaders. We know that Jesus completely lived up to God's perfect standards in every way, so how was His anger consistent with God's character? What do you think was the reason for His feelings and why were they not wrong? Do you think that there is any context in which we, likewise, can be righteously angry, or is that a contradiction?

3. The Narrative does not give many clues, but knowing what we do about God's character, how do you think Jesus would have related to Judas? Do you think that, just like everyone else, He would have been genuinely offering Judas the opportunity to repent and put His faith in him or, knowing the future, would Jesus internally have already written him off as a lost cause?

1.43 Jesus calmed a storm & released a man from the control of demons

 OBJECTIVES OF THIS TUTORIAL

Learners will continue to explore and discuss the themes and the truths presented in God's Narrative. The portions of Scripture referred to in this tutorial are: **Mark 4:35-41, 5:1-20**

Last time

Back in Capernaum some people brought a crippled man to the house where Jesus was staying, but when they couldn't get him in because of the crowds they broke through the roof and lowered him down. Jesus healed the man and said his sins were forgiven because of his faith. Jesus went to the house of a tax collector, Matthew, who became his disciple.

The religious leaders became increasingly hostile towards Jesus and conspired to find a way to have Him killed. Jesus chose 12 apostles, companions who He would equip, then send out to teach.

Jesus calmed a storm on the sea of Galilee

Hanging out with Jesus for the disciples is an incredible experience. Mark describes two incidents from the same afternoon which demonstrate His awesome power and authority for them. It has been a long day already. Jesus has taught crowds of people on the rocky shore of the lake for hours. (Mark 4:35-41) Late in the afternoon Jesus suggests that they go over to other side of the lake, visible a number of kilometers away. They climb into the boat and push off. Obviously exhausted, Jesus lies down in the back and goes to sleep. As they draw away from shore, the fishermen among them are nervous. Conditions are right for one of the storms they know can come so quickly. On a warm day, when cool air is coming down onto the surface of the lake from the nearby eastern mountains, it's a recipe for sudden violent storms. And sure enough, that's what happens. One moment it is fine, the next they're fighting for their lives. The wind has whipped up waves that are threatening to swamp the fishing boat. Everyone is bailing madly but they're losing ground. Incredibly Jesus is still back there asleep. Desperate they call Him, "Teacher, what are you doing? Get up. This is serious. Don't you care if we all drown?"

Now, a little bleary eyed, Jesus is on His feet, facing into the wind. He's saying something. He's not yelling, but it's clearly audible over the wind and waves and thunder. He's telling the storm to be quiet, to calm down, to be still. What are words going to do at a time like this? The only time people speak to storms on this lake is with curses. But look, what's happened? Before He's finished speaking it stops. The silence is deafening. It's calm, almost eerily still. And Jesus quietly asks them why they were afraid. Haven't they learned yet to trust Him? Don't they have any faith?

No one, including the tough fishermen who've lived beside and on this lake all their lives, can believe what they just saw. What kind of person is this? An hour ago He was clearly exhausted. They were concerned for the Master: all the teaching, the questions, and people's demands for healing... they were glad He could rest, get some sleep.

The next moment that same person has the wind and waves obeying Him! Who can make a storm lie down like a mongrel dog? It's almost more terrifying than the storm, being with someone like this. What Jesus is allowing them to glimpse, the reality they would later be willing to live, and die for - a mystery but no less real for that – was that this man who need sleep and food and air to breath is the Creator God who designed and created the universe he was now a natural part of. He could speak to and be obeyed by the wind and the water because He had spoken them into existence in the first place. But He had also come into the creation and become part of it, allowed Himself to be vulnerable within it - to be hungry, tired, to experience physical weakness and pain – so that He could fulfill the great Rescue Plan for God's lost race that the One-God-Who-Is-Three had put into place.

Jesus freed a man from the control of evil spirits

Mark describes a second incident from the same afternoon that further demonstrates Jesus' authority and must have filled the disciples with awe again. (Mark 5:1-20) Their landfall after the storm is near the village of Gergesa... also often identified by another well-known city nearby, Gadara (modern day Jerash). On the steep hillside running down to the shore were burial caves used by the community. Living among the tombs was a man who had become totally controlled by the spirit beings, formerly God's messengers, now Satan's evil followers.

People had tried to help this man, to subdue him, even to chain him up so he wouldn't harm himself. But under the control of the evil spirits he had the strength to break whatever they used to constrain him. He spent his days and nights in misery, "howling and cutting himself with sharp stones" the text says. The man's condition provides a powerful and confronting analogy of the real state of human beings. The common myth might be that we've got it together and things are improving, but the reality is we live in a society spiraling out of control.

People keep finding new ways to inflict pain on each other, often children are the victims. Marriages have a less than even chance of lasting. Popular culture is obsessed with what's twisted, ugly and dark. There's widespread addiction to video violence and online pornography. People try to escape by getting into the latest thing, by hoarding stuff, by masking reality with alcohol and drugs, or eating themselves to death. Huge numbers of normal people deal daily with overwhelming panic and debilitating depression. Is it any wonder really that so many, often young, take what seems the only escape, suicide?

Satan's role in our society, and its desperate plight as a result, might not be as obvious as it was for the man living among the tombs then, but it is no less real. In fact, the sophisticated packaging of his control today makes it perhaps even more insidious. Certainly people in our society are no less in need of Jesus' liberating, life-giving intervention than that desperate, naked, filthy man on the hillside above the lake that day.

Mark describes how the man runs to meet Jesus. The evil spirits – and they were numerous, it turns out - using the man's voice, identify Jesus as "the Son of the Most High God". Clearly they're terrified of this one with absolute authority over them. The account of this incident hints at some things about the spirit world which God does not elaborate on... no doubt because we're not equipped to understand. When that happens, and when other parts of His Word don't shed a lot of light, we're best off to just accept His Narrative without too much unnecessary speculation. The spirits, fearful of whatever alternatives Jesus might have planned, beg Him to send them into a herd of pigs feeding nearby. He agrees, but when they come out of the man and enter the pigs, the entire herd – about 2,000 – go thundering down the steep hillside and drown in the lake.

The Narrative does not elaborate on what happened next to the evil spirits, who of course, not having a physical existence, could not drown. Some men who were responsible for the pigs have watched all this happen. Now they run off to tell everyone what they've seen. A crowd soon gathers. They can hardly believe their eyes. Isn't that the possessed man? But this is impossible. He looks so calm and composed. And someone's given him some clothes. He looks normal. The story is retold by the eyewitnesses, each trying to be heard. "I saw the whole thing... It was this man, His name's Jesus, He did it... The man was screaming... suddenly the pigs go crazy... drowned, every one of them." But the disciples observe that the people are not thrilled, as you might expect, by the man's release from the terrible bondage. Not excited that this notorious crazy man from their neighborhood is back to normal. And after this incredible demonstration of His authority over the powers of darkness, you'd think they'd want to know more. Ask Jesus questions. Want Him to teach them. Instead, they're obviously fearful. And they plead with him to go… to leave them alone. Whoever He is, whatever He stands for – they don't want any part of it. They don't want to be disturbed, to have their perspectives challenged. They just want to go on with their lives. But the man himself, the one who has been freed from the torment of possession, he wants to be near Jesus. However Jesus tells him to go home and tell his family about what the Lord has done for him… the mercy he has experienced.

This follows a pattern that emerges from the Narrative. When God saves someone from eternal death, he also gives them a purpose to live. He draws them into His Rescue effort by sending them out to tell others about Him and the good News about what He has done for them.

? DISCUSSION POINTS

1. Make any observations you can about the connections between (a) the creative power of God's speech in the beginning ("God said…") (b) the authority of Jesus' commands (to the storm, to evil spirits etc.) and (c) the power of God's Narrative, His Word (Note Jesus' comments to Nicodemus about the role of God's Word in the new – spiritual – birth.)

2. Comment on Jesus' challenge to His disciples about their lack of faith in Him during the storm. Based on the Narrative so far, explain what you understand He meant by this. What might it have looked like if they had trusted Him more in that situation? Reflect on your understanding of the relationship between faith and things like: good judgment, careful planning, taking precautions etc.

3. Describe some of the main strategies you feel Satan and his spirit-followers have used effectively in our society to capture people and to keep them from the truth.

1.44 Jesus fed 5,000 people

✓ OBJECTIVES OF THIS TUTORIAL

Learners will continue to explore and discuss the themes and the truths presented in God's Narrative. The portions of Scripture referred to in this tutorial are: **John 6:1-35**

Last time
One afternoon Jesus was asleep in the back of a boat as He and His disciples were crossing the lake. A fierce storm threatened their lives but the wind and waves calmed immediately when Jesus told them to do so. On the other side, they encountered a demon-possessed man who lived among the graves. Jesus commanded the evil spirits to leave him. They entered a herd of pigs nearby which ran into the lake and were drowned. The people in the area didn't want Jesus around and begged Him to leave.

Jesus miraculously provides food for a huge number of people
We continue with the story of the life of Jesus the Messiah, this time with John's description of another astounding incident. (John 6:1-15) Through everything Jesus says and does, God is continuing to reveal Himself. All His characteristics – His power, righteousness, grace, faithfulness etc. – are being perfectly communicated in the person of Jesus of Nazareth. We again find Jesus crossing the Sea of Galilee with His disciples. John places the incident on the calendar, just before the Jewish Passover – the annual remembrance of God providing their ancestors with a way to escape the death that came to every Egyptian family. By now, a huge crowd is following Jesus everywhere, drawn by the healings and other miracles.

Sitting on a hill with His disciples, He sees a huge crowd of people coming toward them. Jesus turns to one of the disciples, Philip, and asks where they could possibly buy food for all these people. John notes that Jesus already knows full well what He's going to do, but He wants to use it as a teaching opportunity for the disciples - to show them the gaps that still exist in their understanding of what He can *do*, who He *is*. As we've seen a number of times already, God is committed to teaching, equipping and involving faithful followers in every aspect of His purposes. Indeed, Philip's response shows that he still has a long way to go – "what can be done? They are small in number, the people's need is huge, there's no money, no resources, forget it, it's hopeless." The Narrative doesn't say, but you have to wonder if the others laugh at Andrew when he mentions that he's come across a young boy with five small bread rolls and two fish. Of course, he quickly adds, what use is that among so many? But the presence of the One who first created wheat and fish and even the hillside they are all sitting on changes everything. Normal rules and limitations don't apply. He is the Creator, Provider, the One in whose hands not even close can become more than enough.

Jesus takes the food into His hands, thanks God His Father for what they're about to eat, then starts passing it on… soon the thousands of people sitting around are eating bread and fish. After everyone has eaten all they can, there's still lots left over. The crowd is gripped by a sense of amazement, excitement, anticipation. "This must be the One! God's prophet, David's descendant. Let's declare Him King. We won't take no for an answer. We'll depose Herod, throw out the Romans. It'll be great, no one will ever be sick, and we'll always have plenty to eat." Jesus, of course, knows what is being said, what they are planning. He knows that most of the people are not wanting to follow him because of spiritual hunger. They're not drawn to Him by a sense of their immense need before God. The miracles, the healing, feeding them in such an amazing way – these are not ultimately about meeting people's physical needs, much less their desires. He cares about them deeply, but His purpose in coming to earth is not to make them contented and comfortable. The signs and miracles are about demonstrating his authority, they are statements about *who He is*… to draw those who've been waiting for the Messiah to provide the final solution for their debt of sin before God. The great Story God is writing in history, and Jesus' role in it, does not call for Him to be a king on earth at that point, like the people want. So He quietly slips away into the nearby hills.

Jesus walks on the top of the water

John now relates yet another amazing incident… in a fairly matter of fact way. It's almost as though by this point the disciples have come to expect astounding things from Jesus. (Jn 6:16-21) After the thousands of people have been fed, the disciples wait for Jesus on the shore. When it gets dark and He still hasn't shown up, they head back across the lake to Capernaum.

Before long they're caught in a storm, fighting huge waves. It's tiring, paddling on and on, hour after hour. Then someone catches sight of something in the darkness. "Look, what is that? Where? Over there. Looks like a figure… a person. But out here on the water? You don't think it's a spirit, like a ghost or something? It's coming this way. Hurry, row away…"

Then a familiar voice, "Hey, stop worrying. It's me." Relief. "Oh, it's the Master. Look at that! He's walking on top of the water. Incredible. Yeah, well it's Jesus, nothing's difficult for Him.

Welcome, Master. Get in the boat with us. Wow, are we glad to see you. We were terrified."

Suddenly they've arrived, safe and sound... with the comforting sound of the keel running up onto the pebbles at Capernaum.

Jesus declares that He is the Bread of Life

The next morning the crowds from the day before come to Capernaum looking for Jesus. But He's not flattered by the attention or excited by His growing popularity. He tells them up front that He knows very well they haven't understood the underlying, important things He's demonstrating through the miracles. Basically they just want Him to provide more food. They're thinking of physical desires, not spiritual needs. (John 6:22-35) But even though He knows their motivation, He doesn't send them away. He patiently tries to help them understand the truth. He challenges them not to be consumed with physical, transient things like food. They should put their energy into understanding how He can give them eternal life. He can do this, He asserts, because He comes from God, is approved by Him. They claim - perhaps not very sincerely - that they want to do things that will please God... and ask what they should do. This is the same mistake we've seen through the Narrative that humans always make, beginning with our ancestors when they originally rebelled against God. Their first impulse was to *do* something, to somehow make things right, to cover up their shame, to try to look okay in God's eyes.

But to the crowd on this morning in Capernaum, Jesus replies that there's only one thing God wants from them... that is, to believe in Him, the One God sent. We don't know if there were individual exceptions, but the crowd is not in a mood to humbly accept Jesus' words, nor to give up their hopes of another miraculous feed."Well if you want us to really believe you're from God, you'll have to come up with something amazing... how about more food... yeah, on a regular basis. Moses gave our ancestors bread from heaven. How about something like that? Like manna." But Jesus points out that Moses didn't give them bread from heaven. That was God who did that. It was *His* mercy, *His* grace. And that was only physical bread anyway. Now God is offering them the real thing. Bread from heaven that gives life to the world. *What* is it? *Who* is it? It's Jesus Himself. He's the Bread of Life, He tells them. He's the one who fills every real need, who satisfies the real hunger and ache that humans have in their hearts... the great void that has been left by their turning away, the very real sense of guilt before God, even if they don't recognize it. When people realize their need, realize they can't *do* anything for themselves, when they look to Him, the One sent from God, then He'll never turn them away… He'll give them eternal life and satisfy the deepest spiritual hunger in their hearts.

The crowd though cannot, or are unwilling to, see beyond their small concerns. They refuse to look past their small self-absorbed worlds. And so tragically, they miss the fact that God's Son is standing before them, offering them everything they so desperately need. The same thing, of course, has happened countless times down through history. He never stops seeking, but only a handful accept what He's offering, Himself, the Bread of Life.

? DISCUSSION POINTS

1. What do you think Jesus was hoping to teach Phillip and the other disciples in the process of feeding thousands of people from just a few fragments of food? What assumptions and limitations in their worldview do you suspect He was exposing? Do you feel you might share any of those assumptions and limitations? If so, can you pinpoint any ways He challenges those things with you?

2. Reflect on your understanding of what Jesus offers those who follow Him. If someone was considering becoming a Christian and asked you whether or not that would mean greater safety for them and their family, more financial security, or an increased chance of being treated fairly by others… how would you respond?

3. Expand in your own words on the concept of Jesus as the Bread of Life. Consider the background understanding of the Jewish crowd He was addressing. With that in mind, describe any difficulties you can imagine in trying to explain Jesus' statement about being the Bread of Life to someone in our society who has no Narrative foundations.

➡ ACTIVITIES

1. Review the Narrative covered so far and note any evidence you can find in support of the proposition that God is committed to drawing faithful followers to His purposes and equipping them to be effective.

1.45 The Pharisees rejected God's way

 OBJECTIVES OF THIS TUTORIAL

Learners will continue to explore and discuss the themes and the truths presented in God's Narrative. The portions of Scripture referred to in this tutorial are: **Mark 7:1-7, 14-23, Luke 18:9-14**

Last time
When a crowd of thousands followed Jesus and His disciples across the lake, He fed them in a miraculous way - starting with a very small quantity of bread and fish. The people wanted to declare Him their king but He slipped away. Later that night, He came walking across the waves to the boat where the disciples were caught in a storm. The next morning, in response to the crowd who came back wanting more food, He declared that He is the Bread of Life... anyone who accepts what He offers will be given eternal life.

Jesus contrasted religious legalism with genuine faith
As we follow the Narrative and understand the message Jesus is bringing from God, one thing that stands out is how He targets the religious hypocrisy that is so entrenched among His people, the Jews. He condemns the religious legalism of those who lead that system in contrast with the genuine, humble, repentant faith that God wants from human beings. We'll see this first from an incident Mark records, then from a story, or parable, that Luke wrote down.

Mark tells how one day some Pharisees and teachers of religious law come from Jerusalem to see Jesus. (Mark 7:1-7) From their track record and the subsequent conversation, it seems very unlikely they've come wanting to learn from Him, to find out the truth. We've already heard in the Narrative how these religious leaders and so-called experts in the Law are consumed with trying to follow the letter of the Law God gave to Moses. They had created an elaborate religious system which they control, adding numerous other requirements on top of God's commandments and trying to impose them on the people. They're not around Jesus very long before something happens to surface the underlying error in their view of God and of themselves.

They notice that some of His disciples fail to follow the Jewish ritual of hand washing before eating. Mark gives some background here, explaining that the Jews, and particularly the Pharisees, have very strict and elaborate rules governing the washing of hands, particularly before touching anything that goes in the mouth. These Pharisees and religious experts from Jerusalem challenge Jesus on this point, asking why His disciples don't follow these traditions. But Jesus clearly isn't interested in debating the finer points of doctrine or theology. In fact, He's not even particularly polite. He calls them a bunch of hypocrites. Of course, He's the one person qualified to make this evaluation of others because He can see their "hearts" - their thoughts and motivations. He quotes from the prophet Isaiah who talks about people who claim to honor God even though they prioritize other things... whose so-called worship is a farce because it's based on their own ideas about pleasing God.

Having called to the nearby crowd to come and listen, He continues to expand on His point. (Mark 7:14-23) He targets another whole area the religious experts are obsessed with - dietary laws - and dismisses it as foolish legalism. What we eat, when, how it's been prepared, by whom... those are not things that impact God's view of us. They don't make us good or evil.

What does betray our evil natures and condemns us before God is what comes out of our hearts - desires, attitudes, thoughts, words and actions. Even those who are able to keep all the edges tucked in, who seem like *nice*, respectable, even noble people...at the end of the day no one's heart is free of pride, selfishness and wrong motivations.

So Jesus exposes the hypocrisy of these religious leaders, but they just serve as an extreme example of the mistake that everyone in the crowd makes (including His disciples).

Indeed it's the mistake that most... no, all, humans fall into! We tell ourselves we're not really *that* bad. We find others who we consider worse than us and compare ourselves favorably to them. And those who have any notion of God, often comfort themselves with the thought that surely He'll do the same... He's reasonable, He can see that they're not as bad as so-and-so, definitely not evil like murderers or terrorists for instance! Surely at the end of the day the good they've done will outweigh any mistakes! But of course this is human thinking, part of the same mindset that produced the elaborate system of rituals and rules of orthodox Judaism (along with most other religions). It is what has made the word *Pharisee* synonymous with hypocrisy.

Jesus told a parable about a tax collector and a Pharisee

Jesus used many parables in His teaching. This, as we know, is the traditional English term for these brief stories that are fictional but not fanciful... they could well happen. Parables illustrate important truths, but the underlying message, and certainly its applications, are not always immediately obvious. Luke records one (Luke 18:9-14) that vividly portrays the conceited, legalistic pride that God rejects, in contrast to the humble, repentant faith He's looking for.

Speaking one day to an audience of people He knows are self-righteous and dismissive of others who don't live up to their self-imposed religious standards, Jesus tells the following parable. Two men go to the temple to pray. One is a Pharisee, and the other is a despised tax collector. The Pharisee stands by himself and prays this prayer: 'I thank you, God, that I am not a sinner like everyone else. For I don't cheat, I don't sin, and I don't commit adultery. I'm certainly not like that tax collector! I fast twice a week, and I give you a tenth of my income.' But the tax collector stands at a distance and is too fearful to lift his eyes to heaven as he prays. Instead, he hits chest in sorrow, saying, 'O God, be merciful to me, for I am a sinner.'

So how does God view the two contrasting players in this story Jesus told? There's no denying that the tax collector is a sinner... everyone knows what those guys do, what their lifestyle is like. Certainly God knows all about his sin. There's no doubt he's guilty, condemned to eternal punishment. But the point Jesus is making here is not who's the worst person. It's about who recognizes their sin. And this tax collector does. He's crushed by the weight of it. He realizes there's no way for him to avoid the consequences. He can't do anything to pay for his sin-debt. And so he throws himself on God's mercy. It's not as though his prayer itself *does* anything... but it's the kind of approach God is looking for. Someone knowing their desperate need and throwing themselves on His mercy... saying, "God, if you don't help me I've got nothing else. I'm dead meat."

The lifestyle of the Pharisee, in contrast, would no doubt have appeared pretty good. Super religious, doesn't swear or drink, gives to charity, a pillar of society. The kind people might say about, "If anyone's going to get into heaven, it will be that guy." But again, the point Jesus is making is that, at the end of the day, no matter how hard someone tries, they're still hopelessly short of God's perfect standard. There's a record kept of the Pharisee's sin as well... and every single entry, on its own, condemns him to eternal punishment.

Good-living religious people desperately need God's grace - need to have their sin-debt dealt with - just as much as any loser who society condemns. And so Jesus concludes the parable with the statement that, as these two men head home from the temple that

THE PHARISEES REJECTED GOD'S WAY

day, it's the tax collector, not the Pharisee, who is justified - whose sin-debt God has canceled and who is now acceptable according to God's righteous standard.

❓ DISCUSSION POINTS

1. Would you agree that our society doesn't think it's good to be overly religious, any more than it is to be a real "no-hoper"? So what are the things by which people are judged in our culture? Make a list of the positive and negative qualities by which individuals are accepted. Also consider whether that list would vary with different generations.

2. Do you think that a prayer is necessary for someone to be saved? If not, why not? If so, why? Also describe the elements you feel are needed. As much as possible support your perspective from the Narrative we've covered so far.

3. How would you answer someone who put forward an argument like this: if it's true that "good living" people and really bad people are just as condemned by their sin in God's eyes, then what point is there for someone in society to "do the right thing"? Doesn't it make good sense to just live as you like and then repent when you're old?

➡ ACTIVITIES

1. Write an answer to the first discussion point above, and support your answer with a combination of research and a survey of some people you know.

2. Write a version of the parable about the Pharisee and tax collector that is contextualized for our culture.

1.46 Jesus is the Christ, the Son of God

 OBJECTIVES OF THIS TUTORIAL

Learners will continue to explore and discuss the themes and the truths presented in God's Narrative. The portions of Scripture referred to in this tutorial are: **Mark 8:27-38, 9:1-10**

Last time
When some Pharisees from Jerusalem challenged Jesus about His disciples not following Jewish religious regulations, He exposed their hypocrisy. He said that it's what comes out of people's hearts that condemns them before God. He told a story, a parable that contrasted a self-righteous Pharisee and a repentant tax collector praying in the temple.

Jesus asks the disciples who they believe He is
Mark records some events that serve as important landmarks in the disciples' journey toward understanding who this person is that they are following. (Mark 8:27-30) The account of what they hear and observe is no less important for us as we follow God's Narrative and consider the implications for ourselves and others we interact with. Mark says that Jesus and the disciples leave Galilee and head north to the area around Caesarea Philippi, a town at the base of Mount Hermon.

As they are walking along Jesus asks them what they've been hearing...who are people saying that he is? He, of course, already knows the answer to the question, but He asks these kinds of things in order to get them thinking, to challenge their existing paradigms, and then to communicate truth with them. The disciples reflect on some of the rumors and wild speculation about Him that have been going around. Some people are saying that He is John - the one who baptized so many in the Jordan - come back to life after Herod executed him. Others say Elijah, the Old Testament prophet who didn't physically die. Other prophets have been suggested as possibilities. On a number of occasions Jesus has clearly stated that He is God's Son and proved it by the incredible miraculous things He'd done. But it seems very few people are believing He is actually who He says He is.

Jesus isn't going to allow this pivotal question of His true identity to stay in the theoretical or the third person for His close companions - just a matter of what *others* think. The issue isn't finally about how their friends or their family or the majority of people would answer this question...it's who *they*, individually, believe He is. He puts it to them directly, "But who do you say that I am?" It's the question that God wants every human being to have the opportunity to answer...having heard His Narrative of what has lead up to Him graciously sending His Son to the world, for them to then stand before Jesus, as it were, and declare who they believe He is. Answers like, "A good, wise man", or "A prophet" are irrelevant. People need to have heard enough of His Story to either accept His claim to be God's Son who came to save the world, or reject the whole thing as a fabrication, a pack of lies. There's simply no middle ground on this issue.

Peter - always the first to speak up - says, "You are the Messiah". In other words, the long-promised, anointed or chosen One from God. His ultimate Storyteller, his *Prophet*, the great *High Priest* and the eternal *King* in the line of David. It's a bold statement for this humble fisherman from Capernaum. But after hanging out with Jesus for some time now, watching His life day after day, hearing Him teach and seeing the amazing things He's done...he is confident he knows who Jesus is, and we can assume he speaks for the other disciples.

Jesus tells them not to be sharing their perspective on His identity with others... He doesn't want people just jumping on the bandwagon. If they come to the point of saying that He is God's promised Deliverer, He wants it to be something they've really believed for themselves, in their own hearts.

Jesus foretells His suffering, death and resurrection

Jesus then lets them in on some things that are shocking to these men who've identified themselves with Him and made at least some level of commitment to His cause. (Mark 8:31-33) Haven't they, after all, just said that He's the Messiah? Doesn't that mean they've made a wise choice when they became His disciples? Okay, so far there hasn't been much in the way of obvious rewards or benefit, but surely things will get better. Soon He'll get the recognition and honor that are His right... and when He does, well, naturally things will also improve for His closest companions, right?

So now they listen in horror as He tells them that the religious leaders are going to vehemently and violently reject His claims. At their instigation He's going to be tortured and put to death. He does tell them that He'll come back to life after 3 days, that doesn't really register or make sense. It's all the other grim things He's told them that are playing on their minds. Peter pulls Him aside and tells Him not to say things like that. It's unsettling Master, unnecessary...all this negative talk about rejection, suffering and death. Let's be positive here...lay out a proactive strategy for the kingdom. But Jesus rebukes Peter in the strongest terms. That's the story Satan has deceived humans with all along - that somehow things can be made right in this sin-cursed, pain-filled, death-soaked world, without suffering and death. That's not how things *are* in God's true rescue Story for His lost race. Jesus' coming to earth and what He has committed to do are the climax of that Story and He won't listen even for a moment to any alternatives, no matter how nice and positive and reasonable they might sound.

Jesus presses the point home, calling over the crowd that has inevitably gathered when He turns up somewhere. (Mark 8:34-9:1) He makes some profound statements about what becoming one of His followers involves. He wants no one under any illusions. Certainly it will be a journey, and the realities cannot all be understood from the outset, but those setting out to follow Him need to weigh up the realities. He's looking for people who grasp the fact that what they've built their lives around - their goals, their right to tell their own story, their whole "world" in fact, is seriously misaligned. And even though the realignment will take the rest of their lives and be a less than comfortable process, they are at least willing, by faith, to acknowledge His right to lead them through it.

Three of the disciples get a glimpse of Jesus' true glory

The whole matter of Jesus' true identity is further highlighted in yet another remarkable incident that Mark relates next. (Mark 9:2-10) It's six days after the conversation about who people say He is and how they, the disciples, identify him. Despite His strong words to Peter less than a week before, Jesus specifically invites him, along with James and John, to walk together up what the text calls "a high mountain". Traditionally this has been identified as Mount Tabor in lower Galilee, but there's no way to be certain.

On the summit, things are as normal until at some point the disciples notice that Jesus looks different. What is it? Teacher, what's happening? Suddenly His whole being is glowing: His clothes, everything... is luminous, shining. It has an unearthly quality that they can only feebly define in human terms as "white". But a white like no white they've ever seen before. Then, there are two figures who they somehow recognize as Moses and Elijah talking with Jesus.

James and John are speechless, but Peter, being Peter, just has to say something. In his amazement and confusion he's babbling about how great this all is, and that they should put up some kind of monumental structures... But his foolishness is quickly forgotten when they see a cloud cover Jesus, Moses and Elijah and they hear a voice come out of it that says, "This is my dearly loved Son. Listen to Him".

When they look again, only Jesus is there, looking like normal again. On the way down He tells them not to tell anyone about this until after He has risen from the dead. This will prove to be a defining moment…when these three of His closest companions for a very brief time are given a glimpse of who He truly is. They are left grappling with the mystery that his very normal human body is actually a container or vehicle, in a sense, for the being of God Himself. In physical terms He is just like them, but He also contains within Himself all the amazing glory of God, the Creator of the universe. They can look over and see Him right there next to them, walking down the mountain on two legs that are no doubt getting weary like theirs, in sandals that are just as dusty as theirs. But they'll never quite see Him the same way again, because up there on the mountain they caught a glimpse of His glory and they heard God identify Him - just like after His baptism - as His Son who completely pleases Him.

As the Narrative will show, there are many struggles and low-times ahead for these three men… but whatever anyone else says about who Jesus is, they *know*. No one can take away from them or make them doubt what they've seen with their own eyes and heard with their own ears. And despite failures and very real human struggles they'll face, they will go on to give up everything to be His storytellers, to help others to also realize who He really is.

❓ DISCUSSION POINTS

1. As you reflect on Jesus' interaction with people so far in the Narrative, are there any specific points or principles that have been highlighted or that you've noticed yourself in how He went about communicating truth? Also make any applications you can that would be a help to us as we attempt to be His witnesses in this society.

2. (a) For someone to be saved - born again - how accurately and completely do they need to answer the question Jesus asks, "Who do you say that I am?" (E.g. Do they need to know He is God's Son? God in human form? The Messiah? David's descendant? Born of a virgin?)
(b) How much background from the Biblical Narrative does someone need in order to know enough about who He is to be saved?

3. Why do think it is that many people - even many religious systems - are happy to acknowledge that Jesus was a good, wise, caring person, even a prophet of some kind, but refuse to even consider the possibility that He was God in human form?

4. What features of God's character stand out when you think about the two declarations He has made that Jesus is His Son who He is completely pleased with?

➡ ACTIVITIES

1. On a map, find historical Caesarea Philippi, Mount Hermon and Mount Tabor. Trace Jesus and the disciples' possible route as they first went north from Capernaum then south to Jerusalem - as is likely if they went there for the obligatory Feast of Tabernacles that occurred soon after.

1.47 Jesus is the only door to eternal life

 OBJECTIVES OF THIS TUTORIAL

Learners will continue to explore and discuss the themes and the truths presented in God's Narrative. The portions of Scripture referred to in this tutorial are: **John 10:7-11, 14:6**

Last time
On a trip north to the slopes of Mount Hermon, Jesus discussed with His disciples who people were saying He was. Then He asked them who *they* believed Him to be. Peter responded by declaring that Jesus was the Messiah. But when Jesus revealed that His future held suffering and death, Peter protested. Jesus firmly rebuked him, saying that Satan was behind that kind of human perspective. Later Jesus took Peter, James and John to a mountaintop where for a brief moment they were allowed to glimpse the glory of His *deity* that was normally hidden by His humanity.

Jesus uses a compelling metaphor about *sheep & shepherds*
As the Narrative unfolds, Jesus continues to challenge people's view of Him and helps them to understand His role. To do this, He uses a number of metaphors taken from everyday life… familiar, concrete things that help His audience understand the abstract truth He's communicating.

John records some of these. In the first, (John 10:7-11) Jesus likens Himself to the *gate* of a sheepfold. To the people listening that day, everything to do with raising and looking after sheep is commonplace. Each morning for part of the year, a familiar sight is the local shepherds leading their flocks out to wherever grass and edible shrubs can be found for grazing. In the evenings you can see and hear them bringing the sheep back to the enclosures on the outskirts of the towns and villages. In the hot summers they probably won't be around as they've led the sheep up into the cooler hills. Again, in cold winters you won't see them because they've taken their flocks for warmth and shelter down to lower valleys.

But even out in the wilderness, they have enclosures with walls made out of rocks and whatever else comes to hand... perhaps some thorn bushes. Some of these are built against a cliff face, particularly if there's a handy cave... To let the sheep wander at night is a sure way to lose many to thieves and to wild animals.

In fact, a conscientious shepherd knows that he can't just get the sheep into the sheepfold and then disappear into his tent or cave and assume everything's fine for the night. What he does is get them in then lie down in the gap, the entrance... to be, as it were, the gate himself. Then, even if he does go to sleep, it's like half of him is awake so that at the slightest disturbance he's ready to keep any wandering sheep *in* or to keep anyone else *out*.

So the audience immediately has this very familiar picture in mind when Jesus starts talking about shepherds and gates.

Yes, certainly everyone has seen what He's describing... on their way out in the mornings or back at night, the flocks often mingle. But it all gets sorted gradually as the different sheep recognize their own shepherd's voice calling out to them and eventually gather around him.

And it's true that only the true shepherd of a flock goes through the gate, anyone sneaking over the wall must be up to no good. But clearly Jesus is using it as an illustration of something. What's His point? Teacher, what are you trying to tell us? We don't understand...

But as He continues and expands the illustration His meaning starts to emerge. He's saying that they, we, all people, are like sheep. In other words, rather foolish creatures, prone to aimless wandering, badly in need of rescuing, care and protection. In this picture, *He* is the gate for the sheep... the entrance into peace with God, protection from his Enemy, and purpose in this life and beyond. The sheep that are drawn to His voice come to Him and to Him alone because they realize that His offer is completely genuine. All other claims are false. They are made by imposters - Satan, his spirit helpers, and often unknowing human collaborators - who care nothing for the sheep. They want to steal and kill... to entirely destroy all life and hope. In contrast, Jesus cares deeply for the sheep; He wants to lead them to where life can be rich and satisfying, now and forever.

In fact, as a shepherd, He loves the sheep so much He's willing to give His life for them. Were the listeners that day reminded of the prophet Isaiah's words, written centuries before but clearly pointing toward the man now speaking to them? "... He was pierced for our rebellion, crushed for our sins. He was beaten so we could be whole. He was whipped so we could be healed. All of us, like sheep, have strayed away. We have left God's paths to follow our own."

Jesus stated that He is the way, the truth and the life

A little later in his record (John 14:6) John recalls Jesus making another statement about who He is. His claims here are so *definitive*, so *exclusive*, that anyone who actually engages with them has to accept them as truth, OR to dismiss them as the pathologically conceited ramblings of a madman. Again, He leaves no middle ground... no neutral position regarding who He is. Speaking to His disciples one day, and specifically addressing Thomas - the proverbial skeptic among them - Jesus says, "I am the way, the truth, and the life. No one can come to the Father except through me."

So first of all, Jesus is saying that He, and He alone, is **the way** that anyone can relate to God. All other attempts whether under the banner of "Christianity", another organized religious system, or some other vaguely "spiritual" ideology, are dead-ends...they don't lead to God. Even if these activities make people feel temporarily peaceful, comforted, uplifted, "in tune with God" or whatever... Jesus categorically states that unless it is through Him, it is definitely not God they're relating to.

Secondly, He says that He is **the truth**. It's important to note that this, like the other claims Jesus makes, are not just - to use philosophical terms - *epistemological*, i.e. about how things are *known*. Rather, He is making *ontological* statements - what things are in their very essence, their existence... in other words, who *He* actually is.

So while it's perfectly true that He teaches truth and through him truth can be known, even more fundamentally, he is saying that He *is* the truth. Truth has no external existence apart from Him. Nothing can accurately reflect reality if it doesn't accurately reflect who He is.

Any worldview, ideology, belief, thought pattern, opinion or statement that is not aligned with the Truth that He is, is by definition false. But this is not just a theoretical statement... and truth is not just some cold, detached propositional doctrine or dogma.

Because He is the good shepherd, because as well as being Truth He is also Love and Grace, He shares Himself - the Truth - gladly and willingly with those who come humbly to listen and learn. He takes on Himself the burden of reaching out to us and patiently leading us in the journey of truly knowing Him and the Father.

Because, as His third statement makes clear, as well as being the way and the truth, He is also **Life**. Again, this is an *ontological* statement. The concept "life" is meaningless without Him. All existence that is not part of Him, part of His life, no matter how great it might look, is a fake - as Adam and Eve began to find out in that bitter day in the garden. For one thing, "life" apart from Him is just a brief pathway that is leading to physical and then spiritual death - eternal punishment and separation from Him. But His statement about Him being *Life* goes infinitely further than just offering a way to escape the horror of death. It also includes the incredible, mind-blowing possibility of living now and eternally without ever being separated from Him... of walking through life beside Him while He progressively opens up to us all that God intends for His image-bearers to experience in this gift called life. It does not mean any kind of escape from the bumps, and problems and real pain of life on earth. But it does mean that those who come to him for life - who accept him as life - have the opportunity to experience a purpose and hope that is absolutely real and limitless... because He is.

DISCUSSION POINTS

1. Why do you think Jesus used so many analogies and illustrations from everyday life rather than just laying things out in a straightforward point form? Can you think of any overarching characteristics of God that this demonstrates? Are there any principles about communicating truth we can glean from this?

2. How does it make you personally feel to consider Jesus' description of Himself as the loving shepherd who is willing to give His life for the sheep?

3. How would you answer someone who objected to the idea that Jesus' claims are exclusive - that He, and He alone, is the way, the truth and the life. How would you respond to the challenge that anyone who says that about Jesus is not being respectful toward other beliefs... and that it leads to intolerant fundamentalism?

ACTIVITIES

1. In no more than 6 Power Point slides, put together a presentation you think would help someone understand what Jesus was teaching through the illustration of sheep, shepherds, gates, thieves etc.

1.48 Jesus raised Lazarus from the dead

 OBJECTIVES OF THIS TUTORIAL

Learners will continue to explore and discuss the themes and the truths presented in God's Narrative. The portions of Scripture referred to in this tutorial are: **John 11:1-54**

Last time
Jesus used an extensive illustration about sheep that would have conjured very familiar images for His audience. He said that He is a good shepherd, one who cares for the sheep, protects them... indeed, gladly lays down His life to save them and offer them a rich and fulfilling life. This is in contrast to others who make false claims but who are really thieves and who ultimately want to destroy the sheep. In another statement He made some remarkable and very exclusive claims about who He is: the way, the truth and the life.

Jesus has some friends and followers in Bethany
By now, opinion about Jesus has become very divided. The authorities are increasingly antagonistic and are obviously waiting for an opportunity, any excuse they can find, to arrest Him. There are not many places where He is safe, very few family homes - certainly not in the southern areas near Jerusalem - where He is welcome. An exception is in the town or, more accurately, village, of Bethany.

Just a few kilometers' walk from Jerusalem, on the slopes of the Mount of Olives (in today's West Bank) there two sisters and their brother who are only too glad to have Jesus visit their home. Luke introduces them earlier in his account, focusing on the sisters, Mary and Martha. They are very different in character from each other, but Jesus obviously counts both as dear friends as well as followers. Despite the storm of controversy and danger gathering around Jesus, these courageous ladies are devoted to Him, and their home provides something of a base for Him and His disciples when they are in the Jerusalem area. Now John records an incident that involves their brother Lazarus, and which will prove to be one of the truly outstanding events from Jesus' time on earth.

Lazarus becomes sick and then dies

The two sisters have sent word to Jesus, "Lord, your dear friend is very sick". Jesus, who of course knows exactly how things are going to work out, makes the observation that this has happened so that God and His Son will receive glory. (John 11:1-16) Knowing the danger that awaits them anywhere near Jerusalem - in the province of Judea - the disciples are no doubt a bit surprised but also relieved that Jesus does not immediately head down to Bethany at the news of His friend's serious illness. So why now, after two days have passed, does He suddenly want to go? "Teacher, we're only thinking of you, but it would be crazy to go to Judea now. Only a few days ago people there were trying to stone you to death." "What's that you say Lord, Lazarus has fallen asleep? Surely you don't need to go and wake him. If he's having a good sleep, no doubt that means he's on the mend."

But Jesus tells them straight out that Lazarus is dead. He also adds that He's glad He wasn't there, because the way things are going to happen will help them to believe. This is all very disturbing... does He mean to go down there and let the authorities kill him so He can join Lazarus? Thomas, always the pessimist but also loyal, says, "Well, if He's going down there to die, I guess we might as well go too."

Jesus speaks with Martha & Mary after their brother's death

By the time they get to Bethany, it's already four days after the burial. There are still quite a lot of people hanging around who've made the short walk from Jerusalem, supposedly to comfort the sisters after their loss. As the story unfolds, it's questionable how close many of them were to Martha and Mary, or how genuine their concern. But one thing is for certain, the events that take place will be seen by a lot of eyewitnesses, and their account cannot help but spread like wildfire in the nearby capital. (John 11:15-32)

Hearing that Jesus is on His way, Martha goes out to meet Him, no doubt in tears, "Oh, we kept waiting, and waiting, hoping you'd arrive. Right up to the end.... Now... well God would give you whatever you ask... but, no of course it's too late, isn't it, Lord?"

"Martha. Your brother will be brought back to life."

"Yes I know... it will be some day far in the future - at the end of time, when God raises everyone for the final judgment."

"Martha, listen. *I* am the resurrection and the life. Anyone who believes in me will live, even after they have died. Everyone who lives in me and believes in me will never ever die. Do you believe that?"

"Yes, Lord, I have always believed you are the Messiah, the Son of God, the one who has come into the world from God."

At this point Martha goes and finds Mary and discreetly lets her know that Jesus wants to see her. Mary immediately comes to where He is but her first grief-stricken words, like her sister's, are about what might have happened… "Lord, if only…" Even though they believe in Jesus, their earth-bound, time-restricted, human view, limits their understanding of how and towards what objectives He is moving events.

Jesus calls Lazarus back to life again

John now records something that must have impacted he and the other disciples deeply as they later recall this whole remarkable incident. He describes how Jesus is very obviously distressed, even angry in some sense, as He sees Martha and her friends crying in their grief.

For a moment He allows His true emotions to well up and be seen. There's no indication that he's directly angry with them…although perhaps He is frustrated in some ways at their lack of faith in Him. But mostly it seems He's angry about death itself and the despair it brings to humans who were not originally created to die. Jesus asks them to take Him to where Lazarus is buried. As they head towards the grave, their emotion touches His heart again and everyone can see that He is crying. (John 11:33-44)

When they arrive, much to their alarm, Jesus wants them to roll away the large stone that is used to block the small cave that is the family tomb. Martha protests but He reminds them how He'd promised that they would see God's glory if they would believe. After they've rolled the large stone disc away Jesus prays to His Father. Then He stands and shouts into the dark mouth of the cave, "Lazarus, come out!" Everyone holds their breaths… they're frozen, watching.

No way, this is impossible. It cannot happen. But wait, what's that? Was that a noise from inside? They crane their necks to see, crowd in behind Jesus. And there is Lazarus - it has to be him of course. He's feeling his way out because he can't see - his head is wrapped up…and he's stumbling a bit from the cloth all bound around his legs. For a moment no one knows what to do. Jesus has to tell them, "Come on. Unwrap him and let him go!"

In the most dramatic and emphatic way Jesus has further defined who He is. He has said He is *Life*… also that He is *The Resurrection* - the one who brings people back to life from death.

And He's proven those things to be true with overwhelming evidence for the first-hand witnesses and those who accept their account by faith. The way in which it happened is a vivid reminder of Creation.

In the beginning, God spoke into the dark chaos and called all things into existence, to life. Now, into the darkness of the cave mouth with death inside, and into the dark despair of human beings as they try to deal with death, God's Son in human form speaks. With the same authority and power with which the One-God-Who-Is-Three created originally, Jesus calls someone out of death and back to life.

Opinions about Jesus polarize even more

John goes on to describe how those who've been there with the sisters through these events and who know what actually happened - from that moment believe in Jesus… that He truly was the long-promised Messiah. Others, even though they can't deny what they've seen, incredibly, refuse to believe in Him. Some go to the religious leaders and tell them what they've witnessed. (John 11:45-54) At a crisis meeting of the Sanhedrin, the Jewish ruling elite are increasingly desperate and vehement. "Something must be done! If stories like these about this Jesus of Nazareth continue to grow and circulate, it's inevitable, the people are going to declare Him king. There's already lots of talk on the streets about it. And then what? The Romans will call it a rebellion, they'll send in the troops. There will be violence… and who knows, they might destroy the temple. One thing's for certain. Our role of wisely leading the nation on God's behalf won't survive something like that. The Romans will take the opportunity to do away with this Council and run everything themselves. We owe it to the nation, to God, to do something about this Jesus. Better for Him to die than for the whole nation to be destroyed, right?"

Jesus, knowing what they are saying, at least for a time steps back from public prominence and leaves the Jerusalem area.

❓ DISCUSSION POINTS

1. Put yourself in the place of the disciples. Based on what they knew from the Old Testament and what they'd heard and seen from Jesus up to this point, what principles should be guiding them in thinking about caution and safety vs. risk and danger? Were there unique elements to their circumstances as they followed Jesus then, or can those principles be applied in exactly the same way for us today?

2. How do you think you would have felt if you were Martha or Mary as you waited for Jesus to arrive while you watched your brother dying? How would you have prayed to God? Faced with similar circumstances a few years later, do you think your prayer would be fairly much the same, or would your perspective have changed significantly?

3. Some estimates say that by the time someone is 18, they will have viewed 40,000 murders on TV. (Note that this is only violent deaths in one medium.) What impact, if any, do you think this massive exposure to images of death has on the worldview of our society... and therefore on people's ability to understand Jesus' view of death?

4. Think back through the Narrative and identify any principles that have emerged which can help to guide the way we view the government and the laws of this country. Are they universal principles or might they not apply in another place? Are there circumstances under which it is okay to go against the laws of the government? (As much as possible base your response on what has been covered in the Narrative so far.)

1.49 Jesus taught that we need to humbly admit our guilt

 OBJECTIVES OF THIS TUTORIAL

Learners will continue to explore and discuss the themes and the truths presented in God's Narrative. The portions of Scripture referred to in this tutorial are: **Mark 10:13-24, 12:30,31**

Last time
When word came from devoted followers, Martha and Mary, that their brother was very sick, Jesus didn't immediately rush off to their home village of Bethany, near Jerusalem. He and His disciples eventually went, but arrived four days after the burial. After speaking to Martha and Mary and seeing the despair of the people who were mourning, Jesus was visibly angry and moved to tears because of all that death implies for humans. The cave-tomb was then unsealed and Lazarus emerged after Jesus had brought him back to life by the authority and power of His command.

Jesus teaches about the importance of child-like faith
We now return to Mark's account and take the chance to gain more insights into God's character and perspective as we observe Jesus interacting with people - first some children, then a rich guy who talks to Him.

One day some parents bring their young children to Jesus. (Mark 10:13-16) There's no indication that these people are in the very small minority who believe He is the Messiah... more likely they are among the bulk of the common people who view Him as a teacher, a Rabbi... perhaps even a prophet from God with some miraculous power. So it's not out of the ordinary in that culture for them to be bringing their children to Jesus so He can lay His hand on their heads and speak some words of blessing or pray for them. People do this regularly with Rabbis or those considered holy men.

On this occasion though, the disciples are anything but welcoming toward these parents and their children. "Why are you bothering Him? Can't you see He's very busy with lots of important things to do? Take your kids and move away." When He notices what's happening Jesus rebukes His disciples and also takes the opportunity to address a bigger issue... along the lines of: "Hey, you guys, what are you doing, stopping them like that? Let the children come over here to me. Listen, the people who have submitted to God's rule over their lives, are in many ways those who are just like these kids. Really. I mean this. If someone wants to be one of God's people, to come under His rule and authority, they have to first of all put aside their assumptions and pretensions and realize that they are helpless, like a child. There's no other way to be under God's rule and to enjoy the rich rewards."

The point Jesus is making is consistent, of course, with what God has been saying to human beings since Adam and Eve rebelled against His authority over them in the first place. That happened when they believed the false picture Satan had painted: that God was keeping them in some kind of childishly dependent state, and that they could only come to their full adult potential if they exerted their independence from Him. People's view of what it means to be a mature, adult human being has been skewed ever since.

Adulthood, in the way we normally define it, is when someone is no longer reliant on their parents for everything. We say "they are their own person"; in other words, they now have their own opinions, relationships and resources. That's not without truth in a human sense, but the problem is in how people apply it to their relationship with God as Creator and Father. As we know from His Narrative, God created human beings for a specific reason and for a particular kind of relationship with Him. In fact, that's what it means to be human - someone created for that relationship with God. Again, as has been clearly demonstrated by the way the Father and now His Son, Jesus, relates to people, His intention was for the relationships to grow and mature. But, in what seems like a paradox, given the normal human view of *maturity* and *adulthood*, growth in the relationship of a person with God is marked, not by less dependence, but by more.

This is a very difficult thing to grasp for a person who has been conditioned by their society, and who has always heard that being a responsible adult is "standing on your own two feet".

Jesus is fully aware of all of this - He knows the misconceptions in the minds of His disciples and others around, and so He takes the opportunity here to press the point home. His message then and today might be: "See these little children. Look how this one is simply sitting in her father's arms. Why? Because she trusts him completely. She isn't thinking she has to look after herself, doesn't doubt for a moment that he cares for her and will look after her. That's the way you need to come to God. That's the correct approach. You can't come under His rule and protection if you come with all your pride and preformed ideas, asserting *your* rights, *your* self-worth, *your* individuality. He's God. *He* can take care of you far better than you ever could. *He* knows what's good for you. *He* values you far more than you or anyone else possibly can. He made you an individual, He knows you, and He loves you, as you. Someone growing in a childlike dependence on Him and submission to His authority is someone headed towards wisdom and maturity…is actually becoming a true adult."

Mark records that Jesus does go ahead and takes each child in His arms and, in the traditional way, puts His hand on their head, while He blesses them.

Jesus challenges the assumptions of a young, wealthy guy

Soon after, as Jesus is heading off to Jerusalem, a man - who we find out elsewhere is young, as well as wealthy - comes rushing up. (Mark 10:17-24) He kneels down in front of Jesus and says, "Good Teacher, what can I do to get eternal life?" In this encounter, Jesus is going to challenge a number of this guy's assumptions and He starts out by questioning the words he uses, "What do you mean when you say I'm good? Only God is truly good."

Jesus' rhetorical question and statement might appear simple on the surface, but He's actually digging into some important worldview issues: does the man's concept and standard of *good* match up with God's? Does he think he and Jesus are *good* in a similar way? He sees Jesus as a Teacher, but does he also recognize that He is God? But in answer to the question itself, Jesus mentions some of God's laws that the guy obviously already knows…about not killing anyone, committing adultery, stealing, lying, and being disrespectful to parents. Of course as God's Narrative has shown, Jesus isn't saying that the guy can somehow follow every commandment and live up to God's perfect standards. What He wants him to realize is the very thing God gave the Law for in the first place. He, like everyone, falls far short… he doesn't have the slightest hope of earning eternal life through anything he does, or doesn't do. But his response shows that he's based his whole life on a false assumption. In fact, he says that he's obeyed all the commandments since he was a kid.

A little bit later in Mark's account (Mark 12:30,31) we hear how, in response to a question from the religious experts, Jesus sums up God's Law like this, "You must love the Lord your God with all your heart, all your soul and all your mind, and all your strength…and love your neighbor as yourself." Now, as He looks at this young guy, His heart goes out to him. What is the best way to demonstrate to him that his easy confidence in his own ability to fulfill God's Law is misplaced… that he doesn't even come close to loving God and other people as he should? "So, you've followed God's Law? Okay, here's just one more thing you need to do. Go and sell everything you have and donate the money to charity. It will be put to your account in Heaven. Then come and follow me."

JESUS TAUGHT THAT WE NEED TO HUMBLY ADMIT OUR GUILT

Again, we know that Jesus doesn't mean that the guy can earn salvation by doing this. What Jesus was doing was putting His finger on the thing that was most important to him - his stuff, his money, his career. He was saying in effect, "You say you follow God's Law perfectly. But to really do that you would have to always prioritize God above everything else in your life. And, as a result, you would have to care about other people in every way more than you do yourself. Is that the reality? Do you do that?" Mark records that when he heard this, his face fell and he went away sad because he had a lot of possessions. Perhaps the reality was striking home that his money and stuff really was more important to him than anything else... in effect, that was his god, and he was not - at least at that moment - willing to turn away from it. Or maybe he was realizing that all his efforts to follow the Law had been futile. As the guy leaves, Jesus makes a comment to His disciples that it is a really difficult thing for rich people to enter the Kingdom of God. It's not that God holds someone's wealth against them, but when someone has attained what most others in the society are after, has "made it" so to speak, it is often very difficult for them to see themselves as needy. Often they've built their whole lives around having enough money and stuff so they feel secure and free of need. It is usually only through a very painful process that someone like that comes to the point of recognizing their really desperate situation and bowing to God's authority over their lives.

❓ DISCUSSION POINTS

1. Describe anything you care to about the circumstances that have shaped your concept of independence, being grown-up, "standing on your own two feet" etc. In general do you feel your experiences have helped you to have a correct understanding of what maturity looks like in your relationship with God (the picture that is emerging in the Narrative), or have there been some major obstacles to this?

2. Based on what we've heard in God's Story so far, what do you think might have been some of the things Jesus said when He blessed the children?

3. Limiting yourself to what we've heard in the Narrative so far, in your own words describe what you understand Jesus meant when He used the term "Kingdom of God".

4. Make some observations about Jesus' statement that it is difficult for rich people to enter the Kingdom of God. Do you think that it is appropriate then to make corollary statements that it is easier for poor people to be saved? Is it valid to draw any principles from this about the kinds of people we should be trying to share His Story with, or not?

➡ ACTIVITIES

1. Ask three people - at least one of whom is a non-Christian - the following questions, then record their answers (summarize if necessary):

(1) Do you think it is valid if people are attracted to Christianity by the idea that God will help them with financial security?

(2) How would you respond to someone who says that true followers of Jesus should be materially poor like He was?

(3) Do you think there are many really wealthy people who are also Christians? Share any observations you have about this.

(4) Do you think Christianity is a religion that is generally attractive to poor people? Can you suggest any reasons for your answer?

1.50 It is foolish to give material things pre-eminence over God

 OBJECTIVES OF THIS TUTORIAL

Learners will continue to explore and discuss the themes and the truths presented in God's Narrative. The portions of Scripture referred to in this tutorial are: **Luke 12:15-21, 16:19-31**

Last time

Jesus was upset with the disciples when they tried to stop some parents from bringing their children to Him to be blessed. He used the opportunity to teach about how people cannot come to God in pride and self-confidence. Instead, they need to come realizing their need and responding with child-like faith to what He says. He also spoke with a rich young man who was confident he had fulfilled God's law. By identifying what the guy was unable to give up - his money and stuff - Jesus showed that he had no hope of living up to God's perfect standards.

Jesus told a parable about a rich but, ultimately, foolish man

Jesus focused on the issue of materialism a number of times. Luke records two stories Jesus told in which He vividly illustrates the results of being preoccupied with money and stuff. Just after His conversation with the rich young guy, Jesus gives everyone listening a blunt warning, "You really need to be careful that your life isn't being run by greed…and greed comes in a lot of subtle forms. The value of your life is not measured by how much money or stuff you have." Then he tells them this parable - it's fictional in a sense, but it certainly could, in fact actually *has* happened many times in real life. (Luke 12:15-21) It goes like this:

There's this guy who owns a farm on really rich soil. It's highly productive in terms of yield. The owner has harvested and stockpiled so much already that he's filled up all his barns and can't fit in the surplus. He decides the only solution is to pull down the existing barns and build even bigger ones, and then fill them up as well. *Then*, he thinks, I'll have enough. It will be really cool. I can kick back, chill out, have absolutely anything

IT IS FOOLISH TO GIVE MATERIAL THINGS PRE-EMINENCE OVER GOD

I want. I'll have people over all the time and we'll have a great time." But God says to the man - who can't hear, because he's not listening - "You're a fool. You're going to die tonight...then who's going to enjoy everything you've worked for? Because it certainly won't be you." Jesus sums up, "Yes, a person is a fool to store up earthly wealth but not have a rich relationship with God." The picture Jesus paints of this man is one that is very familiar to the people. Maybe there are even one or two prosperous farmers in the crowd that day. But really, He could have chosen someone from any occupation or way of life to illustrate the point. Certainly wealth is no prerequisite for greed, nor vice versa. Poor people can be preoccupied with getting more. Middle class folk are just as likely as anyone to look for their security in material possessions.

The foolishness of the man in the parable is not in him being wealthy per se. Clearly he has no sense of proportion. He's never satisfied. Having plenty doesn't stop him wanting more. This is not a symptom of what he already has, but rather of the assumptions he's built his life on. He thinks that when he's filled his even bigger barns, he'll be happy and contented. But no doubt he thought the same at each previous stage. His worldview orientation is the same as the majority of human beings. Even those whose lives have been realigned to God's Story still regularly find themselves functioning according to this predominant paradigm.

This *materialism*, is closely linked with a *materialistic* worldview. Even if people say they believe in something beyond themselves and this world, in their daily lives they function as though there *is* nothing else. What they have, or more often, what they don't have yet but would like to have, defines them and their world in a way that they tell themselves is complete. It leaves no room to consider anything beyond their world or this life. A relationship with God, if considered at all, is only valued for the help they believe - are told to believe - He might give them in their pursuit of physical comfort, security and entertainment. Thoughts of death are pushed aside. They don't fit, they're unhelpful, disturbing, a "downer". But at the end of the day, no matter how tightly someone has crammed their world with stuff, whether they've been rich, comfortable, or "battlers", death explodes the whole thing and brings them face to face with God asking them the questions they've so carefully avoided in life.

Jesus told a story about a rich man and a poor man

A little further on in his account (Luke 16:19-31) Luke records another story Jesus told to expand on the points He's been making about materialism. He describes a rich man who is able to afford really expensive clothes, eat good food and generally live a luxurious lifestyle. In the audience that day are some Pharisees, and this guy is probably meant to represent their class of Jews who are self-righteous but also greedy and preoccupied with money. Every day a man can be seen lying near the gate of this rich man's house. He's too sick and frail to work so - and this is not uncommon in that culture

- he lives near this wealthy household in a precarious dependence on their charity. He survives on any leftover scraps that are given to him. Jesus gives the destitute man's name as Lazarus - a common name in that society. He doesn't name the rich man. Apart from the huge gap in their standard of living and status in the community, there's another even more fundamental difference between them: Lazarus is a true believer... he's realized that he can never please God by his own efforts, he has repented and turned to God in faith for salvation. The rich guy, on the other hand, has never come to this point...so the debt and judgment for his sin is still in place. Whether or not he's religious, we're not told, but regardless, he stands condemned by God's perfect standard. We know this because the consequences of this fundamental, spiritual, difference between the two men are about to play out... they both die. In death, their bodies are no doubt treated very differently.

A rich person in the society is honored with a long and lavish funeral and then buried in a special tomb. The corpse of a beggar, on the other hand, is often thrown without ceremony onto the town tip to be eaten by wild animals. But neither of these men could care less about all that now. Now the disparity in wealth and material security they've had on earth doesn't matter. The gap in their previous standing in the community is irrelevant. They both face eternity, and what that will look like for each of them is determined by God's criteria, a world away from human standards.

So because Lazarus' sins have been forgiven, he is taken to the peace and comfort of heaven.

For his Jewish audience, Jesus describes this as being taken by God's spirit messengers - angels - to where Abraham is. The rich man, on the other hand, whose sin has never been dealt with, finds himself in a place of terrible torment. Jesus stresses the terrible nature of this existence without the presence of God. The man faces an unbearable eternity that he can do nothing but bear. He cries out for mercy...but it is too late. There are no more chances. He entered eternity with his sin-debt owing, and he'll now be paying forever. His wealth when he was alive, and even his lack of compassion for the poor, dying man at his gate are not, in themselves, the reason why he's now suffering - any more than Lazarus' poverty and suffering on earth is the reason why he is now enjoying freedom from any pain or suffering.

God's true story does not include the concept of *karma* - that we earn what we get in the next life - good or bad - by what we've done in the previous life. The reason why the rich man is now in an eternity of anguish, cut off from God and all that is good, is because he lived his life as though there was no eternity. He left no room in life on earth for God, much less for others in need. He allowed his felt needs, his comfort, his ambitions, his future, to crowd out the reality of his real need before God. He never turned to God in humble repentance and faith in the way that God provides for sin to be forgiven. And those moments in his life when God the Great Communicator, the One who tirelessly seeks for his lost race - when He did get through the self-indulgence, the elaborate defenses, the clutter of all the *stuff*... in those few unguarded moments when it struck the man that perhaps he'd been sold a lie... each time he had ignored God's voice. Or he'd put it off... "Maybe I'll think about it when I'm old, when I have time, when I've got all the money I want." The terrible thing is that now he, and billions of others like him, will spend eternity remembering and regretting the times they turned away from truth.

That is the true horror of eternity in hell.

DISCUSSION POINTS

1. As you think about the different strategies Satan has adopted for keeping people from listening to God's Story, how do you think materialism rates in terms of effectiveness? Do you think it is more effective with some parts of our society than others? Why?

2. Reflect, if you care to, on any ways in which you feel you might sometimes fall prey to materialism in your own life. Are there any principles you can draw from God's Narrative so far that might help to establish and maintain a healthy balance or "tension" in this area?

3. Have you heard Jesus' story about the rich man and Lazarus used to support the idea that our eternal destiny is determined by whether we've been a good or bad person in our lives? (If not, can you see how this could happen?) How can we avoid making such incorrect interpretations and invalid applications from portions (pericopes) of God's Word?

ACTIVITIES

1. Think through and write descriptions of materialism expressed in these three different, but related, ways: a) As a defined philosophical system, b) As a worldview and overriding cultural value, c) As an everyday, real-life preoccupation for most people.

2. Imagine moving into a community where you are far wealthier than anyone else. Describe any challenges you feel this might present as you attempt to be one of God's Storytellers in that community; also how you might go about approaching those challenges.

1.51 Jesus rode into Jerusalem. They celebrated the Passover

 OBJECTIVES OF THIS TUTORIAL

Learners will continue to explore and discuss the themes and the truths presented in God's Narrative. The portions of Scripture referred to in this tutorial are: Mark 11:1-10, 14:1-26, Zechariah 9:9, 11:12,13, Psalm 41:9

Last time

Jesus told a parable about a prosperous farmer who thought he'd be happy and content after he'd built bigger barns to store his latest harvest. But God called him a fool because He knew the man was going to die that night and all he'd worked for would be worthless to him.

Jesus also told a story about a rich man and a beggar called Lazarus. When both died, the huge difference in their material possessions proved to be irrelevant. Lazarus, a believer, will enjoy eternity with God. The rich man, who ignored God in life, will spend eternity in a torment of regret.

Jesus is given a royal welcome as He rides into Jerusalem

We now continue with Mark's account of events that are building towards the climax of Jesus' life here on earth. Everything that happens is going to be according to God's plan and with Jesus' full knowledge of where this is all heading. One day, not long before the celebration of the Passover, He and His disciples approach Jerusalem. On the slopes of the Mount of Olives He sends two of them to get a donkey He says they'll find tied up in a village just ahead. So when Jesus enters the city this time, He's riding on a donkey. He's . Some people gather, then more. They crowd around and line the road. Suddenly He's in the middle of a shouting, singing, dancing procession. People are taking off their outer cloaks and spreading them on the road in front of Him, others laying down branches. The rumors fly. "It's Jesus of Nazareth. Haven't you heard the stories? The Pharisees and Sadducees hate Him. But He's a great healer and teacher. Could He be the

Promised One from God? Maybe He's going to throw the Romans out? Come on, let's follow, see what happens."

Remarkably all of this fulfills something the prophet Zechariah wrote centuries before (Zechariah 9:9), when he encourages the people of Jerusalem to shout in triumph because their king is coming to them, humbly riding on a young donkey. The procession sweeps Jesus into the city where He heads to the temple. But the excitement is short-lived. The crowd fades away. (Mark 11:1-11) They're hoping for a king, even for the Messiah, but Jesus has come to meet a much greater need than their short-sighted desires and ambitions.

One of the disciples, Judas, agrees to betray Jesus

The Jewish religious leaders are disturbed by all of this. Then, over the next few days, Jesus says and does some things, which infuriate them even more. He's here in Jerusalem on their turf, so they're determined to take the opportunity to arrest Him and kill Him, in secret if necessary.

But they're really concerned about doing it while everyone is gathered in the holy city for the Passover celebrations... they know that Jesus has a lot of populist support and they're worried about a riot. It could go badly for them and who knows how the Romans will respond. (Mark 14:1-11)

They need some way to get to Him when there's no crowd around. But how? Although they've never been able to catch Jesus out in a sin or even a technicality of the law, they rationalize their evil intent... they even self-righteously tell themselves that they're doing it for God and for His nation. Of course it's not difficult to see the hand of Satan in all of this, as he spurs them on, using their pride, resentment and desire to hold on to power.

Likewise, God's Enemy has been at work in the heart of one of Jesus' disciples. Judas originally followed Jesus for what he thought he might get out of it...a position and perhaps some material gain. He's always loved money. Through his own cunning - so he thinks - he's been able to snag the job of looking after the communal funds. He's taken the opportunity to dip into the kitty for personal use every now and then... "Who's going to know? They're all so naïve and trusting." But recently he's become disillusioned and resentful. This disciple thing isn't leading him to the position and wealth he'd dreamt of. By now he should be treasurer of the kingdom, but Jesus just isn't ambitious enough. And sometimes, when Jesus looks at him, Judas wonders if sees through him... if maybe He really does know what's going on in his heart.

So when he gets the chance, he slips away and finds some of the top priests. He offers to betray Jesus... to tell them when they can get Him without the crowds around, and to give a sign so they'll definitely get the right man. They agree to pay him - an amount that Matthew tells us is 30 silver coins. We can only assume that Judas doesn't realize he's fulfilling King David's prophetic words about the Messiah - that a trusted friend with whom He's shared food will betray him. (Psalm 41:9) Or the prophet Zechariah's prescient mention of someone's wages that come to 30 pieces of silver. (Zechariah 11:12,13)

Jesus celebrates the Passover Feast with His disciples

As visitors in Jerusalem, the disciples know they need to find somewhere to celebrate the Passover... a lamb has to be sacrificed and then the ritual meal eaten together. (Mark 14:12-26)

When they ask Jesus, He sends two of them off with detailed instructions. They find a man, just where Jesus says he'll be. They follow Him to a house where the owner has already prepared a large room on the second floor... prepared for them! "But how? We've been with the Master the whole time. How did he arrange this? How did He know? Oh, but of course, we keep forgetting..."

It's evening now, and they're together in the room... around the table eating. Suddenly, Jesus looks around at them, rather sadly some notice... and then He drops a bomb-shell. "This might be hard to believe, but it's true. One of you guys eating this meal here with me is going to betray me." They're stunned. They can't believe what they're hearing. Surely not! How can that be? Maybe someone will go insane and do it without even knowing. "Master, it's not me is it?" "Please say it's not me either." "I couldn't, could I?"

"Well, I'm sad to say, it's definitely one of you twelve who've been dipping bread into this bowl of sauce with me. The Scriptures spelled out long ago that as God's Son who's also a man, I'd have to die, but that's no consolation for the traitor. In fact, he'd be better off if he'd never been born." It's unthinkable. They've heard from childhood that it's one thing to have open enemies. But to share a meal with someone as though they're your friend and then stab them in the back - that's disgusting, it's Gentile treachery!

Jesus is, of course, fully aware of what has been building in Judas' heart... knows that he's gone to the leading priests and arranged to betray Him. He loves Judas and he's deeply hurt at the treachery of his close companion for the last few years. But why does He make it clear He knows about it, but without naming Judas? We can only conclude that He was giving him a final opportunity to draw back from the brink...to recognize the terrible thing he was doing and the evil heart that it came from... to repent and throw himself on God's mercy. Jesus was making the same genuine, gracious offer to Judas that He made to Adam and Eve, Cain, the people in the time of Abraham, the Egyptian Pharaoh... and to everyone else who has opportunity to know about Him.

JESUS RODE INTO JERUSALEM. THEY CELEBRATED THE PASSOVER

Only the true Author can give people the opportunity to make genuine choices about the role they'll play, while retaining absolute control of how His Story will turn out.

Despite the pain of Judas' betrayal, Jesus is committed to a path that will lead to His death.

He now does something which on the surface is unremarkable, but the circumstances and Jesus' words fill it with meaning... although that meaning won't become clear to the disciples until much later. Picking up some bread that was there as part of the Passover meal, Jesus prays to the Father and then breaks it into pieces and passes it around to the disciples.

In the bread being broken, He says, they are to see His body being broken. Later it will be a very vivid reminder as they remember... indeed as they intentionally remind themselves by regularly re-enacting this simple ceremony together.

His enemies are about to cause severe injuries to His body which, being a normal human body is vulnerable and susceptible to pain. Once they've eaten the bread, Jesus picks up a cup of wine from the table, gives thanks to God, then passes it around for them to drink from.

He says that in the pouring out of this wine as they drink it, they are to picture His blood being poured out. He adds something astounding that, again, will only fully strike home later... He says that His blood will seal a covenant between God and man. Also that it will be a sacrifice for many. But what does this mean? Isn't there already a Covenant in place? The one God made with their ancestors, through Moses. It has its laws, its priests, the temple, and the whole system of sacrifices. So what will this new Covenant be? And what does Jesus' death that He keeps mentioning have to do with it? How will His body being broken and His blood being poured out bring about this new Covenant? The questions swirl in their heads as they sing a song of worship to God. But there's no time to ask Him more. They're on the move. Through the streets, between the houses - they can hear murmuring voices, and see candles flickering in windows were others are celebrating Passover - then beyond the houses, along a path between the trees on the slopes of the Mount of Olives.

? DISCUSSION POINTS

1. Why do you think Jesus entered Jerusalem as He did this time - in a way that seemed to encourage the crowd to cheer Him as a possible King, even as the Messiah - and then afterwards obviously rejected that kind of populist support? Do you think He toyed with the idea of pursuing that path and then decided against it, or did He have another purpose in mind all along? If so, what was it?

2. How do you think it was possible for Judas - who'd interacted closely with Jesus, seen His life and heard His teaching - to end up doing what he did? How do you picture him? As: (a) some kind of psychopath (b) probably demon possessed (c) just a fairly normal person who'd continually turned away from the truth (d) some other description.

3. Imagine yourself in the place of one of the disciples...say John. As a Jew, you know quite a bit from the Old Testament, and you've just spent three years with Jesus. What do you make of His statements about dying as a sacrifice for many and validating a new Covenant with His blood? What questions would you like to ask Him?

➡ ACTIVITIES

1. In about half a page, write a description in your own words of what takes place at Passover in an orthodox Jewish household. (Try to find out if it is basically the same today as it would have been in the time of Christ.)

1.52 Jesus was arrested by His enemies

 OBJECTIVES OF THIS TUTORIAL

Learners will continue to explore and discuss the themes and the truths presented in God's Narrative. The portions of Scripture referred to in this tutorial are: **Mark 14:32-65, 15:1-20, Psalm 27:12, Isaiah 50:6, 53:3,7**

Last time

Jesus entered Jerusalem riding on a donkey. People gathered around Him on the road and soon there was a procession with the people honoring Him as a king, even as the Messiah. The religious leaders wanted to arrest and execute Jesus. They paid Judas to betray Jesus by leading them to Him when there was no one around. Jesus celebrated the Passover meal with His disciples. He used bread as a symbol of His body which would be broken, and wine for His blood which would be poured out to seal a new Covenant between God and His people

Jesus spends time in prayer before He's arrested

Mark continues with his account of the events leading up to Jesus' betrayal and arrest. Jesus and the disciples are on the slopes of the Mount of Olives walking through the orchard. (Mark 14:32-51) In the general area is a cave, still there today, which for centuries housed an olive oil press. There is evidence that this was within a walled, cultivated area known as Gat-Shemanim (transliterated to English as Gethsemane). Even though the Narrative doesn't specify, it seems likely that the cave is a place Jesus and His disciples regularly use for sleeping when they are in the Jerusalem area, and that it is their destination this night. The disciples can sense that whatever is about to happen is weighing terribly on Jesus. When they arrive Jesus draws His closest friends among the disciples - Peter, James and John - off to one side and tells them frankly that the knowledge of what He's facing is so overwhelming that it is crushing Him physically.

He just doesn't know how He can survive what He's going through at this moment. "I realize you guys are tired, but I need you right now. Will you stay awake and just be here for me...ask God for His help? Please." He moves a bit away from them and falls down with His face on the ground. The thought of what's coming is unbearable. Always, always, always, in every single thing, He and His Father have been together. Yes, there have been challenges, even terrible disappointments - like Judas - but the Father has always been there to give strength, wisdom and fellowship. Now this terrible, dark path looms ahead, and He has to walk it alone, cut off, rejected, even shunned as an enemy. That's the real price that has to be paid. "Oh dear Father, is there any other way? Please. But no, I'm willing. I want your plans to be fulfilled... I reject the whole idea of me wanting anything else."

The disciples desperately want to stay awake and support Him, but after the big meal, the wine, the emotion...they just can't keep their eyes open. But now it's too late for sleep. What's that Jesus is saying? He's been betrayed? What's going on? There are voices, the clash of steel on steel, flickering lights coming through the trees. They're up, rubbing their eyes, "Hey, it's Judas. Yes, where has he been, anyway? Why is he leading those men? Look, they've got swords and clubs." Now Judas is walking up to Jesus. He says, "Rabbi" and kisses Him on both cheeks... immediately the armed men surround Jesus, pinning His arms.

He doesn't look at all surprised, it's as though He's been expecting them. In the confusion, someone trying to protect Jesus is wildly swinging a sword. Who is that? Wow, he took that guy's ear off, blood is pouring everywhere. (In his account, Luke, the doctor, mentions that Jesus heals it with a touch.) Best to get out of here. How can we help Jesus if we're all locked up? All the disciples have the same thought...they're off, running into the darkness. Jesus is left alone among people who want to see Him dead.

Jesus was tried first by the Jewish Council

Peter has run away with the rest of the disciples but now, hanging back in the darkness, he's able to follow as they take Jesus the short distance to the high priest's house in the upper part of Jerusalem. (Mark 14:53-65) Here it's all hustle and bustle... there are torches burning, servants running around. It's cold and a fire has been lit in the courtyard. Peter slips in unnoticed among the guards.

Above, inside, a trial is going on - a mockery of justice if ever there was one. The main religious leaders are all here, desperate to find some evidence against Jesus that will justify having Him executed... but it's not going well. Certainly they'd had people to testify against Him, but their evidence is so petty and obviously fabricated that it won't stand up, even in this farcical court.

Without realizing it, they are fulfilling something David wrote centuries before in a Messianic psalm (Psalm 27:12) that they probably know well, "...they accuse me of things I've never done; with every breath they threaten me with violence."

Caiaphas, the high priest, is frustrated. If they can just get Jesus to say something, maybe He'll condemn Himself. But He remains detached, silent, unwilling to dignify these proceedings by defending Himself. Finally Caiaphas gets the kind of answer he's after when he asks Jesus if He is the Messiah, God's Son. Jesus responds with a resounding "I AM", and adds that one day they'll see Him sitting in a place of power and authority beside God. The high priest expresses outrage, but inwardly he's delighted, "We don't need any other witnesses. You've heard His blasphemy. What is your verdict?" As one they call out, "Guilty, He deserves to die."

Now they're jeering, spitting on Him, slapping and punching as He's led out. Despite these religious experts' familiarity with the Scriptures, it seems unlikely they remembered Isaiah's words that predicted this, and more that was to come, "I offered my back to those who beat me and my cheeks to those who pulled out my beard, I did not hide my face from mockery and spitting." (Isaiah 50:6)

Jesus was tried before Pilate who sends Him to be crucified

The limited powers of the Jewish Council under Roman rule do not allow them to implement the death sentence. So the next morning they take Jesus to Pilate, the Roman governor, hoping he'll be convinced that Jesus should be executed. (Mark 15:1-20) The governor, of course, is not interested in the Jewish religious traditions... his role is to serve Rome by keeping the peace in this far-flung outpost of the empire and seeing that their taxes are flowing into the imperial coffers. He probes to see if Jesus really does pose a serious treat, as the Jewish leaders are saying: "Are you the king of the Jews?" Jesus' answer is cryptic, "As you say it" - It is true, Jesus *is* the legitimate King of God's chosen people, but their definitions of kingship are very different.

The leading priests accuse Him of all kinds of crimes. Pilate is surprised at Jesus' calm refusal to defend Himself against their charges. The religious experts should, but don't, recognize the fulfillment of yet another messianic prophecy playing out before their eyes. Isaiah says (53:7) that the One from God will remain silent in the face of abuse and unfair treatment... not unlike how sheep go without protest to be sheared or even slaughtered. It doesn't take Pilate long to realize that Jesus is not guilty of any crime - the impassioned, almost hysterical, demand by the Jewish leaders for the death sentence is clearly driven by envy and hatred.

In his account, Mark explains that during the Passover celebrations it is traditional for the Jews to select one prisoner for the governor to release. Pilate sees an opportunity here... he suggests to the assembled crowd that this year he release Jesus, who he facetiously calls "King of the Jews". Presumably some of the crowd were in the procession just a few short days before, when Jesus was exulted as King as He rode into the city. But they have proven to be fickle and their adulation short-lived. Now, angry and disillusioned because He has not met their expectations, and urged on by the leading priests, they ask for another prisoner to be released instead.

When Pilate, at a loss, asks what he's to do with Jesus, they demand death. In fact, they're screaming out that He should be crucified. One of the most painful and demeaning forms of Roman execution, crucifixion is reserved as a punishment for traitors, captive armies and the worst criminals. Performed in a public place to discourage crime, the victim's hands and feet are nailed to a stake or crossed timbers. The excruciating ordeal can last for days until exhaustion inevitably results in suffocation, heart failure and death. The crowd's demand for Jesus' death is difficult enough to fathom, but their insistence on this excruciating and humiliating form hints at something else...this is deeper and more sinister than just a mob baying for blood. It's obviously spiritually motivated, but it seems to also involve a physical, even pathological, compulsion to be rid of Him and all He represents. They are rejecting Him, in the most brutal and conclusive way they can. "He's not one of us. He doesn't even deserve to die as a Jew. Give Him to the Gentile filth to kill. That'll shut Him up, cut Him down to size."

Again, seven centuries before, Isaiah was given words from God to describe this national rejection of their Messiah: "He was despised and rejected - a man of sorrows, acquainted with deepest grief. We turned our backs on him and looked the other way. He was despised, and we did not care." (Isaiah 53:3)

Pilate makes a political decision. He doesn't believe Jesus is guilty of any crime, but he's more interested in pacifying the crowd and keeping the Jewish religious leaders on-side than he is in justice. He orders Jesus to be whipped, as is customary before crucifixion. The Roman guards are efficient and merciless. The sharp lead spikes tied to the strands of the whip leave His back deeply lacerated and bleeding. The soldiers enjoy the moment...they try to outdo each other in cruel jokes at His expense. A cloak is draped on Him, purple - the color of royalty, someone else weaves thorn branches into a crown and rams it on His head. As the blood runs down His forehead and into His eyes, they mockingly bow down before Him, "Hey, King of the Jews!"

The thorns provide a vivid reminder of the curse God placed on the earth after man's rebellion. The One who has come to break that curse quietly stands with its cruel symbol wrapped around His head. Finally the soldiers tire of their cruel game. They lead Him away to be crucified.

? DISCUSSION POINTS

1. As you think about what Jesus did and said in light of what He was going through that evening in Gethsemane, what stands out to you the most? Consider particularly how He related (a) to His disciples and (b) to His Father in those particular circumstances and describe anything specific this tells you about Him.

2. Describe some of the differences you can think of between what Pilate, the Roman governor, would think when he used the term "King of the Jews" and the truth that Jesus had in mind when He acknowledged that title.

3. As you contemplate being Jesus' representative in a hostile context, are there lessons to be gleaned from the way He faced His accusers? Based on this account and on what we know of Him from the Narrative, what attitudes did He have towards these people who hated Him and wanted Him put to death?

4. From what we've heard in the Narrative, are there features of Jewish religious culture that explain the Jews' violent rejection of Jesus as Messiah? Does any of that relate to people's attitudes towards Him in our society today, or was it an entirely unique set of circumstances at that place and time that resulted in them turning away from Him in the way they did?

➡ ACTIVITIES

1. Familiarize yourself with a map of Jerusalem so that you can find the key locations from the events surrounding Jesus' arrest, trials, and crucifixion. (Gethsemane, the likely site of the High Priest's house, The Praetorium, Calvary, etc.)

1.53 Jesus was crucified

 OBJECTIVES OF THIS TUTORIAL

Learners will continue to explore and discuss the themes and the truths presented in God's Narrative. The portions of Scripture referred to in this tutorial are: **Mark 15:21-26, Luke 23:39-43, Isaiah 53:12**

Last time
After the Passover meal, Jesus and His disciples went to a garden area on the Mount of Olives called Gethsemane. Although in spiritual, emotional and physical agony as He contemplated what was ahead, He prayed that the Father's will would be done, not His own. Judas brought armed men who arrested Jesus. A mock trial took place before the Jewish council that, without evidence, said He must die for blasphemy. The Roman governor found He had broken no law, but to pacify the Jews he handed Jesus over to be whipped and then crucified.

Jesus was nailed to the cross
Before they leave the fortress that is the Roman governor's headquarters in Jerusalem and the regimental barracks, the timber for the cross is located. Jesus is forced to carry it as they leave and head out towards the area where the crucifixion is to take place. He shoulders it without complaint, but stumbling under the weight and near collapse after the terrible whipping, He clearly won't make it. The soldiers randomly grab someone passing by to carry the cross - his name is Simon, from Cyrene in modern day Libya - probably in Jerusalem for the Passover. By now a large crowd is trailing them. Some are Jesus' family and friends. They don't have to go too far to reach their destination: a place just outside the city walls called Golgotha - "place of the skull" in Aramaic - some say because it was a hill that resembled a skull (English translations in the past often used the Latin transliteration, *Calvary*). When they arrive, He's given wine mixed with myrrh...the aromatic ingredient in incense and ointments that also contains anesthetic properties.

History records that women of Jerusalem prepared this concoction as a mild sedative and to dull the pain, at least a little, for those being crucified. But Jesus has no intention of trying to escape this ordeal, either physically or mentally, and he refuses the offer. It's about 9 in the morning when a detail of four soldiers proceed with the process of crucifixion that even in those brutal days was called "the most cruel and disgusting penalty" by the Roman philosopher and statesman, Cicero. First they strip His clothing off… which they divide between themselves, using some kind of dice to decide who gets what. Then they hammer long metal spikes through the flesh of His hands and feet, leaving Him hanging upright on the crossed timbers.

These callous soldiers have no idea that their actions are fulfilling what one of Jesus' human ancestors, another King of the Jews, David, wrote prophetically centuries before, "My enemies surround me like a pack of dogs; an evil gang closes in on me. They have pierced my hands and feet… They divide my garments among themselves and throw dice for my clothing."

It is customary for the criminal charges to be displayed above the head of the person being crucified. But Jesus, of course, has not been found guilty of anything under Roman law, so His sign simply says, "The King of the Jews". In his account, John notes that the leading priests object to this, but Pilate refuses to change what he has written. No doubt he's using it as an opportunity to insultingly press home to the Jews the futility of anyone trying to lead a rebellion against the might of Rome.

People's response to seeing Jesus on the cross varies a lot

And so Jesus is suspended there on the cross for all to see. This is exactly what He'd told the Pharisee, Nicodemus, would happen… that He'd be lifted up just like Moses lifted up the brass snake for the Israelites to look at if they'd been bitten by the deadly snakes infesting their camp. Now He is hanging high on a cross, visible to people in the area that day. But in a much broader and even more powerful way, because God has preserved this account in His Narrative - indeed it is the climax and what makes sense of the entire Narrative - millions of people down through history have been given the chance to *look* at Jesus, as it were, on the cross.

The way they see and respond to Him, however, varies hugely - that's the case this particular morning just outside Jerusalem, as it has been ever since. This difference is nowhere more apparent than in the attitudes of two men who are being crucified at the same time, one on each side of Jesus. They are convicted criminals, possibly revolutionaries, which would explain why they've been sentenced to this terrible form of execution. One of them obviously rejects the possibility that Jesus is who He says He is. Luke records his mocking, "So you reckon you're the Messiah do you? Prove it by saving yourself - and us, too, while you're at it!" But the man on the other side has a totally different view. We don't know if he's met Jesus before, but as he turns now to look at Him it's not the congealed blood, the grime, the humiliation he notices… what he sees is truth, holiness, and access to God for a sinner like himself. He can't believe the other criminal's attitude, "Man, you're about to die, aren't you afraid of God? We're guilty, we deserve it. But He has done nothing wrong."

Even in these, the most extreme of circumstances, Jesus demonstrates God's grace and mercy. Seeing the faith of this convicted criminal He forgives his sin, assuring him that that they'll meet again soon in God's presence. Yet again, some very specific things foretold by the prophet Isaiah are playing out here. He wrote (53:12), "He was counted among the rebels. He bore the sins of many and interceded for rebels."

Others too that morning are seeing Jesus and either coming to conclusions then or functioning according to their existing worldview commitments. Part of the reason for the Roman's choice of Golgotha as a place of crucifixion is because it is in a very public place. They are keen for as many people as possible to see the horrendous execution as a deterrence against crime.

Mark describes people passing by on a road and shouting out abuse at Jesus, "Yeah, right. Look at you now. What was all that about you destroying the temple and rebuilding it in three days? If you're so great, save yourself and come down off that cross." This is in reference to something Jesus had said some time earlier that helped to build His notoriety. In the temple one day He vented His outrage at this place, that's supposed to be dedicated to the worship of His Father, also being used widely as an animal market and currency exchange. There is quite a scene as He drives the animals out and tips over tables stacked with coins. The leading priests, who have vested commercial interests, angrily demand some kind of miraculous sign as evidence for His authority to do this. He responds, "Okay, here's a sign for you. You destroy this temple, and in three days I'll raise it up again." The leaders, looking to discredit Him, have made sure this quote is passed around Jerusalem as a preposterous, even blasphemous, boast.

What they don't realize is that this is actually a prediction about something infinitely greater than the stones and timber of Herod's Temple. By "temple" He is referring to His own body which he knows will be brought back to life three days after they put Him to death. Now, at Golgotha, lifted up in view of everyone walking past, Jesus is an easy target for their mockery. They think they're superior and quite witty as they get a laugh from the crowd by throwing His own words in His face. In fact, what they're showing in this rather pathetic way is just how sinful and unbelieving they are. Because what they're unable or unwilling to recognize is that this is their Messiah. This is the Creator of the universe who's voluntarily submitting to the pain and humiliation of crucifixion.

And the irony - if that's what it is - is that He's doing it for *them*... dying to make a way of escape for His pathetically blind and lost race, so they have the opportunity to live in the relationship with God they were designed for. When they're brought to account, people like this might plead their ignorance, but the Jewish religious leaders there that morning certainly won't be able to. They are very familiar with God's Story up to this point, but they don't recognize the One who it is all about. They know the words of their nation's storytellers appointed by God - Isaiah, David and all the rest - but they refuse to see that it was Jesus of Nazareth these prophets were pointing toward. Their prior worldview commitments blind them to the truth even when it's right in front of them. They join in the mockery "Look at Him. He saved others, but He can't save Himself. Let this Messiah, this King of Israel, come down from the cross so we can see it and believe Him!"

Even this was specifically echoed in the past by David, "I am scorned and despised by all! Everyone who sees me mocks me. They sneer and shake their heads, saying, 'Is this the one who relies on the LORD? Then let the LORD save Him! If the LORD loves Him so much, let the LORD rescue Him!" God most certainly does love His Son completely. But there will be no rescue, no dramatic last moment escape from the cross. Because finally, the determining thing is not people's view of Jesus, or whether they recognize Him as Messiah and Saviour. It's not their response to Him, one way or the other, that shapes this Story.

Looking down through the pain He can see the Roman soldiers eager now to get back to their barracks. On the road people are walking by, some totally indifferent, others taking the chance to mock. In front, the self-righteous religious leaders, voicing their hatred, thinking that now they've shut Him up, that finally they'll be rid of Him. He can hear the groans of the criminals on either side. And over there, fearfully huddled to one side, a small group of His followers - His mother among them. Then, looking out beyond that time and place, He can see all the people who will live and die on this planet... and it's *His* view, His love and His Father's love for us all that keeps Him there.

 **DISCUSSION POINTS**

1. What are your thoughts about different traditions and depictions of the crucifixion that focus graphically on the physical aspects of Jesus' suffering? (The movie "The Passion of the Christ" is a modern example, but a great deal of religious art and iconography from the past also demonstrates this.) What beliefs at a worldview level might be involved? Does this seem to be consistent with what God is communicating through His Narrative?

2. If you were to meet these possible eyewitnesses to Jesus' crucifixion a day or two after in Jerusalem, how do you think they might each describe it?

(a) Simon from Cyrene who carried Jesus' cross

(b) The Pharisee, Nicodemus

(c) One of the four Roman soldiers who crucified Him

(d) A trader from a pagan community in Ephesus

(e) Lazarus, brother of Martha and Mary

1.54 Jesus was buried and was raised from the dead

 OBJECTIVES OF THIS TUTORIAL

Learners will continue to explore and discuss the themes and the truths presented in God's Narrative. The portions of Scripture referred to in this tutorial are: **Mark 15:33-47, 16:1-8, John 19:30,38-42, Isaiah 53:9, Psalm 16:10, Luke 24:8-12**

Last time

The detail of soldiers tasked with Jesus' crucifixion took Him to a place called Golgotha, outside the city walls. They crucified Him there between two convicted criminals, one of whom Him as the Messiah. Fulfilling His earlier prophecy to Nicodemus, Jesus hung there on the cross for all to see. Some of the people passing by stopped to mock Him. As did the religious leaders who'd come to enjoy what they thought was a victory over a dangerous rabble-rouser from Galilee.

The sun is darkened as God turns away from His Son

One of the terrible things about crucifixion compared with almost every other form of execution, is how it draws out the cruel ordeal for so long. It was not uncommon for victims to live on for two days before death mercifully came. Jesus was nailed to the cross at nine in the morning and at midday He is still there alive.

At this point, a remarkable thing happens. Mark records that for three hours darkness comes across the whole land. Whether or not a naturalistic explanation can be made - such as a solar eclipse - the circumstances and timing clearly point to God's hand. For the benefit of the eyewitnesses and all who hear this Account, God is giving a physical demonstration of what is happening in the spiritual realm. As we know, millennia before, Adam and Eve's rebellion triggered an unstoppable epidemic of death in the world. From then on their physical bodies were dying, they were spiritually separated from God, the Source of life, and after death they faced a terrible eternity of separation from Him. What's more, every single one of their descendants is likewise infected.

God, as we know, is absolutely holy and righteous - it's not just something He sometimes does, it's who He is in His very being, His existence. Because of that, he can't associate with this now corrupted evil race of rebels. But He loves us, and His grace isn't diminished or obstructed by our sin. So even in the terrible moment when He is separating us from Himself, He's also promising that He'll make a way for us to come back to Him. But how? What is desperately needed is another man to take Adam's place as representative of the human race. But it has to be someone very different...someone who does not inherit Adam's sin and who voluntarily chooses to obey God, who lives up to God's perfect standards.

So as we know, God chooses His own Son, and the Son willingly, gladly, volunteers to be that man. He's born and lives as a human being. As we've heard, He fully demonstrates His obedience. He refuses to be tempted by God's Enemy, to rebel like Adam did. He is everything God created man to be and God is delighted by Him. But now, the last chapter is being written. On the cross, Jesus is representing all of Adam's lost, corrupted, sinful race. He is absorbing in Himself the death and separation that all humans deserve. And so now when the perfectly holy, righteous God sees Jesus there, He rejects Him...He turns His back on Him... and Jesus is alone, cut off from His Father with whom He has always been in perfect harmony.

So now, God demonstrates just what a momentous and terrible moment this is by shutting out the light of the sun. His face is turned away from His Son who is now the world's sin-bearer, and the sun's face is turned away as well.

Jesus gives up His life, declaring that "It is finished"

After three hours of this, in the middle of the afternoon, Jesus calls out in His agony and despair, "My God, my God, why have you abandoned me?" Soon after, He calls out again, and then stops breathing.

It's important to note that no one took His life from Him. From the moment the ordeal began in Gethsemane, through the trials, the abuse, the whipping, the crucifixion itself, and now as His life slips away. He has not been a victim - not of Judas, the armed men who arrested Him, the Jewish leaders, Pilate, the Roman soldiers or even of physical forces. He has been fully in control. He allows it because of His obedience to the Father, His love for us, to fulfill the prophecies, to redeem His lost race... He lays down His life as a sacrifice. The blood of animals that have been sacrificed can never pay for sin - they can only cover it temporarily and point towards Jesus' sacrifice that will satisfy God's perfect requirements.

Mark doesn't give Jesus' words when He speaks again just before death, but in his account John records that He calls out loudly, "It is finished." We know that what is finished is the payment for sin. God's rescue effort put into place so long ago is now complete. A way has been made for humans to be forgiven and have the relationship with God He's always intended. Whoever repents - agrees with God that they are sinners with no hope of making themselves acceptable to Him - and believes in Jesus and His death, is born again into God's family... forever.

Mark records something incredibly significant that takes place at the moment Jesus declares "It is finished" and gives up His life. The thick, heavy curtain in the temple that divides off the Most Holy Place is torn from the top to the bottom. As we know, God's glorious presence on earth has been there. No one has had access except the High Priest once a year when he brings the blood of a sacrificed animal to sprinkle on the covering of the ark of the Covenant. But now Jesus has paid the final sacrifice and through Him humans can have access directly to God. The curtain is ripped from above, by God, to show that He is completely satisfied with the payment Jesus has made for sin. Just as Jesus had foretold to His disciples during their Passover meal together, a new Covenant has been brought into place, sealed by His blood.

The Narrative includes a fascinating side note. One of the eyewitnesses to Jesus death is a Roman army officer. He watches Jesus' death intently and when it's over exclaims, "This man was truly the Son of God!"

A number of women are also mentioned who have been watching Jesus' crucifixion and death from a distance, no doubt too timid to come closer.

They have been part of the group who've followed and supported Him in Galilee, believing that He is the Messiah.

Jesus is buried but is resurrected after three days

Mark explains that Jesus dies on a Friday. This makes things urgent for His friends who want His body to be properly buried - nothing, of course, can happen on the Sabbath, which officially starts at sunset the day before. The other complication is the concern about what the authorities will do to anyone showing their sympathy with Him or His cause. But someone boldly takes the risk. His name, Joseph, is a common one, so he's also identified by his home village, Arimathea. He's wealthy and a member of the Jewish Council, who has been a secret disciple of Jesus.

When he goes to Pilate to request the release of the body, the Roman governor is shocked that Jesus is already dead by this first afternoon. But after verifying the death with the officer who was present at the crucifixion, he allows Joseph to take charge of the body. John tells us that his fellow Councilor, Nicodemus, helps to take the body down from the cross, and wrap it in cloth according to Jewish custom. Then, in some haste no doubt because of the time, they carry it to a nearby garden and place it on a stone shelf inside Joseph's own previously unused tomb. Yet another of Isaiah's very specific prophecies is fulfilled - this one predicting that the Messiah will be buried in a rich man's grave (Isaiah 53:9). A large disk of flat stone is sitting in a sloping groove beside the entrance. They take out the wedges and allow it to roll down, sealing the tomb. Opening it again will be difficult, requiring the strength of a number of men.

Early on the Sunday morning, three women who Mark mentioned as being present at the crucifixion, go to the tomb to anoint Jesus' body with the customary burial spices... something left undone perhaps in the hasty burial on the Friday afternoon. On the way, they wonder out loud who's going to help them move away the large stone from the entrance. But when they get there, much to their surprise, it has already been moved and the burial cave is wide open. Wondering, they stoop to enter. Inside their astonishment turns to fear. Instead of a body lying there, as they expect, they see a young man dressed in a white robe. It turns out this is one of God's spirit messengers, an angel, who is here in physical form in order to speak to them. Actually, both Luke and John record that there are two angels, but Mark only mentions this one, probably because he's the only one to speak. He tells them not to be afraid and then passes on some incredible news. The one they're looking for - Jesus of Nazareth who was crucified - has risen from the dead. They are to tell the disciples that He's gone on ahead to Galilee and that they are to meet Him there.

This should not really be a surprise - the angel reminds them that Jesus had predicted His death and resurrection a number of times. Perhaps beforehand the reality just never really sank in. No doubt they didn't want to even contemplate the possibility of Him dying, and so they'd never pictured him rising again. But the fact is, this had been prophesied hundreds of years before by King David. In a Psalm or worship song to God (Psalm 16:10) he wrote, "You will not leave my soul among the dead or allow your holy one to rot in the grave." The women run from the grave too scared to mention what they've seen and heard to anyone. But Luke tells us that they do go and tell the disciples.

Later, Jesus appears to many people, including His disciples, on a number of occasions. On the cross, Jesus took the sins of the human race on Himself. God turned His back on Him and judged Him for our sins. As the holy and righteous Judge, He passed sentence on Him and the sentence was death. But that sentence has now been completed, the penalty paid in full. And God, completely satisfied with the payment Jesus made for the sin He bore, has raised Him again from death, never to die again.

The Story, including the written Narrative, still has many chapters to be completed. But everything before has been leading up to this point... everything after, flows from it.

Jesus, God's Son, the Christ, the Deliverer, the crucified sin-bearer now resurrected, *is* the Story.

❓ DISCUSSION POINTS

1. How would you respond to someone who objects to the concept of God as the sovereign Judge who is willing to punish His own innocent Son for other people's sin? Can we really say that a truly loving God would reject and abandon His Son who is clearly in such agony of body and soul?

2. Reflect on Jesus' statement just before death that "It is finished", then:

(a) in your own words, describe some of the enormous implications of this declaration.

(b) describe what an individual actually has to do so that "it is finished" for them, i.e. for their sins to be forgiven and to be born again.

(c) answer the potential objection that it is contradictory to say Christ has finished everything necessary for salvation while also saying that an individual still has to do something personally to be saved.

3. Picture yourself as one of the disciples hearing the women describing what they saw at the tomb on the Sunday morning. How do you think you would have reacted? Confused, excited, dubious? Thinking back to what you know of Jesus and the things you've heard Him say, would you immediately believe He has been raised from the dead or would you be looking for some other explanation for the empty tomb?

➡ ACTIVITIES

1. Since Jesus' death and resurrection, many different teachings have been put forward that contradict the straightforward reality of the Narrative that He actually died physically and then was resurrected. Briefly describe two of these erroneous teachings and comment on the potential confusion they bring to anyone exposed to them.

www.ingramcontent.com/pod-product-compliance
Lightning Source LLC
Chambersburg PA
CBHW061925290426
44113CB00024B/2823